The Reader in Modernist Fiction

This book is dedicated to my nephews and nieces, Leon, David, Sara, Melvin, Shoham, Nathan, Mishka, Lida, and Ishaan.
Keep reading, and read critically.

The Reader in Modernist Fiction

Brian Richardson

EDINBURGH
University Press

Edinburgh University Press is one of the leading university presses in the UK. We publish academic books and journals in our selected subject areas across the humanities and social sciences, combining cutting-edge scholarship with high editorial and production values to produce academic works of lasting importance. For more information visit our website: edinburghuniversitypress.com

© Brian Richardson 2024

Edinburgh University Press Ltd
13 Infirmary Street
Edinburgh EH1 1LT

Typeset in 11/13 Adobe Sabon by
IDSUK (DataConnection) Ltd, and
printed and bound in Great Britain.

A CIP record for this book is available from the British Library

ISBN 978 1 3995 2836 8 (hardback)
ISBN 978 1 3995 2838 2 (webready PDF)
ISBN 978 1 3995 2839 9 (epub)

The right of Brian Richardson to be identified as the author of this work has been asserted in accordance with the Copyright, Designs and Patents Act 1988, and the Copyright and Related Rights Regulations 2003 (SI No. 2498).

Contents

Acknowledgements	vi
Preface	viii
Introduction: Modernist Hieroglyphics and the Implicated Reader	1
1. From James to Conrad and Ford: Suppressed Narratives, Subaltern Reading, and the Drama of Interpretation	26
2. The Fate of Reading in the Work of Joyce: Illusion, Demystification, Sexuality	52
3. "Books Were Not in Their Line": The Use and Abuse of Reading in Katherine Mansfield and Virginia Woolf	77
4. The Dangers of Reading from Edith Wharton to Ralph Ellison	105
5. Reading Ruins: From Modernism to the Illegible Texts of Postmodernism and Beyond	132
Conclusion: The Stories of Modern Fiction, the End(s) of Misreading, and the Other Reader's Response	164
Bibliography of Works Cited	181
Index	195

Acknowledgements

A number of friends, colleagues, and editors have assisted me in the writing of this book; for their valuable editorial and critical advice I wish to thank Jan Alber, Claire Battershill, Melba Cuddy-Keane, Gerri Kimber, Zoran Kuzmanovich, Todd Martin, Vara Neverow, Emily Orlando, Nels Pearson, James Phelan, Peter Rabinowitz, Ray Stevens, Leona Toker, Christina Walter, Andrea White, and Annjeanette Wiese. I offer special thanks to Jackie Jones, my superb editor at Edinburgh, who deftly navigated this work to its home.

I have presented portions of this material on a number of occasions at several universities and I appreciate the many comments I have received from audience members at the University of Tübingen, Aarhus University, the University of Bologna, the Hebrew University of Jerusalem, Groningen University, the Freiburg Institute for Advanced Study, the University of Warsaw, the Catholic University of America, and the Ludwig Maximilian University of Munich. I am similarly appreciative for suggestions received at conferences of the Joseph Conrad Society of America, the James Joyce Symposium, the International Virginia Woolf Conference, the International Society for the Study of Narrative, and the Modern Language Association. I wish to thank my graduate students at the University of Maryland who have discussed these ideas with me in courses I have taught featuring reading and modernism. I thank the University of Maryland College of Arts and Humanities for a GRB grant that helped me greatly at the beginning of this project. I also offer my gratitude to my colleague and friend, Caroline Eades, who lent me her apartment in Paris for a month where I drafted significant sections of this book.

Earlier versions of material in this book have been published in the following venues: the pages of Chapter 1 on "The Secret Sharer": Copyright © 2001 University of North Texas; this article first appeared in *Studies in the Novel*, Volume 33, Number 3, Fall

2001 and is republished with the permission of the Johns Hopkins University Press. Parts of Chapter 3 appeared in *Virginia Woolf and the World of Books*, edited by Nicola Wilson and Claire Battershill (Clemson University Press, 2018) and *Katherine Mansfield and Virginia Woolf*, edited by Christine Froula, Gerri Kimber, and Todd Martin (Edinburgh University Press, 2018). The paragraphs on Graham Greene and Tayeb Salih in Chapter 4 were published in *The Conradian* 36.1 (Spring 2011). Earlier versions of portions of Chapter 5 and the conclusion first appeared in *Criticism* 39.1, published by Wayne State University Press. I thank all of these publications for permission to reprint this material.

Preface

Between 1890 and 1938 a large number of significant works of fiction appeared that foregrounded the effects of reading, usually the reading of narrative fiction. My primary project in this book is to assemble and analyze these instances and explore their implications concerning an intersecting range of subjects including the articulation of modernist poetics, the implicit construction of the modernist reader, the contestation of Victorian mores and official social doctrines, the web of intertextual allusions, the reading of the narrative itself, and even perception in general. Though several approaches to the figure of the reader can be discerned, what is most intriguing is the insistence with which Joseph Conrad, James Joyce, Ford Madox Ford, Katherine Mansfield, William Faulkner, Katherine Anne Porter, and other high modernists regularly created dramas in which reader-characters misread and then come to a painful end, while other, more skeptical interpreters thrive. By dramatizing the dangers of misreading, these authors helped create an alternative interpreter, whom I will call the critical reader, who evaluates discourse more suspiciously and can therefore elude the errors that condemn the more naïve, complacent, or uncritical figures in the work.

The appearance of such a large group of these sorts of texts at this historical moment is of course no accident. By the end of the nineteenth century, the very concept of human knowledge had begun to change. Rather than an ever increasing accumulation of facts and transcendence of earlier errors that led humanity inexorably closer to the truth, a new cluster of radical thinkers argued instead for a skeptical epistemology in which traditional repositories of knowledge were shown to be likely sources of illusion. This new hermeneutics of suspicion, spearheaded by Marx, Nietzsche, and Freud, is well known; it is in fact something of a critical idée reçue. What has not been adequately explored is the extent to which the high modernists were actually reproducing the conditions of human knowledge and error by embedding important patterns within texts that were, at first encounter, difficult to decode. This practice can explain in part the reason behind the opaque nature of many modernist texts and the interpretive difficulties they are notorious for creating. As Wolfgang Iser observes, the reader of the modernist text, "in striving to produce the aesthetic object, actually reproduces the very conditions under which reality is perceived and comprehended" (*Act* 103). Intriguingly, in a wide range of modernist works, figures of an underprivileged group—women, workers, non-whites, gays, children—emerge as privileged interpreters of the social world enveloping them. Many of the central characters of these works also imagine (and try to influence) how the events of their lives will later be read as a narrative, a topic that has not been analyzed in a sustained manner in literary studies. Tropes of hidden or obscured meaning are frequently invoked as the surface narrative is complemented (or undermined) by another, partially submerged progression; in this process, official positions are frequently demystified.

A central referent of dubious signs, secret codes, and difficult knowledge is, of course, sex. In fact, sex first becomes a subject for scientific inquiry during this period. Not surprisingly, sensual knowledge is often interwoven within or directly produced by various reading experiences, as a character's discovery of the actual order of the world is complemented by new knowledge of the possibilities of bodies. This pairing is variable; it is intermittent in the first part of the century: there is relatively little in Conrad or Woolf, while for Joyce, Ford, Mansfield, and Wharton, reading usually includes a highly sexualized element. As the twentieth century continues, the sexualization of reading proliferates. I will trace out this trajectory through the decades and identify the changing fate of the coupling of reading and eros, including the ways it is inflected by violence or death.

My account will advocate a more generous historical span than is generally allotted to modernism, identify intercontinental geographical parameters, and point to a significant neomodernist presence today. The readings of major and canonical works in this study are in addition intended to impact interpretation of the individual texts themselves; my reading of "The Secret Sharer" suggests the novella is charged with an ironic skepticism more profound than that argued for by any previous interpreter. Similarly, my accounts of reading, misreading, and nonreading in *A Portrait of the Artist as a Young Man*, *Ulysses*, *To the Lighthouse*, and Katherine Anne Porter's "Old Mortality" are intended to contribute to the reinterpretation of central issues of these works, particularly concerning the act of reading and the nature of interpretation. This book is designed to contribute to current debates over the nature, extent, and social implications of modernist literary practices. In it, I offer a general portrait of modernism that underscores its complex, progressive, multivalent, and interactive nature.

This study also attempts to contribute to critical theory. I will discuss various models of reading and reception in an attempt to do justice to covert, multiple, oppositional, ambiguous, and divided audience responses in a range of twentieth-century narratives. In particular, we find that high modernist works are frequently addressed to a dual audience, one that comprehends and one that fails to perceive the central interpretive nodes of the text. A revised model of the reader is needed to articulate the dual, ambiguous, or polymorphic response regularly produced by both modernist and minority authors. In addition, I hope to identify a distinctively modernist strategy of intertextuality and discuss the implications inherent in different narratives of the history of modern literature. Finally, I will engage with recent debates concerning "surface" and "symptomatic" reading, arguing that the modernist practice I describe tends to elude both of these models of interpretation as they are currently configured.

The Reader in Modernist Fiction begins with an introductory chapter that outlines some of the basic impulses behind and dynamics within high modernist narrative texts. I suggest that modernist practices typically frustrate many expectations appropriate for Victorian narrative. These texts move to create a new kind of reader that can participate in a more engaged kind of narrative reconstruction. I demarcate how modernist misreading differs fundamentally from ostensibly similar earlier treatments from Cervantes to Mark Twain, contrast my approach with some earlier critical accounts of the use and abuse of reading, and examine recent debates over reading and critical interpretation, such as surface reading and reparative reading. Lastly, I set the stage for the analyses that follow by identifying the different status of the figure of the reader in early twentieth-century fiction prior to the development of what I call the critical modernist stance. This includes a brief consideration of Wells' *The History of Mr. Polly*, D. H. Lawrence's *Lady Chatterley's Lover*, and E. M. Forster's exploration of the value and limits of high culture in *Howards End*, a narrative that culminates in the death of Leonard Bast, the impassioned autodidact of the lower orders, who is killed when a bookshelf falls on him. I also point to key intellectual transformations across the disciplines at the time (from the skeptical hermeneutics of Nietzsche to the rise of archeology to developments in biology like the germ theory of disease transmission) that make the search for a deeper, underlying meaning a significant break from the past and a defining feature of modern knowledge.

Several critical readings of major modernist texts follow that illustrate the challenges of interpretation and dangers of (mis)reading. Chapter 1 begins with an overview of the representation of readers in the work of Henry James, with particular attention given to "The Figure in the Carpet." The rest of the chapter explores the effects of reading and the theme of interpretation in Conrad, especially as it appears in *Lord Jim*, and unearths the hidden narratives cached within "The Secret Sharer." I argue that these versions are significant counters to the narrator's discourse, present the point of view of the seamen, and provide an alternative interpretation to the main events of the narrative—one that has consistently eluded interpreters who do not take the epistemology of class perception (as well as relevant historical antecedents, in particular the alleged mutiny on the USS *Somers*) into account. This tale embodies a high modernist poetics more fully than is generally recognized: its narrator is more fallible and its drama of misinterpretation more extreme than Conrad criticism has acknowledged. I end with an analysis of the deleterious consequences that befall individual readers in Ford Madox Ford's *The Good Soldier* (the adulterous Ashburnham was a "sentimentalist, whose mind was compounded of indifferent poems and novels"). Here, the kind of situations we find in Conrad also appear, though with an intensely sexualized form.

Chapter 2 discloses Joyce's fascination with and repeated examination of the act and theme of reading and misreading. In *Dubliners*, an enhanced *Bovary*-type model prevails, as characters regularly misapply the conclusions found in fiction to situations in the real world. A paradigmatic example is found in "An Encounter," where the passionate reading of Westerns engenders a day of truancy that turns into a very different kind of adventure from the one the boys had imagined—an encounter with a self-identified "bookworm" pederast. The trajectory that appears in *A Portrait* is rather different, and offers two kinds of reading. One indicates that books can provide substantial solace, though they often prove to be inadequate or illusory. The other suggests that words, forbidden or obscene, crude or Latinate, written out or carved by furtive hands, provide a searingly powerful vision as they articulate the unspeakable. In *Ulysses*, one finds a sustained drama of misreading, hidden reading, and demystified reading. Printed words are repeatedly set forth as potentially or typically

xii *The Reader in Modernist Fiction*

deceptive signs that critical readers are urged to see through. In addition, we find entire cycles of furtive readings, particularly as sexually charged materials are hidden and read in isolation. The topic of reading, reception, and (mis)interpretation within Joyce's work has been discussed at various points in earlier criticism; my chapter attempts to provide a more global interpretation of this practice, situating it within the construction of the modernist reader and standard reception theory, which it tends to destabilize in interesting ways.

Chapter 3 explores the act of reading in the work of Katherine Mansfield and Virginia Woolf. I begin by describing the role of reading, misinterpretation, and sexual connection in several of Mansfield's stories, such as "Bliss," "A Cup of Tea," and "Marriage à la Mode," noting Mansfield's critique of misread texts, signs, and allusions. I then note how this wider lens of non- and misinterpretation plays out in the works of Woolf, especially *To the Lighthouse*, where I observe that the major events of the narrative center on actual or apparent acts of reading. It is Mrs. Ramsay's reading to James that arouses the jealousy of Mr. Ramsay at the beginning of the novel, and that act serves as a site of contestation between the boy and his father for Mrs. Ramsay's attention. It is also the partial subject of the painting Lily Briscoe is creating. The painting, however, cannot be "read" by Mr. Bankes, who doesn't comprehend the work's meaning or reference. The text being read to the boy, the fairy tale "The Fisherman's Wife," a patriarchal story warning of the dangers of unchecked female desires, has long puzzled Woolf scholars. I argue that it offers a prescient image of the situation of the Ramsay family, though it is one that none of the characters is able to perceive. The drama of reading continues as the site of reading, so often a pretext for a wide range of very different activities, finally turns into a space of deep engagement that produces unexpected connections and concludes as the reader and Mr. Ramsay both finish the volume they literally hold in their hands.

Chapter 4 offers a much broader perspective on staged dramas of reading and misreading as it situates my extended discussions of individual texts earlier in the book within general modernist practice from the 1920s to the early 1950s. I begin with an analysis of the covert semiotic drama of books, signs, and amorous relations in Edith Wharton's *The Age of Innocence* (1920). William Faulkner raises the stakes of the fate of interpretation and adds a crucial racial context by disclosing the fatal consequences of Joe Christmas' naïve reading in *Light in August* and by dramatizing the effects of an exegesis of a slave owner's damning account book in "The Bear." Katherine

Anne Porter aligns deadly sexual repression with constricting master narratives that are uncritically recirculated in "Old Mortality." The novella takes its name from a romantic novel of Walter Scott; Scott's work serves Porter (as it did Joyce, Ford, and Woolf) as a model and source of the nineteenth-century literary and social values that needed to be overturned. I then follow Elizabeth Bowen's exploration of the ethics and dangers of reading in *The Death of the Heart* (1938), as the sophisticated readers within the novel are shown to be morally deficient; the way they respond to real or potential writings of the protagonist reveals the limitations of each. In *The Heart of the Matter* (1948), Graham Greene redeploys Conradian tropes and scenes of reading in a colonial, West African setting. Here too, uncritical reading proves deadly. Its protagonist, Major Scobie, wonders at its end whether he would understand the woman he loves if she were simply a character in a book, and is forced to conclude, "But I don't read that sort of book." Next I examine how Ralph Ellison discloses the material effects of reading and being (mis)read in *Invisible Man* (1952), laying particular stress on the reading and writing of history and the documentation of those who are usually written out of its pages. This chapter concludes with a discussion of Tayeb Salih's *Season of Migration to the North*, a rewriting of Conrad's "Heart of Darkness" that performs a postcolonial interrogation of reading and sex.

Chapter 5 chronicles the radical transformation of the figure of the reader that accompanies the rise of postmodernism. It begins with an analysis of Vladimir Nabokov's *Lolita*, a text that both extends and deforms high modernist practice as it has appeared up to this point. Throughout his fiction, Nabokov is deeply concerned with the act of reading and consequences of misreading. In *Lolita*, "well-read Humbert" is pitted against Charlotte Haze, who places "blind faith in the wisdom of her church and book club" as well as author Clare Quilty, whose hidden identity Humbert cannot deduce despite all the clues he has left. Reading and the quest for obscured meaning become a major focus of the plot as the novel revolves around the construal of behavior, casual words, notepads, and hotel registers, to mention only a few sites of occluded signification. In this book, the construction of a modernist "aesthetic" reader is performed with a theatrical flair, though not always in conformity to the logic of modernist reading as I have described it. Designed to provoke a number of conventional readers, this work also contains depictions offensive to minority readers, and thereby puts into sharp relief the question of the nature and extent of divided, multiple, and oppositional audiences. I suggest that *Lolita* is a transitional text, largely within the high modernist camp but also edging toward a number of postmodern positions which Nabokov would develop in his later works.

I go on to discuss the postmodern rejection of the basic terms of modernist reading strategies. After the advent of postmodernism, reading is no longer what it used to be: misreading is difficult or impossible and books themselves are dubious commodities. Postmodern techniques also include exaggeration and parody; both are prominent in postmodern depictions of physical volumes and their effects. Nevertheless, Italo Calvino in his narrative of readers and reading, *If on a winter's night a traveler*, finds it necessary to embody a dialectic between high modernist and postmodern stances. Based on the depictions of fictional readers, the move from modernism to postmodernism is not simple, thorough, or definitive. In addition to identifying some particularly compelling or destructive depictions of reading and books in postmodern texts by Ishmael Reed, David Toscana, and others, I also look back at earlier prefigurations of these stances in the work of Borges. I end this chapter with a brief glance at the revivals of two other traditions. One is the enlightenment model, represented by Bernhart Schlink's *The Reader* (1995) and Jhumpa Lahiri's *The Namesake* (2003). The other is that of neomodernist fiction, which I analyze in two recent novels: John Banville's *Eclipse* (2000) and Ian McEwan's *Atonement* (2001), as we observe the paradigm outlined by Flaubert continuing to flourish in the twenty-first century.

In the conclusion, I note the persistence of the drama of misreading over such an extensive period and summarize the results of this study—thematic, ideological, theoretical, sexual, and intertextual. I reflect on the nature(s) of the modernist reader that so many of these texts have helped construct, noting its parallels to and differences from rival conceptions of audiences and general accounts of interpretation. Drawing on feminist, queer, and African-American practice, I develop a theory of the dual implied reader to help explain the effects produced by numerous modernist works. By tracing the creation, development, and final transformation of the modernist reader(s), we can appreciate their repeated alignment with significant minority literary practices, progressive ideological positionings, and dramatic affirmations of the sexualized body.

Though centered firmly in the modernist tradition in the British Isles from 1898 to 1938, I occasionally stray geographically, as salient representations of the reader continue to appear in fiction by authors from the United States, Latin America, and elsewhere. My central subject, once again, is the effect of reading as presented in works of modern fiction, as well as the larger implications of such reading for understanding the poetics of modernist fiction and of interpretation in general. This book does not present a new theory of modernism, though I hope that its conclusions might be drawn on by future theorists of the field. It does however provide an intervention into widespread conceptions of the history of twentieth-century narrative: I argue that what we call modernism in fiction is more diverse than is generally accepted, that it extends much longer than is acknowledged, and that postmodernism has an earlier origin than its theorists usually allow.

Lastly, a terminological caveat: there are, as Peter Nicholls has compellingly established, many modernisms; consequently, there are many implicit modernist readers. I will be focusing on what has been called high modernism, in this case the overlapping narrative poetics of Conrad, Joyce, Mansfield, Ford, Woolf, Faulkner, Porter, and Bowen (and, to a lesser extent, Wharton and Greene). These authors regularly employ a poetics that stresses temporal fragmentation and rearrangement; unconventional, unusual, or multiple narrators; extensive and extreme representations of consciousness, nonconventional narrative sequencing and endings, and a web of oblique allusions. To this well-established cluster I will suggest we add interpretive contests that often feature partially obscured meanings that the reader is intended to discern. I will call this particular figure the critical reader or the modernist reader. To reiterate, I am focusing on one major strand of modernism, one that has a number of common features but differs significantly from the modernism and the implied readers of other authors, including Gertrude Stein, Wyndham Lewis, and Franz Kafka. These too offer representations of reading, its effects, and interpretation in general—in the case of Kafka, one thinks of "In der Strafkolonie" (1919), where the prisoner's sentence is carved into his flesh, but which is entirely illegible. I acknowledge their presence and importance, but my focus is on a different, sustained tradition.

Introduction: Modernist Hieroglyphics and the Implicated Reader

In this book I argue that dramas of misreading—literal, social, sexual, and intertextual—are a central feature of many modernist narratives, and are as important as other better known aspects such as fragmented subjectivities, nonlinear temporality, or nontraditional gender constructs. Joseph Conrad, James Joyce, Ford Madox Ford, Katherine Mansfield, Virginia Woolf, William Faulkner, and other modernists regularly created a series of interpretive dilemmas that lead central characters into painful dramas of misconstrual in which a faulty or naïve reading leads to disappointment, failure, or death. At the same time, these authors regularly restage the same interpretive challenges for the reader to experience and thereby invite the construction of an alternative "modernist" reader who is intended to see beyond such errors. Modernism teaches readers how to comprehend misleading statements about the world and unusual constructions within the text.

Throughout modernist fiction, authors repeatedly create partially hidden layers of meaning within their works that reflect the suspiciously opaque new world around them. As Joyce explained to Arthur Power, "Previously, writers were interested in externals and, like Pushkin and Tolstoy even, they thought only on one plane; but the modern theme is the subterranean forces, those hidden tides which govern everything" (Power, 54). A central project of literary modernism might well be described as the oblique presentation of these hidden tides, often through their re-presentation in a form that, like experience, partially obscures them from a superficial view. As Maurice Blanchot states, "if the book is a replica of the world we must assume that the world is not merely the result of creativity but equally of the powerful ability to fake, feign and mislead from which all works of fiction necessarily derive—the more so when this ability is carefully concealed" (223). From this perspective, modernism's occasional obscurity is a challenge that must be successfully negotiated by alert interpreters. Stephen Dedalus points to the dialectic of knowledge and opacity early in *Ulysses*: "*You find my words dark. Darkness is in our souls, do you not think?*" (3.420–21).

2 *The Reader in Modernist Fiction*

Discussing this general interpretive dynamic, Vicki Mahaffey explains that "the idea of the author and reader engaging in a virtual conversation (above the heads of the characters) gradually changed the underlying structure of many modernist texts. This is not necessarily or immediately observable in the text itself; instead, the reader is confronted with an unpredictable format, verbal virtuosity, and a prolonged delay before the design and meaning of the whole begins to become apparent" (124). This is an accurate depiction of the general hermeneutic practice of modernism. She goes on to note that "such delays frustrate and distract the reader, confounding his or her expectations, but they also draw attention to the multiple ways in which the written material can be interpreted" (124). I also suggest that different readers will respond very differently; knowing to wait to learn the deferred meaning is an essential part of becoming a reader of modernist narrative. And so is knowing which information is unlikely ever to be divulged.

An exemplary incarnation of interpretive challenge appears in *Mrs. Dalloway*, where the characters are literally trying to decipher a message in the sky produced by an airplane. "Only for a moment did they lie still; then they moved and melted and were rubbed out up in the sky, and the aeroplane shot further away and again, in a fresh space of sky, began writing a K, an E, a Y perhaps?" (29). Here, modern commodity culture turns the heavens into a space for writing out ads; unfortunately for the advertiser, the message is indecipherable: the letters K, E, and Y hint at the retrievable hidden meanings in Woolf's text as they mock the faulty reception of the ad. Another viewer, the shell-shocked Septimus Smith, believes the letters are signaling to him (22). The discourse of advertising is as it were transformed into a parodic version of symbolist writing: instead of literally inscribing an unmistakable meaning across the sky, it becomes an opaque text in need of interpretation. Woolf concludes her episode of open air misreading by turning the plane that produced it into an emblem for another observer: "away the aeroplane shot, till it was nothing but a bright spark; an aspiration; a concentration; a symbol (so it seemed to Mr. Bentley . . .) of man's soul; of his determination . . . to get outside his body, beyond his house, by means of thought, Einstein, speculation, mathematics, the Mendellian theory" (41). Or, one might add, to get *within* the nature of things. Modernist reading, like modern living, is a continuous contest where savvy interpreters are generally rewarded while uncritical readers are left disappointed and feeling manipulated.

The character of Septimus also represents the deformed double of the modernist interpreter—the paranoiac who finds meanings that are not there. Such a figure is a regular sort of shadow presence in major modernist texts: we find it in the imaginatively overwrought governess in "The Turn of the Screw," the disturbed Denis Breen puzzling over the letters "U.P.: Up" in *Ulysses*, and Doc Hines proclaiming a delusional, supernatural causalism in *Light in August*, as well as in the more gently unhinged characters in the fiction of Chekhov ("The Black Monk"). Conrad provides many deranged interpreters that counterpoint his more skeptical readers: the mate suffering from *delirium tremens* opposed to Marlow in *Lord Jim*; Kurtz versus Marlow in "Heart of Darkness"; the frenzied mate Jukes versus the unimaginative Captain Whirr in "Typhoon"; and, as I will argue, the credulous narrator against the perspicacious first mate in "The Secret Sharer." A powerful instance of this figure appears in Nabokov's story, "Signs and Symbols," where the protagonist's madness is confirmed by the fact that he believes the natural world reflects his personality and situation. Of course, in modernist fiction, details of the external world *do* reflect the protagonist's situation, but this is something that only competent readers (and never characters) are supposed to know. It should come as no surprise, then, that postmodernism clears a space for itself by valorizing paranoia, as the widespread modernist distinction between madness and art is eroded.[1] As I will discuss at greater length in the fifth chapter, postmodernism and its antecedents constitute an antithetical paradigm by stressing illegibility and the collapse of communication.

A necessary corollary of the new approach to interpretation was exposing the failures of traditional, more complacent types of understanding. Reading in general was increasingly depicted as a mystifying or dangerous activity by writers of fiction. An exemplary instance of this new notion can be found in two consecutive acts of reading by characters in Conrad's early text, "An Outpost of Progress" (1899). The men, who manage a trading station in Africa, find some torn books left behind by their predecessor. For the first time, they read imaginative literature, greedily consuming fiction by Dumas, Fenimore Cooper, and Balzac. "All these imaginary personages became subjects for gossip as if they had been living friends. They discounted their virtues, suspected their motives, decried their successes; were scandalized at their duplicity or were doubtful about their courage. The accounts of crimes filled them with indignation, while tender or pathetic passages moved them deeply" (*Tales of Unrest* 94).[2] In the same paragraph, they are depicted reading imperial propaganda in an old newspaper; here too, they have a naïve and credulous response to the material, their emotions are readily manipulated by the author,

4   *The Reader in Modernist Fiction*

and they are entirely unable to read either text critically: "They also found some old copies of a home paper. That print discussed what it was pleased to call 'Our Colonial Expansion' in high flown language." It spoke of "the sacredness of civilizing work, and extolled the merits of those who went about bringing light, faith and commerce to the dark places of the earth." Enjoying the way they had been cast as significant agents in this impressive narrative of imperial enlightenment, "Carlier and Kayerts read, wondered, and began to think better of themselves" (94–95). Somewhat later they find themselves involved in the more brutal aspects of colonialism and soon they become implicated in slave trading. Later, one man winds up shooting his partner and then hanging himself. Implicit in Conrad's tale is a sustained critique of any simplistically mimetic approach to reading, a keen awareness of the fabricated nature of all writings, the motives behind their production and the methods by which they attain their emotional effects, as well as a more general suspicion toward widely held or officially sanctioned worldviews. The characters' inability to read either kind of text critically—to see through the two related kinds of fabrication—contributes to their deaths. Their ignorance and helplessness are vividly contrasted to the knowledge and pragmatism of the African bookkeeper, Makola. Elsewhere in Conrad and Ford, we will see that uncritical reading is typically associated with delusion, failure, and death. Similar acts of misreading and misinterpretation are found throughout modernist fictions, and these function as something like a touchstone that fuses issues of literary technique and the representation of the social world.

These acts of (mis)interpretation are regularly re-staged for the reader to experience. A classic method is what Ian Watt has described as Conrad's technique of "delayed decoding," in which the author would "present a sense impression and . . . withhold naming it or explaining its meaning until later" (175). Watt uses an example from "An Outpost of Progress" to illustrate this practice: As Kayerts erroneously believes that Carlier is coming to shoot him, he moves around the building until he unexpectedly bumps into the other. "A loud explosion took place between them; a roar of red fire, thick smoke; and Kayerts, deafened and blinded, rushed back thinking: 'I am hit—it's all over'" (*Tales* 113). Soon he realizes that he is still alive; but, having lost his gun, he realizes he is defenseless and is convinced the other man is stalking him. He then gets up and prepares to die. Seconds later, as he turns a corner, he sees a pair of turned-up feet. "Even now," Watt explains, "Kayerts does not decode the visual signs: it is only when he sees Carlier's untouched revolver that Kayerts realizes" that he had shot an unarmed man (175)—a conclusion that the reader has just arrived at a few lines earlier.[3] In this way the reader is positioned to experience Kayert's perceptions as they are narrated and invited to form judgments concerning their import. In the rest of this study, I will focus on the figure of the reader and the frequent failure to read hidden signs correctly as well as the larger interpretive issues, including accurate readings, genuine misreadings, multiple meanings, and the times when an apparent sign is not a sign at all.

Modernist characters and narrators express wonder about the precise meaning of the experiences they undergo with an amazing frequency, at times producing a self-reflexive stance that the critical reader is invited to share. Immediately following the unprecedented "Time Passes" section of *To the Lighthouse*, we are given the sentence: "What does it mean then, what can it all mean? Lily Briscoe asked herself" (145). She is using "a catchword from some book" to examine her feelings on her return to the island after the death of Mrs. Ramsay; these words also reflect readers' uncertainty at what is happening in the text—they have just been given the description of a ten-year period in a largely empty house. What does it all mean? This is a kind of self-reflexive interpretive comment that many other modernist writers would not be able to resist.

If modernism teaches its readers to be suspicious of books that disseminate officially sanctioned pseudo-knowledge, it also points to a hidden, illicit knowledge present in other, unauthorized books, or carefully cached within seemingly innocent works. Sexual love in all its permutations becomes a regular presence. From *Madame Bovary* to *Ulysses* to *The Well of Loneliness* to *Tropic of Cancer*, the history of modern reading is both the story of the daring revelation of embodied, illicit desire and, often, the history of its censorship as well. Sexual desire, regularly forbidden, had been associated with reading in the past: the obvious example is the joint act of reading performed by Paolo and Francesca depicting Lancelot's adultery with Guinevere that precipitated their own adultery as referred to in the fifth canto of the *Inferno*. Richard Brown notes that Joyce's "imagination flew straight to the *Inferno* and to the second circle where those who have died because of their erotic passions are forever whirled" (126). Mary Reynolds estimates that this section of the *Inferno* is the one most frequently alluded to by Joyce (78). At the origin of modernist fiction we find Emma Bovary consuming romantic narratives that will lead to her pleasures and her demise: "she recalled the heroines of the books she had read, and the lyric legion

6   *The Reader in Modernist Fiction*

of these adulterous women began to sing in her memory with the voice of the sisters that charmed her. She became herself, as it were, an actual part of these lyrical imaginings; at long last, she saw herself among those lovers she had so envied" (117).

In *The Picture of Dorian Gray* (1891), Oscar Wilde lovingly depicted the sexual power of reading. Dorian goes to the little yellow book that Lord Henry had sent him and,

> taking up the volume, flung himself into an arm-chair and began to turn over the leaves. After a few minutes he became absorbed. It was the strangest book that he had ever read. It seemed to him that in exquisite raiment, and to the delicate sound of flutes, the sins of the world were passing in dumb show before him. Things that he had dimly dreamed of were suddenly made real to him. Things of which he had never dreamed were gradually revealed. It was a novel without a plot and with only one character, being, indeed, simply a psychological study of a certain young Parisian who spent his life trying to realize in the nineteenth century all the passions and modes of thought that belonged to every century except his own, and to sum up, as it were, in himself the various moods through which the world-spirit had ever passed, loving for their mere artificiality those renunciations that men have unwisely called virtue, as much as those natural rebellions that wise men still call sin. (96)

Gray soon concludes that "It was a poisonous book. The heavy odour of incense seemed to cling about its pages and to trouble the brain," but its effects are irreversible. His reading permanently alters his inner and outer life, for better and worse. As we see from the passage quoted, it also gives him a way to frame and comprehend himself. Concerning this and similar works, Valerie Rohy writes: "when useful images of gay men and lesbians are rare, when visibility is perilous and finding others like oneself uncertain, reading takes on a special urgency. Since the first experience of queer people *as* queer people is so often solitary, cautious, or secret, there is the book" (109).[4]

The practice of hermeneutic dramas cached within high modernist works fits snugly within the language of sexual allusion and covert gay discourse. As Christopher Craft has divulged, Wilde's *The Importance of Being Earnest* is a masterpiece of homosexual innuendo, starting with the name of the wicked Mr. Bunbury. As Jack explains, "One has a right to *Bunbury* anywhere one chooses. Every serious Bunburyist knows that" (44). Nella Larsen's novel *Passing* is extremely interesting in this context. Peter Rabinowitz has pointed out that this secretive text actually has "two different authorial audiences, two assumed, intended and *necessary* targets for the text"; the first one is ignorant of the work's lesbian subtext, while the other "realizes, and even relishes, the ignorance of the first audience" ("Betraying" 203). Here, sexual practices and modernist poetics interpenetrate easily, and form part of a nexus that will stretch from Wilde and James to Tayeb Salih and Ian McEwan.

Twenty-first-century readers may perceive such a conjunction as merely an interesting thematic association, but for audiences of a century ago there could be a powerful and dangerous connection between the reception of literature and "deviant," threatening sexual behavior. In 1918, Wilde's play, *Salome*, was still prohibited on the public stage in England, the Examiner of Plays having found it "half Biblical, half pornographic" (Stephens, 112). A Canadian dancer, Maud Allan, arranged for a private performance of the work to be staged in the spring. A Captain Harold Spencer learned of it and vigorously attacked it in an article entitled, "The Cult of the Clitoris," in which he claimed that Wilde's play "was not only immoral but its current production part of a German plot to undermine British wartime resolve" (McLaren, 9). Allan responded by suing Spencer for libel, but in the end her suit was dismissed. Despite a few counterexamples, we will see that sexuality runs like a red thread through the story of the modern reader.

The interpretive practices I will explore are closely related to the intellectual history of the period. Developments in British empirical philosophy and psychology were of profound importance to this new conception of knowledge. Phenomenalism emerged as a major metaphysical and epistemological position. It stressed the immediacy of perceptions, as opposed to the external entities that they appeared to represent. As John Stuart Mill observed, objects are simply the permanent possibilities of sensation. Hugh Epstein explains that Joseph Conrad's development occurred during the period where a simple concept of psychological materialism was replaced by an insistence on sense data; that is, we don't know things themselves, we know mental perceptions, and must therefore deduce those things from our perceptions. He goes on to state that Conrad works within the encounters of the mind with experience, and is thus "drawn to sensation, to surfaces, to the meeting place of self and the surrounding world." His "novels are novels of inference" (4). Ford Madox Ford stated that he and Conrad "saw that Life did not narrate, but made impressions on our brains. We in turn, if we wished to produce on you the effect of life, must not narrate but render impressions" (*Joseph Conrad* 193–94; see Armstrong 1–15).

8   *The Reader in Modernist Fiction*

One of the central, distinguishing features of modern thought is the discovery of organizing patterns hidden within seemingly arbitrary or random events. Not surprisingly, Freud provides an exemplary case when he recounts the time a woman in polite society made the following assertion: "Yes, a woman must be pretty if she is to please the men. A man is much better off. As long as he has *five* straight limbs, he needs nothing more!" (76).[5] This *lapsus lingua* as analyzed by Freud in his *Psychopathology of Everyday Life* is a typical instance of a widespread phenomenon: beneath the apparent irrational or inexplicable act of making a silly mistake that a child would avoid lies a structure of desire that produces "the mistake" and explains, to those who can read the elusive signs, why it was produced; why, in fact, it was not a mistake at all. This example is of course part of a much larger Freudian network that attempts to explain numerous aspects of human behavior though an interlocking set of partially hidden drives.

Other human sciences at the beginning of the modern period were equally devoted to uncovering the unsuspected pattern or code that lay behind apparent flux, unpredictability, and confusion or, also like psychoanalysis, offered a more persuasive (and more materialistic) explanation than existing idealist sensibilities could allow themselves to imagine. Marx's historical materialism, Nietzsche's analysis of the psychology of *ressentiment*, Saussure's structural linguistics, Fraser's comparative mythology, and Jung's archetypes all attempt to reveal a hidden, genuine order behind or beneath conventional facades and seemingly random conglomerations. Importantly, these discoveries impugned not only the material being disseminated but also the speaker: deliberately or unwittingly, all such purveyors of supposed information became potentially unreliable or obviously suspect. It is no wonder that modern hermeneutics flourished at this period; it could not help but be developed and widely applied. Friedrich Schleiermacher's statement of one of his starting points, a position affirmed and extended by hermeneuticists from Dilthey to Gadamer, could also be readily affirmed by most of the authors in this study: "The more lax practice of the art of understanding proceeds on the assumption that understanding arises naturally . . . The more rigorous practice arises on the assumption that misunderstanding arises naturally, and that understanding must be intended and sought at each point" (cited in Linge, xiii).

Other interpretive challenges abounded. Archeology, which Freud used as a metaphor for his own research into the unconscious, was becoming professionalized and ever more adept at coaxing historical narratives out of the most unlikely masses of apparent scraps, debris, and stray marks. The discovery of the Minoan civilization in Crete during the first years of the twentieth century fascinated the European imagination in a way reminiscent of Heinrich Schliemann's announcement that he had rediscovered Troy less than thirty years earlier. In addition, interest in deciphering codes became pronounced with the attempts to interpret newly discovered Mesoamerican glyphs and the tantalizing yet recalcitrant Minoan scripts "Linear A" and "B," uncovered by Arthur Evans in 1900. The latter may have helped inspire a pregnant image of Woolf's, as Lily Briscoe "imagines how in the chambers of the mind and heart of the woman who was, physically, touching her, there stood, like the treasures in the tombs of ancient kings, tables bearing sacred inscriptions, which if one could spell them out, would teach one everything, but they were never offered openly, never made public" (*Lighthouse* 51).

This kind of inquiry deep beneath the surface was not limited to the human sciences. Darwinian biology and, later, Mendelian genetics eschewed apparent superficial similarities to determine genuine evolutionary proximities, however counterintuitive they may seem, as the suggestive but misleading phenotype was displaced by the actual genotype. Developments in molecular biology, early particle physics, and epidemiology—especially the discovery of disease transmission through germs invisible to the naked eye—further disclosed an unexpected structure of previously unknown aspects of the world.[6] Not since the Middle Ages had appearances seemed to be so misleading; now, however, the world was neither what it seemed to be *nor* what it was said to be.

In short, by the last part of the nineteenth century, knowledge itself was conceived of differently, not merely as seeing but as seeing through deceptive appearances and of finally making legible apparently unconnected elements and events. Since the Renaissance, knowledge had generally been conceived of as a cumulative entity that one could acquire, amass, and extend. As print culture took ever firmer root in the Western imaginary, knowledge came to be increasingly synonymous with reading. The imagined intellectual and political concomitants of this conception were clear: as Voltaire indicates in his essay, "Concerning the Horrible Danger of Reading," a free press, freedom of speech, and the dissemination of existing and newly discovered facts would be enough to secure an informed, rational culture. Of course, history didn't quite turn out that way. By the end of the nineteenth century, books were increasingly seen as another dubious set of partial misinformation to be sorted through critically.

10   *The Reader in Modernist Fiction*

An important feature of the modern period was the rise of literacy in the nations of the industrial West and the unexpected effects that this produced. At first, the extension of literacy was resisted as dangerously destabilizing. Peter Keating observes "earlier in the [nineteenth] century elementary education for the poor had been restricted out of the fear that if the people were literate they would read subversive books"; this of course did not happen very often. What occurred next was that "the poor were to be taught to read so that they would be less easily swayed by radical or socialistic oratory" (143).[7] The proliferation of new publications that materialized to benefit these new readers also produced something different from its anticipated salutary effect. As historian Richard Bessel observes, "It is a paradox of the social history of twentieth-century Europe that the establishment of near universal literacy has been paralleled by a diminution of the literary standards of mass-market newspapers and a vast increase of readily available pornography" (253).

This transformation, which was the primary subject matter of George Gissing's *New Grub Street*, would appear in various guises and form the backdrop to many modernist works: we may adduce Leopold Bloom's use of a story from *Tit-Bits* to wipe himself after a bowel movement. But even in this case the divide is not as impermeable as might appear: David Trotter has pointed out that Joyce, Conrad, and Woolf all submitted stories to *Tit-Bits* that were turned down by its editors (63). None of these authors, in other words, could quite make the transition to dexterous mediocrity. They acted out in their lives the very situation that Henry James had earlier related in his story, "The Next Time" (*Stories* 1895), of the fictional Ralph Limbert, a superb but impecunious novelist who proves unable to write popular prose, since "the perversity of the effort, even though heroic, had been frustrated by the purity of [his] gift" (266). Or as Gissing's Jasper Milvain puts the dilemma in *New Grub Street*, "If I had only the skill, I would produce novels out-trashing the trashiest that ever sold fifty thousand copies. But it takes skill . . . To please the vulgar, you must, one way or another, incarnate the genius of vulgarity" (12). This character, incidentally, goes on to witness the birth of the new, shallow, lower middle-brow journal, *Chit-Chat*, itself clearly modeled on *Tit-Bits*. Virginia Woolf would later comment on the increasingly rigid divergence of types of actual audience in a late, unpublished essay, "The Reader": "as the Habit of reading becomes universal, readers split off into different classes. There is the specialised reader, who attaches himself to certain aspects of the printed words. Again there is the very large class of perfectly literate

Introduction 11

people who strip many miles of print yearly from paper yet never read a word" (Silver, 428).

Describing the transformations of the period from 1870 to 1901, Patrick Brantlinger writes: "never before had there been so many readers, nor so many novels, nor so many literary journals, libraries, bookstores, and publishers—nor so much opportunity for even a mediocre novelist to gain popularity and a decent livelihood through fiction writing" (208). The increase in literacy, and the rise of a new range of publications to satisfy the new readers, is a direct cause of the emergence of "low-brow" periodicals and I suspect is not unconnected to an emergent, potentially contrapuntal hermeticism in modernist texts. To take the example of Ireland, the literacy rate rose from 47% in 1841 to 88% in 1911. Over a similar period, the number of periodicals and newspapers more than doubled. Commenting on these figures, R. B. Kershner points out that they "represent a qualitative shift in the influence of popular literature from marginality, in a basically rural society whose popular consciousness was still significantly influenced by folklore, to centrality" (*Joyce, Bakhtin*, 301). Kershner goes on to observe that this explains why so many of Joyce's characters are *bovaristes*. We might also add that the commercial success of the newly emergent popular literature helped more literary writing identify itself by using a markedly different style that was more poetically phrased, naturalistically detailed, or otherwise resisted easy assimilation and rapid consumption. As such, these works were more likely to be purchased by the emerging public libraries that sought to provide more serious kinds of literature to its readers (see Wexler; Rainey). More importantly for this study, insofar as the rise of popular culture reproduced official Victorian notions of the family, gender relations, the notion of a stable self, and belief in providence, progress, and empire, it became a discursive arena equally in need of critical deflation and skeptical reading.

As modernist literature continued to diverge from accepted or official public doctrine, it saw itself increasingly opposed to the newspaper, a situation nicely emblematized by the fate of novelist Neil Paraday in James's "The Death of the Lion" (1894). Paraday is an excellent but little-known writer who is suddenly "discovered" by a "big, blundering newspaper"; in his ensuing encounter with fame, his masterpiece is lost and his death soon follows (*Stories* 218). Gissing's fictional Alfred Yule avers "that journalism is the destruction of prose style" (*New Grub Street* 161). This period also saw Mallarmé's denigration of the "rag" of the newspaper as opposed to the intricate organism of the book in "Quant au livre" (1895). His dismissal

12   *The Reader in Modernist Fiction*

of journalism was not merely for aesthetic reasons; he also saw the medium as producing incoherence rather than knowledge and specifically denounced the role of advertising.

Journalism at this period was undergoing a comparable but opposite economic transformation as that of literary fiction: by the end of the nineteenth century, the majority of its income came from advertising rather than individual subscribers. Soon, every major newspaper had a business office that systematically screened stories to prevent any annoyance to their advertisers (or in some cases, damaging stories were withheld after the implicated parties increased the amount of their ads). Not surprisingly, modernist authors regularly depicted the ease with which big business insinuated its demands into journalistic forms, as can be found in Decoud's work as the Central American correspondent in Conrad's *Nostromo* or Bloom's negotiations with Myles Crawford in *Ulysses*.[8] This scene continues to be reinscribed in modernist texts up through the squalid journalism that "covers" the final events of Alejo Carpentier's *The Lost Steps*, or that which disfigures the depiction of the 1943 Harlem riot in Ralph Ellison's *Invisible Man*.

Thus, it was only natural that Ford Madox Ford in *The Soul of London* (1905) would excoriate contemporary journalism for abandoning its standards and helping to stupefy the reading public (134–35). He characterized the effects of the Sunday paper as narcotic: "All over the town these sheets, as if they were white petals bearing oblivion, settle down, restful and beneficent, like so many doses of poppy seed" (137). In a similar vein, H. G. Wells in *The Outline of History* "treats mass literacy, with its untrained appetite for mindlessly chauvinistic, war-mongering journalism, as a main cause of the disastrous war-making of the twentieth century" (Brantlinger 205). In Forster's *Howards End* (1910), Helen Schlegel dismisses the Wilcox family, representatives of the new hollow men of capitalism, as a fraud, "just a wall of newspapers and motor-cars and golf-clubs," and she feels sure she would "find nothing behind it but panic and emptiness" (26). Throughout these years, then, we see modernism's joint aesthetic and ideological critique of the increasingly profit-driven capitalist press. This is to say that the days when a man like Anthony Trollope could find himself in the front ranks of living novelists, happily conform to existing social doctrines, write for several kinds of established newspapers, engage enthusiastically in politics, and run for Parliament were effectively over.

Before proceeding to the modernist works themselves, I will briefly survey some superficially similar moments in the history of

Introduction **13**

literature the better to situate and identify the difference of distinctively modernist critiques of misreading. The central such text since the Renaissance is certainly *Don Quixote*, the story of the volunteer knight who has lost touch with reality through the reading of medieval romances and who developed the delusion that the real world corresponds to that depicted in pastoral fictions. The point here is that an extremely artificial genre is utterly unrealistic, and that one who does not recognize this will quickly come to grief. This model—what might be called the evacuation of rival, unrealistic modes or genres—continues for several centuries; it suggests that reality is readily knowable as long as certain obvious fonts of error are avoided. It lies entirely within the Enlightenment paradigm of reading as a steady path to intellectual emancipation. The same is true of Charlotte Lennox's *The Female Quixote* (1752): the cloistered Arabella can have no real knowledge of actual social relations since her entire education has come from the romances she has read.

This general pattern governs nineteenth-century versions of the Quixote story, including Walter Scott's *Waverley* (1814), Jane Austen's *Northanger Abbey* (1817), Flaubert's *Madame Bovary* (1857), and Chapter 35 of Mark Twain's *Adventures of Huckleberry Finn* (1884): in each case, an overly idealized or sentimental conception of the world derived from unrealistic books (specifically, romances or Gothic novels) is shown to founder when applied to life itself.[9] In the last half of the nineteenth century the paradigm shifts significantly. For modernism, all books are potentially suspect. We can readily see this in Flaubert's work as he moves from *Madame Bovary* to *L'Éducation sentimentale* (1869) and in doing so substantially enlarges the object of his critique. Emma's problems in *Madame Bovary* stem from her belief in romantic conceptions of the world derived from books; more specifically, she wrongly believes that the realm depicted in *Lucia di Lammermoor* bears any usable connection to the world she inhabits. It does not, and she is damned. In her defense, it should be noted that the books that deceive Emma are merely implausible and are much more realistic than the extravagant romances or Gothic tales that perturb Don Quixote, Arabella, Catherine Morland, and Tom Sawyer. In *L'Éducation sentimantale*, however, the source of illusion is even vaster: in their early reading, Deslauriers reads philosophers from Plato to the Scottish empiricists and moves on to history and political economy, while Frédéric begins with medieval dramas and volumes of memoirs; soon the latter wants to become the Walter Scott of France, and identifies with passionate romantic figures such as Werther, René, Franck, Lara, and Lélia (25–27). But instead of

14   *The Reader in Modernist Fiction*

leading to another demonstration of the dangers of romanticism, this critique is extended to the realist novel and beyond. Deslauriers urges Frédéric to act like Balzac's character, Rastignac; if he does that, he is sure to succeed, he tells his friend (29).[10]

We are now on the road that will lead directly to *Bouvard et Pécuchet* (1881), that encyclopedic narrative of knowledge and pseudoknowledge that the protagonists are always unable to utilize no matter how much they read. Particularly resonant is the depiction of their attempts to master literature in the fifth chapter. Early on we learn that "after Walter Scott, Alexandre Dumas entertained them like a magic lantern. His characters, alert as monkeys, strong as oxen, happy as larks, entered and spoke abruptly, jumped from rooftops to the street, received horrible wounds that soon healed, were believed dead and reappeared" (115). They find Dumas and Scott full of historical errors, and are disappointed by the fiction of George Sand, Rousseau, and Constant. They are first amazed by Balzac. In his fiction, "new facets emerged from the most banal facts. They had not suspected modern life of being so profound" (118); soon, however, they tire of him as well.

In an impressive survey of some of this territory, Patrick Brantlinger offers a different perspective from the one I am advancing here. Despite his historical focus, he sees attacks on the novel and a general fear of the consequences of reading to be largely co-extensive with the history of the novel, and lumps together the various statements against one kind of novel or another made by characters of Cervantes, Sheridan, and Jane Austen, as well as assertions that appear in the nonfictional prose of Coleridge, Wilkie Collins, Oscar Wilde, and various reactionary religious figures. He explains: "while novelists often express opinions common to anti-novel discourse . . . a major factor underlying the inscription of anti-novel attitudes within novels is the radical uncertainty all novelists share about how the reading public will interpret or misinterpret, use or abuse, the products of their imagination" (3). In the period from the 1790s to the 1890s, his focus is "consequently upon the ways anxiety about mass literacy and the huge, largely anonymous, ever-increasing readership for fiction affected a range" of novels from that century (3).

My argument with Brantlinger is twofold. First, there is a fatal lack of specificity in the general, sweeping nature of his assessment. To use his own examples, while Sir Anthony Absolute in *The Rivals* and Samuel Taylor Coleridge in *Seven Lectures* make similar-sounding claims about the effects of reading fiction, they are actually articulating very different positions: for Coleridge, a work like *Tom*

Jones produces none of the deleterious effects he attributes to inferior kinds of fiction, while for Sir Anthony, Fielding's novel would mark the quintessence of a libertinism he feels it is his duty to suppress. Similarly, *Don Quixote* and *Northanger Abbey* are not joining in or unwittingly sharing in existing anti-novelistic discourse, but instead deprecating (as Flaubert would also largely do) those who live life as if it followed the unrealistic conventions of the romance or the gothic. Their novels were the emetic that would purge their readers, not the *pharmakon* that would both cure and poison them.

His general position leads Brantlinger to misread *Jude the Obscure*: "Jude's book burning represents his rejection of culture and literacy in general, both secular and religious. In a sense, Jude only repeats Arabella's earlier attack on his precious book" (195). This statement is incorrect; it is only the theological and ethical works that are burned. These books represent Jude's attempt at an alternative career once he realizes that he has no chance to make a vocation out of the classics. The "old, superseded, Delphin editions of Virgil and Horace" he retains until the day he dies (321). His actual dilemma is articulated by Sue: "You are one of the very ones Christminster was intended for when the colleges were founded; a man with passion for learning, but no money, or opportunities, or friends. But you were elbowed off the pavement by millionaires' sons" (120).

My second argument with Brantlinger is that he offers too narrow an explanatory framework for his analysis, omitting too many of the other relevant causes and issues in order to concentrate more exclusively on writerly panic over an audience with uncontrollable responses. A much more reliable guide to this territory is Carla Peterson who, in *The Determined Reader: Gender and Culture in the Novel from Napoleon to Victoria* (1986), examines the fates of male and female reader-protagonists in several English and French novels of the nineteenth century. These figures "sought to identify with the fictional characters or historical personages located in texts, or even with the authors themselves, and strove to imitate their experiences in their own lives" (227). Naturally, each of these attempts led to misfortune or disaster; such attempts merely reaffirm the gap that separates fiction from the world of our experience. In the rest of this book, my project is to follow out this drama though its next stage, as much more reading and interpretation become suspect.

In *Unknowing: The Work of Modernist Fiction* (2005), Philip Weinstein argues that modernists like Kafka, Proust, and Faulkner, rather than staging the drama of coming to know, stage the drama of coming to unknow. He postulates that the signature move of modernism is shock, and modernist authors achieved their most compelling experimental effects by undermining the earlier Enlightenment project of gaining genuine knowledge. I argue that modernists instead subvert the typical features and narrative progressions of realist fiction. A modernist work is more likely to produce puzzlement than shock. Weinstein's is an informative and generally impressive work; his focus is on knowledge in general rather than interpretation and still less individual acts of reading. His conceptual framework however is not as capacious as his material. Weinstein is excellent at showing how modernists disrupt conventional hermeneutical practices, but neglects the ways in which they are able to discern (and enable the reader to re-enact) the genuine knowledge they are able to attain. Weinstein chronicles the moment of epistemic failure, but neglects the darker actual knowledge that often follows.

This is perhaps unavoidable since the authors he focuses on are doing very different things with interpretation. Faulkner is a central figure in the high modernist tradition of Conrad, Joyce, Ford, and Woolf, and his narratives do provide genuine, counter-hegemonic knowledge to those who are able to apprehend it. At the end of *The Sound and the Fury*, the critical reader learns much more than Quentin or Jason can ever know. By contrast, Kafka does leave us in a state of unknowing. There are no unambiguous lessons to be learned and no code can be correctly deciphered; character and reader alike are left, at the end, in the dark. His work, like that of Borges and Beckett, looks forward to the unreadability featured in postmodernism. I try to separate these two different and usually antithetical traditions; my chapter on postmodernism attempts to clarify the roots of this alternative tradition of illegibility. Weinstein, I suggest, conflates the high modernist with the early postmodern position.[11]

Dorothee Birke's *Writing the Reader: Configurations of a Cultural Practice in the English Novel* (2016) traces the story of obsessed, Quixote-like readers through the history of the English novel from Lennox's *The Female Quixote* to Alan Bennett's contemporary satire, *The Uncommon Reader*. Birke does a fine job of tracing out new versions of the Quixote figure (and, in the case of Bennett, an anti-Quixote), but does not consider the numerous twentieth-century modernist authors who develop and transform it or the postmodern figures who exaggerate or parody such scenes of misreading. The model I will offer of representations of readers will be more nuanced and will distinguish different types of strategies for depicting characters' reading. Other worthwhile studies that complement my own as they cover adjacent terrain include Kate Flint's *The Woman*

Reader, 1837–1914 (1993), which analyses historical and fictional women readers. More recently, Leah Price's *How to Do Things with Books in Victorian Britain* (2012) explores the uses of books for purposes other than reading; John Lurz's *the Death of the Book* (2016) analyzes novels by Proust, Joyce, and Woolf, stressing their physical formats and tracing the passing of time in the reading of these works; and, in *Victims of the Book: Reading and Masculinity in Fin-de Siècle France* (2019), Francois Proulx shows how reading was considered dangerous to emerging masculinity in young men of that period. Merve Emre's *Paraliterary: The Making of Bad Readers in Postwar America* (2017) examines middlebrow literary culture in the United States, analyzing the kinds of readers that Nabokov and other modernists seem to disdain. Joseph Elkanah Rosenberg's *Wastepaper Modernism: Twentieth-Century Fiction and the Ruins of Print* (2021) focuses on images of tattered and useless paper in the work of James, Joyce, Woolf, Nabokov, Bowen, and others, discussing their implications for the genre of fiction in a period of the rising power of nonprint media. Again, I see my book as complementing these studies.

New work on reading has recently opened up a considerable range of interpretive possibilities that move beyond the familiar, predicable kind of suspicious, "symptomatic" readings that have been dominant for the past forty or fifty years. Especially promising is a new interpretive movement that calls for the development of strategies of "surface reading," an approach that examines "what is evident, perceptible, apprehensible in texts; what is neither hidden, nor hiding" (Best and Marcus 9). These scholars seek to move beyond or transcend what they term "symptomatic reading," which they describe as "an interpretive method that argues that the most interesting aspect of a text is what it represses" and that the interpreter is to reveal the text's hidden meaning by way of a master code, usually derived from Marxism or psychoanalysis (Best and Marcus 3). By contrast, surface reading insists on exploring what is "looked *at* rather than what we must train ourselves to see *through*" (9). Among the surfaces they are eager to explore are those that "locate narrative structures and abstract patterns on the surface, as aggregates of what is manifest in multiple texts as cognitively latent but semantically continuous with an individual text's presented meaning" (11). Surface reading is a helpful addition to the critical repertoire, and promises richer, more capacious, and more varied analyses; more importantly, it insists on a deep engagement with a particular work. It is not without problems, however; in its original formulation, it is too loosely defined

18 *The Reader in Modernist Fiction*

to be of more than heuristic value. In addition, the kind of readings I am performing in this book do not match up well with this approach. The material I explore here is partially hidden and does rest beneath the surface, to continue with these metaphors (which have been critiqued by Toril Moi). But these meanings are present and intended to be uncovered; it is the job of the characters (and the reader) to perceive this and provide appropriate, skeptical inferences.

Other, comparable approaches are also helpful and desirable. Eve Kosovsky Sedgwick in her article, "Paranoid Reading and Reparative Reading, or, You're So Paranoid You Probably Think This Essay is About You," eloquently urges us not to confine ourselves to symptomatic readings: "Subversive and demystifying parody, suspicious archaeologies of the present, the detection of hidden patterns of violence and their exposure: as I have been arguing, these infinitely doable and teachable protocols of unveiling have become the common currency of cultural and historicist studies" (143). Such paranoid (or symptomatic) practices "may simply have required a certain disarticulation, disavowal, and misrecognition of other ways of knowing, ways less oriented around suspicion," she argues. "The monopolistic program of paranoid knowing systematically disallows any explicit recourse to reparative motives, no sooner to be articulated than subject to methodical uprooting" (144). It is reparative readings that we are most in need of now, and the kind of interpretations that I am offering in this book fit well beneath this rubric. Methodologically, we may note that here too, the more limiting kind of reading we are urged not to follow and repeat is delineated much more thoroughly than the type of reading we should aspire to. This has led Michael Warner to doubt whether that reparative reading is a "structured program" or an explication. "For the most part, Sedgwick describes it as local, detailed, and unsystematized. Even the patterns she singles out have this partial character, such as a willingness to describe fragments or passages without a total schematization of the text." He concludes that reparative reading "seems to be defined less by any project of its own than by its recoil from a manically programmatic intensification of the critical" (17–18). In a comparable vein, Timothy Bewes calls for reading "with the grain." Here too we may applaud his practice and intentions, even as we quibble with his metaphors. The texts I analyze here can be said to have occasional knots, splits, imperfect rings, and bits of stray bark. Nevertheless, it is important to attempt to provide the most capacious readings that are aligned with the way the text situates itself as well as to indicate the ways in which such self-situating fails, as I will try to show in what follows. A somewhat

Introduction 19

similar move has been advocated by Rita Felski in her call for post-critical reading. Like Felski and some of the other recent theorists, I am not against symptomatic reading, but only its often "monopolistic program." Together, these new movements are setting forth salutary positions, though understandably somewhat vague in their current formulations. As a movement, they are opening up new space for approaches such as my own.

Before starting the study proper, I will briefly mention some slightly earlier and contemporary figures—H. G. Wells, Eça de Queirós, E. M. Forster, Somerset Maugham, and D. H. Lawrence—who utilized the act or scene of reading for quite different purposes than the high modernists did as they instead reiterated earlier enlightenment, neoclassical, or romantic positions. H. G. Wells discourses on reading in *The History of Mr. Polly* (1910). Alfred Polly, who had always enjoyed adventure fiction, becomes interested in literature once he meets up with two colleagues at one of his jobs. They do not fully appreciate the culture they try to imbibe, but on the whole, apart from a little pretension, it is a salutary experience that leaves the men the better for it. In his middle age, Mr. Polly "still read books when he had a chance—books that told of glorious places abroad and glorious times, that wrung rich humour from life, and contained the delight of words freshly and expressly grouped" (124). He especially enjoys the work of Joseph Conrad (129). Reading is not otherwise developed thematically in this novel, but presented as one more instance of the ways in which British society wastes the potential, aspirations, and happiness of the lower middle class. This work is an embodiment of the enlightenment tradition, and insists that reading, and the time and circumstances to enjoy it, are important aspects of a life worth living for all citizens.

Eminent Portuguese novelist Eça de Queirós, in *A Cidade e as serras* (*The City and the Mountains*, 1901), narrates the story of the wealthy absentee landlord, Jacinto, who lives in Paris on the Champs-Élysées. He believes a man can only be happy if he is "superlatively civilized" (7) and surrounds himself with a 30,000-volume library, subscribes to numerous newspapers and journals, and possesses several modern gadgets, including a powerful telescope, electronic pens, a paginating machine, and a private telegraph. But he is desperately bored, and reads little. His life is transformed by a visit to his estate in rural Portugal. There, his life and his reading are simplified and become intensely enjoyable. He finally is able to read and appreciate Homer and a few other authors, living a slower life connected to the villagers, untouched by modern transformations. This is ultimately a

20 *The Reader in Modernist Fiction*

conservative position that dismisses modern tastes and mechanisms in favor of a few established classics.

Maugham's story, "The Fall of Edward Barnard" (1921), relates a comparable story as it recounts the life of a man who leaves Chicago to go to Tahiti to make money but, once there, "goes native," finally refusing to leave the happy, carefree life he now enjoys. He explains to the man who has been sent to bring him back that in addition to coming to like the new life and the people, "I began to think. I had never had time to do that before. I began to read" (84). When his startled interlocutor protests that he had always read, Barnard responds that previously "I read for examinations. I read in order to be able to hold my own in conversation. I read for instruction. Here I learned to read for pleasure" (84). The strictly instrumental nature of the reading of an American businessman is contrasted with the more leisured and disinterested reading possible in a substantially precapitalist setting.

Other positions were also being articulated. In the first decades of the twentieth century, E. M. Forster was, like Wells, extremely interested in the spread of literary culture; unlike Wells, he was concerned about its fate as it engaged an ever wider audience and was put to previously unanticipated uses. Among Forster's actions in this sphere were his decision to teach Latin at the Working Men's College for several years and his investigation of the fate of the spread of knowledge in his fiction, most notably, *Howards End* (1910). In an early, unpublished short story, "Ansell" (*c*.1903), a classics student visits his cousin's estate in the country in order to complete his dissertation. In a large box are his copious notes and all the books he will be citing. But as they are crossing a steep ravine, the fencing gives way and the cart threatens to fall into the river far below. In the end, all humans and animals are safe: it is only the heavy box of books that is lost. After an initial state of shock, the scholar settles into a bucolic life revolving around the affection of the uneducated young gardener, an old boyhood friend. As the story concludes, it is suggested that this new situation will be superior to the life of a scholar. Early in the text, the protagonist scornfully alludes to Wordsworth's "The Tables Turned," a poem that deprecates scholarship and suggests that nature is a better tutor:

> Books! 'Tis a dull and endless strife:
> Come, hear the woodland linnet,
> How sweet his music! On my life,
> There's more of wisdom in it.

In an ironic reversal, "Ansell" affirms Wordsworth's stance as it goes on to dramatize the familiar Romantic opposition between nature and civilization and, as most of the romantics did, valorize the unlettered life of rustic simplicity (and implicit sexual happiness) above the dubious achievements of modern society—a theme that would also be developed in different ways by Somerset Maugham, as we have just seen, and D. H. Lawrence.

In Lawrence's *Lady Chatterley's Lover* (1928), the emptiness and sterility of the Chatterleys' marriage is symbolized rather crudely by Clifford's war-induced injury that leaves him incapable of having sex and, more interestingly, is also the emblem and cause of his interest in writing. The narrator describes the Chatterleys' life together as being like a dream, a cluster of shadows, a simulacrum of reality. Clifford's modernist style of fiction writing is denigrated as an "endless spinning of webs of yarn, of the minutiae of consciousness." Another character claims there was nothing in the stories and because of that, they wouldn't last. He adds, "Why should there be anything in them, why should they last?" (18). Reading and writing modern literature are equally barren acts for Lawrence; the fact that Clifford's work becomes successful in literary circles only shows how sterile those circles are.[12] After Connie Chatterley has made love with the gamekeeper, Mellors, Clifford asks her whether she likes Proust. No, she responds, Proust bores her: "all that sophistication! He doesn't have feelings, only streams of words about feelings," she explains, clearly being ventriloquized by Lawrence himself (194). The fact that Clifford likes Proust only shows that he is spiritually dead, Connie says—a sentiment no genuine modernist could imagine. Profound sexual love is signified here by an imperviousness to written words.[13] Lawrence is more vehement in his critical prose. In "Surgery for the Novel—Or a Bomb," he feels the pulses of James Joyce, Dorothy Richardson, and Marcel Proust: "You can hear the death rattle in their throats. They can hear it themselves" (*Selected* 155) The modernist novel is "dying in a very long-drawn-out fourteen-volume death agony, and absorbedly, childishly interested in the phenomenon" (*Selected* 155).

Considered together, we see that Forster's Ansell forgoes scholarly study for a simple life in the countryside without books; Maugham's Barnard abandons the life of a capitalist in order to enjoy thought, books, and conversation in a leisurely, tropical setting; while Lady Chatterley walks away from the sterile world of literature and into the vital embrace of the gamekeeper. Even though Maugham's protagonist escapes in order to read while the others

22   *The Reader in Modernist Fiction*

enjoy the release from reading, each work is, in this regard, essentially romantic and escapist, reprising an earlier nineteenth-century critique of the impersonal culture of an emerging industrial society and consequent valorization of natural settings. In chapter three, we will also see a similar move present in Elizabeth von Arnim's *The Enchanted April* (1922).

Forster's *A Room with a View* (1908) contains many of the elements that would appear in later modernist fiction, though it combines them in a different, less compelling manner. Early in the novel, in Florence, George Emerson abruptly kisses the surprised Lucy Honeychurch. Later, she tries to be understanding of this rudeness (which we now would call sexual assault) by explaining that "he looked like someone in a book" of gods and heroes (85). This scene is narrated by Lucy's cousin to a visiting novelist, Miss Lavish, who then includes a depiction of it in her next book. Back in the English countryside, the Emersons (with their library of bracing, modern books, including Nietzsche and Samuel Butler) move in to a nearby house. At a gathering at the Honeychurches', Lavish's novel appears and the kissing scene is read aloud. Afterwards, George gives Lucy, who is now engaged to Cecil Vyse, another unwanted kiss; he tells her "the book made me do that" (194). Ultimately, they are united. The apparent equation of reading and desire, however, does not fully hold since Cecil, an annoying, pretentious snob, says he "is no good for anything but books" (197). When Lucy tells him that she is canceling their engagement, she asserts: "you wrap yourself up in art and books and music, and would try to wrap me up. I won't be stifled" (201–02). Books here seem to be connected with several incommensurate relations: they bring one couple together and they drive another couple apart. With these opposed associations, they lose any specific resonance. It is true that the Emersons, the best educated of the characters, do perceive more than the others do, and they even inform Lucy that she actually loves George. The Emersons, though middle class, are lower in the class hierarchy than those around them. Here, the socially inferior are the most astute perceivers—a kind of dynamic, though rare in Forster, that will regularly be found among the high modernists.

In *Howards End*, we see a more nuanced encounter with reading and education, as Forster probes deeper into a number of seemingly unbridgeable cultural divisions. The central characters are defined in part by their relation to literature: the thoughtful, liberal, well-read Schlegel sisters represent the best of the older English tradition; Margaret is said to inhabit a "backwater, where nothing happened except art and literature, and where no one ever got married or succeeded in remaining engaged" (138). They are juxtaposed to the conceptually hollow Wilcox men, vigorous materialists who are scornful of all cultural interests or egalitarian concerns: they affirmed "that Equality was nonsense; Votes for Women nonsense; Art and Literature, except when conducive to strengthening the character, nonsense" (22). And then there is Leonard Bast, a poor, self-taught clerk, who is intoxicated by the idea of high culture and constantly strives to read and understand more books: "I care a good deal about improving myself by means of Literature and Art, and so getting a wider outlook," he asserts (49). His discourse about this passion for knowledge, however, characteristically ends "in a swamp of books" (110). Neither does he ever seem to be able to break into the closed circle of the truly educated; Margaret thinks: "Culture had worked in her own case, but during the last few weeks she had doubted whether it humanized the majority, so wide and so widening is the gulf that stretches between the natural and the philosophic man, so many the good chaps who are wrecked in trying to cross it" (105). The key figure here is Bast, dedicated reader and sexual interloper; it is most significant that he dies as a shelf of books literally falls on him; his attempts to raise himself up by his reading are not only futile, but perhaps fatal as well. In this culture war, there are three positions, the indifferent philistinism of the new class of wealth and power; the increasingly powerless, female-coded knowledge of traditional culture; and the lower levels of the middle class, with severely limited possibilities of educating themselves. Brian May concludes: "Liberal culture wrecks liberal selves, Forster suggests, because it simply does not 'work'" (88). The enlightenment promise of knowledge and power through reading is here challenged at both ends: it is neither as easily attained nor anywhere near as valuable as it had proclaimed itself to be.

The case of Forster reveals the divide in sensibility and thematics between the Edwardian and more insistently modernist perspectives. Just as there is nothing especially modernist about the narrative properties of *Howards End*, so its ideology turns out to be rather timidly conventional. Perhaps books don't kill Leonard Bast in the end so much as his attempt to rise socially or his sexual liaison with Helen Schlegel. The undifferentiated library at Howards End that falls on him probably represents class more than taste or knowledge. In these works, Forster seems unable to inscribe the possibility of a subversive knowledge. On the other hand, he makes clear that the epistemic center of the novel lies in the knowledge and

24 *The Reader in Modernist Fiction*

judgment of the women: most obviously the Schlegel sisters, but also Mrs. Wilcox and Mrs. Munt. They generally perceive what is going on around them, but are largely unable to affect the course of the most substantial events.

Having discussed these romantic and Edwardian examples, we may now move on to examine Henry James's idiosyncratic practice and the formation of what I identify as the skeptical modernist position by Joseph Conrad.

Notes

1. Tzvetan Todorov, using somewhat different terms, discusses this opposition in "Art According to Artaud" (*Poetics* 205–17).
2. This passage may be indebted to a comparable set of descriptions in Flaubert's *Bouvard et Pécuchet*, which I cite later in this introduction.
3. Watt, it should be noted, does not always stress the reader's participation in this drama, affirming instead that "as readers we witness every step by which the gap between individual perception and its cause is belatedly closed within the consciousness of the protagonist" (175).
4. Rohy also analyzes the feeling of liberation caused by the reading of early sexology in Radclyffe Hall's *The Well of Loneliness* (121–37).
5. "Ja, eine Frau muss schön sein, wenn sie die Männern gefallen soll. Da hat es ein Mann viel besser; wenn er nur seine fünf geraden Glieder hat, mehr braucht er nicht!" (4.86).
6. See Tina Young Choi for a compelling account of the relation between the germ theory of the transmission of disease to the structure of coincidence in Victorian multiplot novels.
7. For an account of the growth of education in the nineteenth century and the changes it precipitated in literature and society, see Alan Richardson, *Literature*.
8. Decoud tells his French journalistic associates, "My friends, you had better write up Señor Ribiera all you can in kindness to your own bondholders" (152); Bloom tells the editor of the *Daily Telegraph*: "I spoke with Mr. Keyes just now. He'll give a renewal for two months, he says. After he'll see. But he wants a par [i.e. a paragraph of "news" about the firm] to call attention in the *Telegraph* too, the Sunday pink" (120).
9. Austen is a bit more complex. As Alan Richardson explains, "Within the pages of *Northanger Abbey*, novel reading emerges as much more than an escapist or self-deluding pursuit: it promotes friendship, contributes to social distinction, forms a common topic and pursuit for men and women and can at best convey the 'greatest powers of the mind'" ("Reading" 400). See also 397–99.

10. Peter Brooks suggests that "the ambitious Dealauriers stands as the figure of the Balzacian novel within Flaubert's novel. And it is part of Flaubert's almost didactic demonstration that however well Deslauriers understands the system of the Balzacian novel, he is doomed to failure in the Flaubertian novel" (173). As Brooks also notes, the Balzacian novel itself stands for a much broader model of realist representation (171–72).

11. I argue that Proust presents yet another model, that of the incommensurability of the written and the real. Life will never live up to its depictions and thus always disappoint, while art can create images and effects that transcend those available in the ordinary realm of our experience.

12. Tony Pinkney points out that Lawrence's critique of modernism increases in each of the three successive versions of the novel; by the final version, Clifford "is now no longer just a modernist epigone, [but] more a notable representative of the movement itself" (124). He further adds that "before she sleeps with her gamekeeper, Constance Chatterley first goes to bed with modernism itself, in the person of the playwright Michaelis, and by the end of the novel she will even become a modernist painting, since her posing for him is the price the hypermodernist abstract artist Duncan Forbes extorts for being named as co-respondent in her divorce case" (125).

13. This relation does not change even after it is revealed that Mellors does have some books in his hut—books on the Russian revolution, even a few novels (212).

Chapter 1

From James to Conrad and Ford: Suppressed Narratives, Subaltern Reading, and the Drama of Interpretation

Before discussing the emergence of the modernist drama of skeptical reading in the work of Conrad, Joyce, and Woolf, it will be useful to have an overview of the figure of the reader in the work of Henry James. James's aesthetic and especially his poetics as delineated in his essays and prefaces articulate distinctive and typical modernist positions, and his writers and readers generally tend to match up rather snugly with the concepts of the implied author and the implied reader that would animate critical theory: his story "The Private Life" (1892) is an excellent illustration of the idea of the implied author *avant la lettre*; concerning the implied reader, James noted, "the writer makes the reader very much as he makes his characters" (*Theory* 321). James of course was deeply interested by the figure of the writer, the nature of literary fiction, and the roles of the unwritten and the unread; he was also concerned with the functions both of reading and of the failure to read. For an author with such interests, however, his depictions of the effects of reading are fairly vague; he rarely depicts the act of reading. Often, we are informed of the public status or genuine value of novels or other writings by fictional authors, but are provided with little concrete description of the precise nature of such works. There is an abundance of missing or lost manuscripts: Henry St. George burns his great novel at the insistence of his wife in "The Lesson of the Master" (1888); the Aspern papers are destroyed before they can be read; the only copy of the great work by Neil Paraday in "The Death of the Lion" (1894) is lost before it can be published; the scandalous letters of "Sir Dominic Ferrand" (1892) are burned instead of being published. In "The Middle Years" (1893), Dencombe expires as he recognizes he has attained his artistic maturity just before he can compose his masterpiece: "the pearl is the unwritten—the pearl is the

From James to Conrad and Ford   27

unalloyed, the *rest*, the lost!" (*Stories* 208).[1] It is the unread rather than the read that figure most prominently in these works.

As the example of Mrs. St. George attests to, reading modern fiction is considered a dangerous activity by some of the more conservative members of society. The wife of Mark Ambient, the charming author of the wicked novel *Beltraffio*, doesn't read what he writes—she finds his work "most objectionable" (*Stories* 72)—and fears that his ideas will corrupt their child. When asked, in front of his wife, whether he thinks young people should read any novels, Ambient responds: "Good ones—certainly not!" (*Stories* 77). When not dangerous, reading fiction can be misleading. Allen W. Menton observes of *The Ambassadors* (1903), "Strether's Parisian experience consists of his attempts to live out the various literary types he associates with Paris. Towards the end of the novel, James figures Strether as 'mixed up with the typical tale of Paris'" (286).

The dominant belief around which James weaves his fiction is that of a remote, isolated aestheticism. Again and again we see examples of exemplary literary brilliance that must wait for an ideal reader. Fairly characteristic is the situation of the fictional author Philip Vincent in "The Real Thing" (1891), an author "long neglected by the multitudinous vulgar and dearly prized by the attentive," who has "the happy fortune of seeing, late in life, the dawn and then the full light of a higher criticism" (174). Several of James's texts focus on the highly desirable yet difficult, rare, or at times nearly impossible union of outstanding author and appropriate readers: in "The Lesson of the Master," St. George states that "not more than two or three people" in England have the discrimination to perceive a work's living up to its full potential (*Stories* 133).

Such encounters are quite infrequent, even extraordinary; this is in fact the primary subject of "The Middle Years" (1893). The ailing author Dencombe rereads his just published novel, *The Middle Years*, and is surprised at how good it is: "He began to read and, little by little, in this occupation, was pacified and reassured. Everything came back to him, but came back with wonder, came back above all with a high and magnificent beauty. He read his own prose, he turned his own leaves, and had as he sat there with the spring sunshine on the page an emotion peculiar and intense" (*Stories* 194). He meets another man, a young doctor, who is also reading a book; "a novel, it had the catchpenny binding" (*Stories* 193), he thinks dismissively, until he realizes that the volume was another copy of his new work. The younger man is effusive in his admiration for it and, not knowing the identity of his new acquaintance, is offended that Dencombe

28   *The Reader in Modernist Fiction*

is marking up his copy with corrections. The writer later muses that "chance had brought the weary man of letters face to face with the greatest admirer in the new generation" (*Stories* 198). Dencombe, realizing he has finally come into his own as an author, hopes to live long enough to produce more in his mature style: "only today at last had he begun to *see*, so that all he had hitherto shown was a movement without direction. He had ripened too late" (*Stories* 203). The first review of his book is also laudatory. Sadly, he will not survive to fulfill his potential.

Two tales in particular indicate James's proximity to and distance from what I am referring to as the modernist drama of the critical reader: *In the Cage* (1898) and "The Figure in the Carpet" (1896). *In the Cage* is the story of a female telegraphist who sits in a "cage" of wood and wire as she sends telegrams for upper-class individuals. She notices two people, Lady Bradeen and Captain Everard, who appear to be having a love affair as they send each other coded telegrams under different names indicating times and places for their assignations. We are told that "she had seen all sorts of things and guessed all kinds of mysteries" (*Eight* 180), though it is the case that in her "world of whiffs and glimpses, she found her divinations work faster and stretch further" (186)—a situation abetted by the fact that she is an avid reader of fiction from the lending libraries (176). Eventually, a telegram goes astray and a scandal is about to break; Captain Bradeen appears and asks her to help him retrieve it. At this point she begins to realize how little she actually knew: "she felt how much she missed in the gaps and blanks and absent answers—how much she had had to dispense with: it was now black darkness save for this little wild red flare" (247). She is able to provide him the help he needs, and the crisis passes. She never sees him again. Later, learning of the subsequent fate of the two apparent lovers, she finally discovers how much she had misunderstood about their positions and relation. The story she had been reconstructing, imagining, and assisting turns out to have been largely her own invention. This kind of story strategy is essentially similar to what we will see in high modernist authors; its results, however, are exactly opposite as the central interpreter, often from the margins of society, is typically able to deduce or discover the hidden relations herself.

"The Figure in the Carpet" is explicitly about the elusive quest for a master design "hidden" by an eminent writer, Hugh Vereker, in all of his works. Though it is elusive, it remains present and in full view of the many readers and critics within the tale. Vereker agrees it is something like a complex figure visible in a Persian carpet; as he explains to those who are seeking the pattern, "My whole lucid effort gives [the reader] the clue—every page and line and letter . . . It governs every line, it chooses every word, it dots every i, it places every comma" (288); it is "the particular thing I've written my books most *for*" (*Stories* 286).

The story has produced a number of divergent critical views concerning the identity of the figure; it is emblematic of the new kind of interpretive tasks being set by the more ambitious sort of fiction, in which insufficiently perspicacious readers are left in the dark. Several critics, narratologists, and theorists of reading have understandably gravitated to this work.[2] Many have taken up the challenge and tried to find, in one form or another, the figure missed by the narrator. In one of the most far-reaching attempts, Tzvetan Todorov sees it as a miniature image of James's work as a whole: "the Jamesian narrative is always based on *the quest for an absolute and absent cause*"; he claims that "the absence of the cause or of the truth is present in the text—indeed, it is the text's logical origin and reason for being" (*Poetics* 145).

Other critics write this quest off as unknowable or illusory, a critical aporia or a kind of joke on the reader who must search in vain for an answer that is unobtainable, though this is a theory suggested and soon abandoned by the narrator early in the tale: "the buried treasure was a bad joke, the general intention a monstrous *pose*" (290). Shlomith Rimmon, whose attention to this work brought it to the center of several debates, argued that the novella supported two antithetical positions: that there *was* a figure in the carpet and that there was *no* figure in the carpet; the text was insistently and irresolvably ambiguous (95–115). J. Hillis Miller agrees that "the meaning of this story is fundamentally undecidable. It presents clues or narrative details supporting two or more incompatible readings" (*Reading* 97). "Therefore," he goes on to conclude, "all the critics who have presented 'monological' readings of it have fallen into a trap set not only by the story itself, in its presentation of an enigma that invites definitive clarification, but also by the critic's false presupposition that each good work of literature should have a single, logically unified meaning" (*Reading* 97). He goes on to give this a deconstructive twist by averring that work is fundamentally "unreadable": unreadability for him is "the generation by the text itself of a desire for a single meaning, while at the same time the text frustrates this desire" (98). But Henry James is not Gertrude Stein or even Franz Kafka; his work is typically predicated on—and, as we have just seen—frequently thematizes the existence of just such a definitive reading by a sufficiently

30 *The Reader in Modernist Fiction*

astute critical consciousness. It is, if anything, more an allegory of the failure of criticism (obsessed critics always miss their mark) than an example of indeterminism. The perspective offered in this study urges us to probe for an answer, albeit an obscure or radical one, and that we look from a marginalized perspective—in this case, a gay reading in which the unspoken figure is the literally unspeakable one of homosexuality, as Eric Savoy has cunningly argued. Having gone too far, Vereker's only recourse is to go still further toward the full flush of embarrassment. His final offer is to equate the "thing" with "the organ of life," Savoy writes, as he develops Fred Kaplan's observation that James's playfully erotic metaphors seem either impossibly innocent or embarrassingly explicit (233).[3]

Even those reluctant to acquiesce in this gay reading will certainly agree with the sexual nature of the cryptic figure, which functions as a jealous lover that demands unwavering fidelity (see Kappeler 77–80). Vereker is a tease about its identity and then urges the narrator not to discuss it with anyone else. The narrator wonders whether some sort of sexual union is necessary for its transmission: "Was the figure in the carpet traceable or discernable only for husbands and wives—for lovers supremely united?" (*Stories* 306). But Vereker denies this, and Corvick discovers the secret only after he has gone away from his fiancée in order to think more deeply about it. Once he has uncovered it, Vereker has him stay with him in Italy for a month. Corvick returns to England but refuses to tell his fiancée the secret until they are married. Shortly after the hurried wedding, he dies before he can write his article that explicates it, the "great intellectual feat that was obviously to have formed his climax" (*Stories* 305). The narrator is determined to learn whether he had divulged his secret: "Had there been a private ceremony for a palpitating audience of one? For what else but that ceremony had the nuptials taken place?" (*Stories* 305). He ascertains that the new widow did learn the secret, but she refuses to divulge it. The narrator even wonders whether he might have to marry Mrs. Corvick in order to solve the mystery (*Stories* 306). They eventually drift apart, and Mrs. Corvick goes on to marry an inferior critic, Drayton Deane. After she dies in childbirth our narrator, as obsessed as ever, tries to learn whether she had divulged the critical revelation to Deane. But she had said nothing to him, and once Deane learns the entire story, he feels she has betrayed him with her silence.

James thus proves to be a highly suggestive but ultimately wayward link in the trajectory from Flaubert to Conrad, Joyce, and Ford. Despite the presence of numerous readers and interpreters in James's canon, only "The Figure in the Carpet"—and then only in the queer reading offered by Savoy—employs something approximating this model of what I call "critical reading." In "In the Cage," James cannot allow his female, lower-class clerk any interpretive insight; his lower-class women can never read between and around the lines they transmit. His position is ultimately that of an aestheticist: he continually stages the drama of a brilliant author hoping to encounter the ideal reader who will perfectly understand his finest strokes, even though death regularly carries off the writer soon after he begins to be fully appreciated. In this regard he is in part the inverse of the other authors I will focus on in this study; James dramatizes the arduous quest for transparent communication of the highest order, whereas Conrad, Joyce, Ford, Mansfield, Faulkner, and Porter point out the deleterious consequences of the uncritical reading of inaccurate, inferior, or mystifying writing.

The other difference is in the relation between literature and sex. For the modernists, these go hand in hand, if that is the proper metaphor. James, for his part, places them in opposition, especially concerning male authors and their wives. "The Lesson of the Master" is precisely the antagonistic relation of the two: in order to produce art, one must renounce heterosexual union; if one falls for the latter (and in James it is a falling), one must renounce the former. As Suzanne Kappeler observes, the "Lion" in "The Death of the Lion" (1894) "divorced his mundane wife in order to live with his art alone; and his devoted disciple, who narrates the story, effectively staves off another woman and potential lover, to prevent her from disturbing the domestic harmony of the Master and his Muse" (79). In this case the narrator suffers: "by choosing to marry the girl himself he is destined to become (only) a literary critic or editor" (79).

Joseph Conrad

The act and theme of interpretation and misinterpretation run throughout Conrad's works. Books and reading also figure prominently as recurrent motifs. Particularly interesting is how often the act of reading proves to be powerless, dangerous, or even fatal. In *An Outcast of the Islands* (1896), we learn that Almayer has insisted on having an elaborate office constructed on the remote island of Sambir, complete with an impressive desk, a revolving chair, bookshelves, and a safe. As the Malays wonder what all those books could be for, an old helmsman explains that they were books of magic which gave

32   *The Reader in Modernist Fiction*

the white men "their wicked wisdom and their strength" (299–300). Almayer, however, soon realizes the uselessness of these artifacts in the remote setting; "he found no successful magic in the blank pages of his ledgers" (300). From the beginning, his books are worthless.

As noted in the introduction, the inability of the station managers in "An Outpost of Progress" (1897) to read critically is both an emblem of their unfitness and a contributing cause of their subsequent deaths. Amar Acheraïou writes: "The bulk of Conrad's [character] readers are given to reading light literature and popular newspapers; they are commonly portrayed as myopic, incompetent readers tied to surface reading and literal meaning. Even when they happen to read serious literature they usually fail to grasp its deeper insights, as shown by Kayerts and Carlier" (95). In *Nostromo* (1904), Pedro Montero's "ability to read did nothing for him but fill his head with absurd visions" (387). In the garrets of various Parisian hotels he would devour "the lighter sort of historical works in the French language"; this compulsive, uncritical reading turns out to be "one of the immediate causes of the Monterist revolt" (387). The opening of *The Secret Agent* (1907) describes the reading material offered for sale in Verloc's shop: its juxtaposition of anarchist journals and pornographic books represents a union of moral and intellectual bankruptcy which will lead directly to Winnie's wish that her brother had never been to school: "He's always taking away those newspapers from the window to read. He gets a red face poring over them" (60). Peter Nohrnberg comments: "Stevie's involuntary bodily response to the anarchist papers aligns their inflammatory political content with the pornographic 'shady wares' of Verloc's shop ... Like the licentious photographs contained within 'very flimsy' envelopes, the 'obscure newspapers, badly printed' show a correlation between shady wares and shoddy goods" (54). At the other end of the spectrum, extensive philosophical reading causes Axel Heyst's father to despise the world in *Victory* (1915).

We find a sustained interrogation of romantic expectations derived from reading in the Marlow narratives; this is especially prominent in "Youth" (1902) and *Lord Jim* (1900). Both texts fuse literary censure of romantic characters, settings, and plots with a social critique of idealism, exoticism, and idealism. In "Youth," the young Marlow admires his ship's motto, "Do or Die." "I remember it took my fancy immediately. There was a touch of romance in it, something that made me love the old" ship (*Youth* 5). After a terrible storm at sea, the ship's crew is wet and miserable, pumping for their lives, but Marlow is exhilarated, thinking "this is the deuce of an adventure—something you read about; and it is my first voyage as second mate" (12). It will come as no surprise that his shipboard reading consists of a romantic novel by Thomas Carlyle and Fred Burnaby's swashbuckling account of his adventures in Central Asia. Once on shore, he acquires a complete set of Byron's works. Marlow's intoxication with things romantic includes Orientalist fantasies of Southeast Asia: "I loved the ship more than ever, and wanted awfully to get to Bangkok. To Bangkok! Magic name, blessed name" (15). The East, frequently exoticized and feminized in the works of Byron that he carries with him, seems "impalpable and enslaving, like a charm, a whispered promise of mysterious delight" (37). As his beloved ship burns and sinks behind him, Marlow remains intoxicated by the images of the Orient that have been constructed by books and other adjacent discourses.

"Heart of Darkness" (1899) can be read as a battle between two rival narratives of the nature of colonialism: one written, public, official, and false; the other largely oral, discussed in private, and accurate. By preserving Kurtz's public image and allowing his discourse on the civilizing mission of colonialism to be published—after first tearing off the incriminating handwritten postscript ("Exterminate all the brutes!" *Youth* 118)—Marlow implicates himself within the public, official narrative even as he exposes its fallaciousness to his friends. Especially intriguing is the drama of misreading that Conrad stages in this work. Originally published in three installments in *Blackwell's Magazine*, a highly prestigious but quite conservative venue, Conrad could not set forth his anticolonial sentiments in a straightforward manner. He establishes a frame narration with a primary narrator who is a proud Englishman and pro-empire, though the examples he cites of England's storied past tend to deconstruct the value he ascribes to them: Francis Drake was a privateer, that is, a licensed pirate who put cities to the torch, while all the members Franklin's expedition died in the Arctic, some after engaging in cannibalism. Marlow's interior narrative entirely undercuts the imperialist ideology of the frame narrator, the other listeners on board the *Nellie*, and the official position of the British government and its various supporters. Conrad's ruse worked: as the reviewer for the *Manchester Guardian* put it, "it must not be supposed that Mr. Conrad makes attack upon colonization, expansion, even upon Imperialism" (cited in Shaffer, 71–72). Intriguingly, as Brian Shaffer points out, "the members of Marlow's *Nellie* audience appear to misconstrue his tale, viewing it a conformist (if also unsuccessful) adventure romance" rather than a biting though often subtle critique of British sensibilities and European colonial practices. Shaffer goes on to argue that "Marlow's audience is built

34   *The Reader in Modernist Fiction*

into the tale in order to implicate Conrad's readers in the imperial crimes and hypocritical habits of mind," thereby demonstrating their culpability (72).

In *Lord Jim*, the protagonist first becomes interested in the sea because of his reading: "after a course of light holiday literature his vocation for the sea had declared itself" (5); Jim was promptly sent to a merchant marine training ship much like the *Conway* in "The Secret Sharer." Onboard that vessel, "he would forget himself, and beforehand live in his mind the sea-life of light literature. He saw himself saving people from sinking ships, cutting away masts in a hurricane, swimming through a surf with a line" and other scenarios, some of which he would in fact go on to experience later in his career (6). Naturally, he has always imagined himself as "an example of devotion to duty, and as unflinching as a hero in a book" (6). But when he actually encounters a life-threatening situation at the side of the training ship, he freezes; others rush past him to perform the rescue.

Once he goes to sea and actually enters those "regions so well known to his imagination," he "found them strangely barren of adventure" (10). An event requiring good judgement, quick thinking, and considerable courage does takes place on the *Patna*, which Jim believes is about to sink with 800 people on board. Jim jumps off the ship into a boat below, leaving the passengers to perish in the darkness. This act defines his public life and haunts him by the characterization it implies. Marlow explains it in relation to the narratives he has encountered: "His confounded imagination had evoked for him all the horrors of panic, the trampled rush, the pitiful screams, boats swamped—all the appalling incidents of a disaster at sea he had ever heard of" (88). Jim himself seems to feel no guilt, only shame, and goes on to longingly imagine the heroic story that would have emerged had he stayed on the ship which, it turned out, did not sink. "I could see in his glance darted into the night all his inner being carried on, projected headlong into the fanciful realm of recklessly heroic aspirations" (83); "with every instant he was penetrating deeper into the impossible world of romantic achievements," Marlow continues (83).

Attempting to flee the widespread narrative of his disgrace, Jim moves ever farther east and into more remote territory. Marlow is happy to assist him, knowing that "Romance had singled Jim for its own—and that was the true part of the story" (282). The final act of Jim's life "is romantic beyond the wildest dreams of his boyhood" (342). In Patusan Jim is able to create the heroic narrative he has always sought; local legend even invests him with supernatural powers. The ring he uses to authenticate messages when communicating with the chief is, he states, "like something you read of in books" (233–34), but as Philip Wegner points out, it is only true of "the kind of books Jim himself reads" (193).[4] When Jim shows Marlow the villagers, he similarly (and revealingly) comments, "They are like people in a book, aren't they?" (260). Fittingly, Jim's demise is brought about by hearing a vague version of his own narrative in the mouth of another, and by giving that figure, the murderous "Gentleman Brown," some of the same trust and exculpation that he had always wanted to have bestowed upon himself. This final, uncritical misreading will cost him his life.

Margaret Cohen, moving beyond the "symptomatic" reading offered by Fredric Jameson, draws attention to the referential aspects of the texts that Jameson's reading ignores. She observes that across the Marlow trilogy, "adventures at sea will yield to the narrator's work of wresting intelligibility from partial information" as "Conrad's experiments with portraying events, characters, and the phenomenal world" become intelligible through a series of "intellectual processes resembling navigation" (69). This is certainly the case, though we need not limit the epistemological model to navigation, or the novels to those set on the sea, but rather should incorporate navigation into Conrad's larger hermeneutical matrix. *Lord Jim* is a novel centrally concerned with interpretation and misinterpretation. In addition to how we read other people and unfamiliar topographies, the novel questions how we construe words ("wretched cur" 70), specific facts ("as if facts could explain anything!" 29), patterns of behavior (individual destinies are as "graven in imperishable characters upon the face of a rock" 186), and the nature of reality (every variety of idealism is always mistaken). Conrad dramatizes the ways in which we construe existence, and frequently restages the interpretive puzzles that obsess his central characters for the reader—especially what Cohen calls "the cunning reader" (66)—to engage in as well.

"The Secret Sharer" (1912)[5] is probably Conrad's most audacious drama of narration and reception; here, the primary battleground is the correct interpretation of oral narratives. The work seems at first to be profoundly multivalent, even to the point of self-contradiction. It is at the same time both a writerly text that invites a wide variety of incompatible interpretations and, curiously, a readerly text that is quite explicitly about accuracy in interpretation as it repeatedly stages and evaluates interpretive acts. The critical literature, however, has generally tended to exemplify the first of these aspects rather than explore implications of the latter. The paradox in this treatment of the

36   *The Reader in Modernist Fiction*

text is that the larger hermeneutical principles it ultimately affirms are ones that cast doubt on the validity of many of the interpretive stances it seems to have solicited. The widely recognized multiplicity of different readings this text indulges is itself threatened by a profound skepticism that the work also invites us to assume. The tale contains several acts and tropes of reading, interpretation, and understanding. At the beginning of the narrative, the ship is at anchor in the Gulf of Siam, far from harbor. The first character that the captain-narrator introduces us to is the first mate, a man who is characterized by his fascination with interpretation: "His dominant trait was to take all things into earnest consideration . . . As he used to say, he 'liked to account to himself' for practically everything that came in his way" (94).[6] Wondering whether his peremptory dismissal of his officers from the deck would be construed not as generosity but rather eccentricity ("Goodness only knew how that absurdly whiskered mate would 'account' for my conduct" [97]), the captain himself walks into a mystery. The side ladder is down; strangely, it can't be pulled up. The captain is astounded and, just like "that imbecile mate," tries "to account for it" (97). In the water at the bottom of the ladder is yet another enigma in the naked figure of a man named Leggatt, who has escaped from the brig on a nearby ship, the *Sephora*.

Just who he is and exactly what he has done are not at all obvious. Among the uncontested facts of the case are the following: Leggatt killed a man on the *Sephora* during a storm, he was imprisoned on board, and he later escaped overboard and swam to the narrator's own ship. The dead man, presented by Leggatt as a contemptible wretch, threatened the survival of the crew and in the crisis had to be dealt with swiftly and decisively. Leggatt claims he saw what had to be done, was trying to set a reefed topsail, throttled the man who tried to hinder him, saved the ship, and was then imprisoned for his efforts. The narrator buys this story *in toto*, and even helps Leggatt produce it. In the dialogue in which the killing is announced, we see the peculiar dynamics of this co-narration. The captain, after hearing Leggatt say he was the mate of the *Sephora*, immediately inquires,

"Aha! Something wrong?"
"Yes. Very wrong indeed. I've killed a man."
"What do you mean? Just now?"
"No, on the passage. Weeks ago. Thirty-nine south.
When I say a man—"
"Fit of temper," I suggested, confidently.
The shadowy, dark head, like mine, seemed to nod imperceptibly . . . (101)

As indeed it might: the captain has just provided the killer with a sympathetic ear and an acceptable motive. Leggatt continues in the vein suggested by the captain—a good man, resolute in a crisis, now in an unfortunate bind. It works well. Within a few more lines the captain states, "He appealed to me as if our experiences had been as identical as our clothes . . . I knew well enough also that my double there was no homicidal ruffian. I did not think of asking him for details, and he told me the story roughly in brusque, disconnected sentences. I needed no more" (102). With the evidence that the narrator has at this point, he has no plausible ground to make such a judgment, either according to the logic of legitimate interpretation already established in the text, or by the ordinary standards of appropriate inference: if one were to meet a largely naked stranger outside a bus depot who admits he has just killed a man, one would certainly not be so quick to offer him clothing, a hiding place, and excuses for his act. Instead, the captain constructs a rather Byronic character and sensibility for the fugitive.

Throughout the piece, the narrator seems determined that no fact or set of facts will tamper with the flattering conception he has so quickly formed of Leggatt. The vast majority of this novella's interpreters have—often equally uncritically—trusted the judgment of the narrator on this point. But despite the fact that alternative accounts of this affair are generally suppressed, they nevertheless leave some significant traces that call into question Leggatt's version. Archbold, the captain of the *Sephora*, tells the narrator that in the course of his thirty-seven years at sea, he has "never heard of such a thing happening in an English ship" (117). This comment does not make any sense when applied to the noble act of impassioned duty described by Leggatt, which is after all an occurrence that would not be so uncommon. Neither is it the kind of act that would normally cause someone to express wonder that Leggatt can sleep at night after what he has done, as Archbold says to Leggatt's face (107). The fact that Leggatt discloses this to the narrator only invites doubt concerning his own account. The same is also true of the unrecorded account provided by the crew of the *Sephora*, which elicits from the first mate the comments, "a very extraordinary story," "horrible enough for me" and "beats all these tales we hear about murders in Yankee ships" (122). These statements too make no sense unless directed to a much more spectacular act of criminality than any Leggatt will admit to. Here too we have to ask why Conrad would include these statements if not to cast doubt on Leggatt's account.

38   *The Reader in Modernist Fiction*

The mate refers to the fact that American ships had a well-earned reputation for brutality in the 1880s and 1890s. Joseph Goldberg writes:

> The "Red Record" of American maritime industry drawn up by the Sailors' Union of the Pacific listed charges by over 100 ships' crews over a period of 11 years of 15 deaths from maltreatment; instances of loss of limbs, eyes, or teeth; other injuries of a permanent character, including insanity; and several suicides attributable to persecution. It was reported that only seven convictions were obtained against the officers involved, with punishments largely nominal. Although flogging had been prohibited by statute in 1850, corporal punishment was not prohibited, the effect being "merely to change its character from the specific to the general: it prohibited the cat; and by implication authorized the use of the belaying-pin and handspike" (11).

It was not until 1898—several years after the setting of the tale—that the White Act prohibited corporal punishment "such as that meted out by the 'bully mates' who hitherto had relied on their fists, belaying pins, and handspikes to enforce discipline" (Bauer 285), often in an arbitrary or brutal manner. Again we must wonder, just what did Leggatt actually do? This of course leads to the corollary question of just how far off the narrator's perceptions and judgments really are.

On purely psychological grounds, the narrator can be described as very strange. As J. D. O'Hara has pointed out, he demonstrates his irresponsibility by leaving his post as watch to go below for a cigar, then leaving it again as Leggatt climbs the ladder unwatched while he goes back for some clothes. This is indeed "wildly improbable as a description of an English captain coping with such a strange visitor in a foreign land" (447); the captain in fact leaves his watch three times that night. Nearly as dubious is the parallel dereliction of his duty to his men when he gives Leggatt half the money intended to buy fresh fruit and vegetables for the crew: these provisions were as important for morale as nutrition on a long voyage before the advent of refrigeration.

The narrator is justly famous in critical circles for his feelings of isolation, of being a stranger; when he says "I felt that it would take very little to make me a suspect person in the eyes of the ship's company" (110), he may well be underestimating the distance between himself and his justifiably apprehensive crew. His odd behavior, starting with his admittedly unusual taking of that fateful watch and continuing with the strange actions designed to protect Leggatt, does cause some perfectly understandable apprehension, most palpably when he feigns deafness while Archbold is trying to apprehend a fugitive and, at the end, when the narrator nearly runs the ship aground for no apparent reason—and for no good reason either, given that Leggatt was such an admirable swimmer and therefore should not need to be so close to the shore in order to reach it.[7]

The captain's discourse is curiously charged with descriptions of his own mental instability: "the dual working of my mind distracted me almost to the point of insanity" (113–14), "It was very much like being mad" (114), "my nerves were so shaken that I could not govern my voice" (128), "I had come creeping quietly as near insanity as any man who has not actually gone over the border" (130). The repeated references to madness strongly suggest that something much more substantial than mere unreliability is afflicting the narrator; coming from the mouth of the one who most desires to maintain his credibility, they would seem to constitute an unwitting admission of genuine and severe mental instability.[8]

In one revealing passage the narrator comments on the mate's tapping his forehead with his forefinger while talking with "a confidential air" to the ship's carpenter. He goes on to explain that although it was too far to hear a word, he nevertheless had no doubt that this pantomime "could only refer to the strange new captain" (128). Again, there is no compelling rational foundation for this inference: there are many other equally plausible explanations for this gesture—one that indeed is unremarkable coming from a man who likes to "get to the bottom of things." The captain's interpretation is closer to paranoia than probability. This is also the case when he hears Archbold's judgement of Leggatt's unfitness as an officer: "I had become so connected in thoughts and impressions with the secret sharer of my cabin that I felt as if I, personally, were being given to understand that I, too, was not the sort that would have done for the chief mate of a ship like the *Sephora*" (119). The captain here admits that his feeling of resentment has its source in his own psychic projections rather than in anything Archbold may have actually implied.

This behavior in turn suggests a nautical intertext that would resonate powerfully in the minds of many of the period, particularly those connected to the sea. I am referring here to the events— real and imagined—on the American brig, the *Somers*, in November 1842, which one historian calls "the most discussed mid-nineteenth century naval episode of any that bore the imprint of mutiny" (Guttridge 116). This is a historical narrative that itself continues to engender and defy interpretation, and involves unreliable narrators, unrecorded counter-narratives, and crucial events that may never

40 *The Reader in Modernist Fiction*

have taken place. As James E. Valle writes: "The Somers mutiny may not, in fact, have been a mutiny at all." It is not clear whether the three men condemned and hanged at sea were really plotting to capture a US vessel and murder her officers, or whether they were simply "the victims of an overwrought commanding officer with a hyperactive imagination . . . The facts we do know are utterly baffling and include evidence to support either hypothesis" (108–09). Some of the damning "evidence," it might be noted, included "a good deal of tense whispering in odd corners of the berth deck" (109). The oddities of the behavior of the captain would thus carry additional ominous overtones to the crew, who might have to pay for his hyperactive imagination with their flesh; I believe that any suspicion they may feel toward the captain is entirely justified. I would like to suggest here that for a seaman of the period, the commander of the *Somers* would likely come quickly to mind as an ominous potential double of the story's narrator-captain. We should also treat the captain's self-serving interpretations with appropriate skepticism, and try to listen to the muted voices of the ordinary seamen whom Conrad so deeply respected.[9]

The vast majority of interpreters of this work have in varying degrees been seduced by the rhetoric of the captain.[10] To get to the other, obscured accounts in the narrative (and to the class-inflected sensibilities of those who utter them) it is necessary first to move beyond the captain's "point of view"—and I use this term in both its psychological and narratological senses. A few critics have offered more skeptical readings. Michael Murphy argues that the captain "is in some important respects an unreliable narrator" (193); Murphy does not claim the narrator "is lying, but simply that he is not telling the whole story" (194).[11] A major piece of evidence for this interpretation (also noted by Robert D. Wyatt) is the determination of the narrator to suppress all rival accounts of Leggatt and his activities on the *Sephora*. As Murphy explains, Captain Archbold "raises his voice to tell his story. What is that story? Oh, 'it is not worthwhile to record that version.' We should be the judges of that, but we do not get the chance. All we get are bits, though Conrad makes sure they are significant bits" (195–96).

One may inquire more deeply into the nature, motives, and appropriateness of the narrator's identification of himself with Leggatt. At the outset, the case made for their similarity is extremely rapid and not particularly judicious. Based at first on what he calls "pure intuition" and "a mysterious communication" (99), the captain quickly imagines an entire psychology and, soon after, a personal

From James to Conrad and Ford   41

history for the brusque stranger before him who is said to speak in disconnected sentences (102). This resembles more the infatuation of an imaginative new lover than the appropriate behavior of a vigilant commander. The captain goes on to innocently believe every statement, claim, and judgment set forth by Leggatt, never wanting to scrutinize the other's discourse critically: "I had not interrupted him. There was something that made comment impossible in his narrative, or perhaps in himself; a sort of feeling, a quality, which I can't find a name for" (109). These kinds of romantic, unnamable qualities, however, often refer to delusive projections.

The descriptive passages in which the narrator identifies physical resemblances between the two men also reveal much about their actual relation. An early mention of their similarity is literally shrouded in darkness: "The shadowy dark head, like mine, seemed to nod imperceptibly above the ghostly grey of my sleeping suit. It was, in the night, as though I had been faced by my own reflection in the depths of a somber and immense mirror" (101). It is certainly a very opaque mirror, through which the narrator can only see darkly and fitfully. The oddest statement of all comes after the narrator, remarking on the expression of Leggatt's face, admits, "He was not a bit like me, really" (105). This disclosure utterly undercuts all other affirmations of identity; I can only conclude that any similarities, physical or psychological, are largely projections of the narrator onto the other man, a series of fabrications that have little or no objective validity. As Robert Wyatt puts it, "there is almost no factual evidence for the narrator's felt sense of identification, other than their shared youth and the coincidence that they are both Conway boys. Whatever identification the narrator feels is more the consequence of his imagination than any similar, objective conditions" (18).[12] There is consequently little reason to wonder why the captain fears Archbold's alternative interpretations, characterizations, and counter-narratives: "If he had only known how afraid I was of his putting my feeling of identity with the other to the test!" (120) the captain writes, and he is right to feel alarm at the idea of such an investigation because it is a test he cannot expect to pass. For similar reasons, Daniel R. Schwarz has observed that the captain's "flattering description of Leggatt is continually modified until it is almost contradicted," and that "the process of idealizing his double . . . is arbitrary and noncognitive" (105).

The ultimate basis of the captain's identification with the fugitive may be simple class prejudice. Cedric Watts points out that both men "are ex-Conway boys, and thus members of a British social and

42   *The Reader in Modernist Fiction*

maritime elite; both have the tone, style, phraseology and assumptions of gentlemen rather than of the working class," and are thus "privileged 'officer material' from the start of their careers" (27). Consequently, they are objects of resentment to both their crews, having been appointed to positions of command by decrees in high places "over the heads of older and possibly more experienced seamen" who instead had to laboriously make their way through the ranks (27). It hardly needs to be added that the same class identification is a common feature of middle-class readers' responses to this narrator, and may partially explain why the captain's version of the events is so rarely questioned in any fundamental way.

Who then is the curious fugitive? If the discourse of the narrator is streaked with images of insanity, that of Leggatt keeps returning to killing: he speaks of "miserable devils that have no business to live at all" (101); affirms "somebody else might have got killed—for I would not have broken out only to get chucked back" (107); states that "[s]omebody would have got killed for certain, and I did not want any of that" (109); and notes, "Do you think that if I had not been pretty fierce with them I should have got the men to do anything?" (124). Ultimately, this language even begins to infect the narrator's imagination: after the steward goes into the captain's inner cabin where Leggatt is hiding, not a sound is heard; the narrator himself can't help wondering, "Had my second self taken the poor wretch by the throat?" (129). Leggatt's allusive self-situating is also very revealing: "What does the Bible say? 'Driven off the face of the earth'" (132). The reference is to Genesis 4.13–14; the question it raises is why would a man who only did what he claims had to be done go on to identify his situation with that of Cain, a jealous and willful murderer? (132). In a practice we will see repeatedly in the course of this study, the allusion made by a central character backfires, and discloses the opposite of what it is intended to do.

We are not able to say for certain what Leggatt is, but we can be sure that he is not nearly as good as the rather romantic, heroic story he provides for himself. Beyond that he is merely a blank slate on which the narrator traces the figure he needs to find. We know, that is, exactly what the narrator wants Leggatt to be, but we can never know what he is in himself. He may simply be a reckless devil with a smooth tongue who is skilled in telling the right lie to the right person. But there is insufficient evidence to determine whether he is or is not "a murderous ruffian," to use a phrase Conrad himself explicitly rejected (*Letters* vol 5, 121). In the end, we have very little more than the captain's "edition" of Leggatt's narrative, itself fairly consistent

From James to Conrad and Ford **43**

but unable to account for the numerous anomalies, elisions, and contradictions that surround it. The narrative of Leggatt's life is both more ambiguous and more amenable to distinctively modernist interpretive strategies than has generally been accepted.

As might be expected in a work that consistently stages and thematizes narrative interpretation, there are a great number of potentially self-reflexive statements concerning speech, tale telling, and narrative genres. Leggatt claims to be motivated by his dread of being trapped within a factual but inescapable story; the mere facts, once related on shore, are certain to be misunderstood and thrust into the service of a very different narrative context: as we have noted, his is a "sufficiently fierce story to make an old judge and a respectable jury sit up a bit," it is hardly a "[n]ice little tale for a quiet tea party" (103). Leggatt's request to be marooned is first objected to on narrative grounds ("We are not living in a boy's adventure tale" [131]) but, as is often the case in Conrad, men do sometimes act as if they lived in such a fictitious universe. At one point the narrator refers to "the chapter of accidents that counts for so much in the book of success" (123), an apt metaphor of the confused action of the tale whose full import the narrator literally cannot imagine.

As the tale ends, the now self-assured captain affirms, "Nothing! no one in the world should stand now between us . . . the perfect communion of a seaman with his first command" (143). He has all the confidence that youth and idealism can engender. He has deserted his watch, alienated his crew, harbored a killer, hidden him from the authorities, given him money that was intended for his crew, and nearly destroyed his first command and marooned his own men for no good reason. He is entirely ignorant of the situation around himself, more so than the young Marlow, gloriously oblivious at the end of "Youth."

The novella's general interpretive situation may well remind one of that of "The Black Mate," in which the hair of Bunter, the first mate, rapidly changes from jet black to pure white. Bunter tells his superstitious captain that the sudden transformation was caused by his having seen a ghostly apparition, when in fact the event actually had a very material cause—Bunter's loss of his bottles of hair dye during a storm. And as Mark Wollaeger writes, since the mate's "story works, readers who miss Conrad's many clues are at least temporarily grouped with the credulous captain as the butt of the joke" (*Joseph* 37). The captain cannot help but believe the fabrication he wants to hear, and goes on to invent a fictitious biography to explain why his troubled mate was chosen for a visit from beyond the grave.

44 The Reader in Modernist Fiction

The narrator of "The Secret Sharer" resembles "Lord" Jim, who could never get the facts of his case to square with his preferred narrative of those facts, and whose death and the destruction of those he loved is directly caused by his unjustified act of identification with "Gentleman Brown"—the latter quite possibly another fine Conway boy or parson's child, if not exactly the baronet's son as claimed by the stories about him—but certainly a master at discerning another's vulnerabilities and then fashioning a discourse to exploit them. The result is a supremely ironic and thus typically Conradian closure, in which the tortuous route between original intention and final state can hardly be conceived by the person who has had to experience it. Perhaps most of all, the interpretive dynamics of this text resemble those of "Il Conde," which Keith Carabine describes as being written in a way to "deceive (say) the readers of a summer number of a magazine, but artfully designed to persuade the discriminating reader to detect another, untold, tale of a homosexual encounter that went badly wrong" (68–69, see also Hawthorn 23–24).

The narrator of "The Secret Sharer" is a prisoner of a hermeneutical circle that he has both constructed and ensnared himself within. He has invented a noble and resolute personality for Leggatt for which there is no compelling evidence, and perceived an identity between them that probably does not exist: "He was not a bit like me, really." He is so obsessed with his own inner drama that he is losing touch with the real events and relations around him. Murphy is right to suggest a parallel between this work and James's "The Turn of the Screw." I believe we may go further, and legitimately find an interesting pairing with Nabokov's *Despair*, in which the protagonist, upon finding what seems to be a double of himself, kills the man, assumes his identity, and starts a new life. He is, however, readily apprehended, since no one else thinks he looks like the strange man he insists is his mirror image. "The Secret Sharer" is not a last, tired reworking of the by then rather hackneyed theme of the Doppelgänger, but instead a skeptical parody of this familiar Romantic topos. I believe that this position, though admittedly at the far end of the range of existing critical interpretations, nevertheless offers the most comprehensive explanation of the relevant events, images, and figures of this rich text.

Such a reading, it goes without saying, has significant implications for other interpretations of this text. It opposes Frederick Karl's claim that the tale is one of Conrad's "most straightforward and obvious works. Its narrative is a model of clarity" (233). On the other hand, the reading I have been setting forth here is perfectly consonant with recent queer interpretations that point to hidden sexual references and allusions that initiates would be able to decipher and comprehend; the hidden meaning of such forbidden discourse is a fitting analogue of the epistemological challenges of modernism, many of whose authors were queer. The gay reading of the text connects interpretation with sexuality in a way that Conrad had largely kept separate up to this point in his career. James Phelan refines the reading first proposed by scholars like Robert Hodges while situating it within a reader-response framework. There are a number of scenes and expressions that make such a subterranean reading very compelling. The narrator states, "At night I would smuggle him into my bed-place, and we would whisper together" (110). Leggatt is equally tender to the narrator; he states that, while naked, "I didn't mind being looked at. I—I liked it." (110). He also notes "'It's a great satisfaction to have got somebody to understand. You seem to have been there on purpose.' And in the same whisper, as if we two whenever we talked had to say things to each other that were not fit for the world to hear, he added, 'It's very wonderful'" (132). As they part, "Our hands met gropingly, lingered united in a steady, motionless clasp for a second" (138).

Critical opinion remains divided on the degree of homosocial bonding implied in this text; the evidence of a gay sensibility is highly suggestive but ultimately inconclusive. Phelan expresses the situation in these terms: "On the one hand, the evidence points to a design on Conrad's part that the authorial audience needs to discern; indeed, without such a pattern of evidence, I would not suggest that this secret is a plausible one. On the other hand, I can't help wondering how much my perception of this secret is [merely] a consequence of my historical moment"; how much, in fact, he has created it (139). If forced to choose between these mutually exclusive positions, he states that he does not know which one is right.

My analysis suggests that the narrator feels a profound connection to Leggatt that is best explained by a deep attraction to him that is independent of any actual facts. Affection, empathy, and closeness are clearly present, though I suspect it is more accurate to designate them as homosocial than homosexual per se: this is the period at which modern conceptions of homosexuality were being formed, and the relation Conrad depicts here is rather a deep same-sex friendship and seems to antedate such formations. Richard Ruppel explains, "it would be ahistorical to describe any of Conrad's male characters—[including] the captain/narrator of "The Secret Sharer" . . . and the other characters whose ambivalent sexuality is

46   *The Reader in Modernist Fiction*

discussed in my book—as 'gay.' It is clear, however, that the acceptable range of male desire within what we would now call 'normal heterosexuality' was greater in the nineteenth than in the twentieth century" (5). Conrad could and did unambiguously depict men who desired other men, such as David Jones in *Victory* and the count in "Il Conde." The case of the secret sharer seems rather different; instead of an obvious instance of homosexual panic, it may simply be a case of sudden, powerful friendship based on class status and the delicate professional situation of the insecure young captain.

The recent debates between advocates of "surface reading" versus the practitioners of prevalent "symptomatic readings" may be instructive at this point. The surface reading model would help open criticism back up to a wider range of legitimate interpretive possibilities. Discussing Sharon Marcus's work on female friendship in nineteenth-century novels in which she resists reading friendship as an unacknowledged symptom of lesbian desire, Best and Marcus write: "Taking friendship in novels to signify friendship is thus not mere tautology; it highlights something true and visible on the text's surface that symptomatic reading had ironically rendered invisible" (12). The same may well be true for "The Secret Sharer"; this is an important interpretive possibility that should be retained and debated. More importantly, a symptomatic reading threatens to entirely erase Conrad's carefully constructed hermeneutical drama centered on the consequences of class perception and prejudice, as a real drama of interpretation and its consequences is dissolved into a familiar and frequently repeated critical masternarrative.

A consequence of my overall reading of this text is that we should take a more skeptical look at the many readings that presuppose an easy correspondence between the author and the narrator; such readers have been as uncritically accepting of the narrator's account as the credulous narrator was of Leggatt's version of events. Nowhere else in Conrad is the distance greater between the implied author and the fallible narrator, and perhaps nowhere is it better hidden. Those looking for a simple autobiographical correspondence should perhaps reflect on the surprise experienced by Conrad's wife Jessie, who had also assumed such a relation to exist: "I remember bitterly reproaching my husband for not having ever spoken of this episode to me before he wrote the story. He gave a hoot of delight, and then as soon as he recovered from his unusual outburst of mirth, gave me a great hug and exclaimed: 'My dear, it is pure fiction. I don't know where the idea came from, but I've taken you in beautifully. Hurrah'" (Jesse Conrad 95).

"The Secret Sharer" both stages and invites basic questioning concerning the interpretation of any sequence of events, as the interpretive choices and class perspectives within the story are doubled by the critical interpretations that the tale engenders. It requires both a more skeptical textual scrutiny and closer attention to the history in which it is situated. A largely neglected concept of Umberto Eco's can help us situate Conrad's text and its functions: it is one of the works that "tell stories about the way stories are built up. In doing so these texts are much less innocuous than they seem: their deep theme is the functioning of that basic cultural machinery which, through the manipulation of our beliefs (which sublimate our wishes), produces ideologies, contradictory world visions, self-delusion" (256). "The Secret Sharer" is a text that inscribes at least two contradictory readings, the most transparent of which is a trap for the unwary. In this, it embodies a gravity and a playfulness typical of modernism; it also demonstrates the range and depth of the deciphering of significant hermeneutical dramas present at the beginning of modernist narrative construction.

As Conrad constructs the modernist reader, we see that he or she (his later works are consciously directed towards a female audience) has above all a critical sensibility, wary of implausible statements made by characters, narrators, or society in general. Readers in his works are to be suspicious of romantic paradigms, idealism in general, government pronouncements, and individuals' self-serving narratives. Insufficiently critical readers within the text will find themselves frustrated, ruined, or dead. Since Conrad stages so many of these interpretive choices for the actual reader to experience as well, an overly credulous one may quickly feel disappointed or worse.

Ford Madox Ford

Ford Madox Ford was fully engaged with the modernist position identified in the previous section. Like his friend and sometime collaborator, Conrad, he was quite explicit in unfolding the more radical epistemological drama of the deleterious effects of uncritical reading. In addition, he sexualizes the effects of reading in a way Conrad never does. In *The Good Soldier* (1915), a novel of the narrator's slow discovery of the long-term affair between his wife and his good friend Edward Ashburnham, reading is ever-present. Most of the principal characters, especially the sexual quintet at the novel's center, are victims of literature, either directly or indirectly. The most

48   *The Reader in Modernist Fiction*

prominent is Ashburnham; we are told near the outset that "poor dear Edward was a great reader—he would pass hours lost in novels of a sentimental type—novels in which typewriter girls married Marquises and governesses Earls. And in his books, the course of true love ran as smooth as buttered honey" (34), a judgment that embraces both ideological and aesthetic critiques. This point is reaffirmed later in the novel; the narrator, Dowell, points out that "even when he was twenty-two he would pass hours reading one of Scott's novels or the Chronicles of Froissart" (161). The most damning assessment of him—and one which explains his otherwise strangely sordid behavior—comes near the end of the novel: "Well, Edward was the English gentleman; but he was also, to the last, a sentimentalist, whose mind was compounded of indifferent poems and novels" (293).

A significant part of Nancy Rufford's sad fate can be blamed directly on reading. As Ashburnham moves closer to her, images from literature confuse her understanding and muddle her judgment: "She remembered chance passages in chance books . . . She remembered someone's love for the Princess Badrulbadour; . . . she remembered a character in a book who was said to have taken to drink through love" (256–57). Suddenly confronted by powerful amorous emotions, she has no sound interpretive frame within which to contextualize them, only discursive scraps from sources ranging from *Arabian Nights* to paraphrases of romantic authors, some of which may well have come from the mouth of Ashburnham: with women, "the fellow talked like a cheap novelist" (131).

The limitations of Florence, Dowell's adulterous wife, derive more from an adjacent literary form, the drama. She takes it upon herself to "educate" Ashburnham; she would do it "three or four times a week," we are informed (48) and would proceed, for example, by telling him the story of Hamlet. Dowell feels she could have "tried to extract from me a new respect for the greatness of her passion [for Ashburnham] on the lines of all for love and the world well lost" (138), an allusion to the title of John Dryden's revision of *Antony and Cleopatra*. She is often on the brink of "theatrical displays" of her love for him (139): "she wanted, in one mood, to come rushing to me, to cast herself on her knees at my feet and to declaim a carefully arranged, frightfully emotional, outpouring of her passion. That was to show that she was like the great erotic women of whom history tells" (139). At other times, she wished to appear like the heroine of a French comedy" (140). When Dowell, to his astonishment, discovers her reading narrative histories of the Renaissance, he "knew that something was up" (49). And so it was. Her actual purpose was, by narrating the excesses of the Catholic Church and the subsequent rise of Protestantism, to stage a scene that would humiliate Edward's wife (a Catholic) and thereby raise the stakes of her affair with Ashburnham. And it succeeds; Leonora is devastated.

The main exception to the trajectory outlined above is Leonora, Ashburnham's long-suffering wife. "Man, for her, was a sort of brute who must have his divagations, his nights out, his, let us say, rutting seasons. She had read few novels, so that the idea of a pure and constant love succeeding the sound of wedding bells had never been very much presented to her" (216). She is also, perhaps not surprisingly, the most accurate interpreter of human actions in the novel, and the one who emerges with the most pleasant fate in the end. It is only fitting that her battle with her husband over Nancy be expressed in novelistic form: "Having discovered what he wanted—that the girl should go five thousand miles away and love him steadfastly as people do in sentimental novels, she was determined to smash that aspiration" (280). Appropriately enough, these interconnected stories of reading are part of a larger hermeneutical drama in which Dowell narrates the series of extended misinterpretations that constitute his married life; in this fashion, the narrator restages the same series of obscure though insidious events for the reader to puzzle over and finally comprehend in all their ramifications. That the resultant textual totality has been itself the object of vigorous interpretive debate over the basic trajectory and general meaning of the work is yet another thematization of the critical drama at its core.

Ford's denunciation of novel reading should not be thought unusual; in his critical prose he is much more extreme. He states that "the best individuals for an artist's audience [are those] who have least listened to accepted ideas" and goes on to affirm "If I had to choose as a reader I would rather have one who had never read anything before but the Newgate Calendar, or the records of crime, starvation and divorce in the Sunday paper—I would rather have him for a reader than a man who . . . had by heart the whole of the *Times Literary Supplement*" (*Critical* 52). Though no doubt hyperbolic, these statements indicate Ford's aversion to false depictions of life as presented in contemporary literature.

Notes

1. Joseph Elkanah Rosenberg notes other similar Jamesian letter-burnings: Kate Croy's destruction of Millie Theale's communication to Merton Densher at the end of *The Wings of the Dove* (1902) and Christopher Newman's burning of the Bellgarde family secret in *The American* (1878).

50 *The Reader in Modernist Fiction*

2. For a critical account of earlier readings of this work, see Shlomith Rimmon (115). Ross Chambers provides an ingenious overview of some of these approaches (167–68).

3. My reading of this story differs diametrically from that of Wolfgang Iser in *The Act of Reading*, who sees the narrator's attempt to find the figure in the carpet to be a typical nineteenth-century reading strategy. Iser's interpretation does not explain how others, such as Corvik, are able to discern the elusive pattern, or how a similar disclosed meaning informs a number of James's works, including "In the Cage."

4. Wegner's account of reading, romance, and space in *Lord Jim* ultimately traces a different trajectory from mine.

5. Parts of this chapter regarding "The Secret Sharer" first appeared in *Studies in the Novel*. Copyright © 2001 University of North Texas. This article first appeared in *Studies in the Novel*, Volume 33, Number 3, Fall 2001. Published with permission by Johns Hopkins University Press.

6. Mark Ellis Thomas briefly discusses various interpreters in this text (224–25), and remarks perspicaciously, "What more fitting double for the careful, critical reader than the chief mate, whose 'dominant trait was to take all things into earnest consideration'" (224).

7. A rare glimpse of the subaltern perspective aboard the ship comes from the captain's sole sympathetic observation concerning his steward: "It was this maddening course of being shouted at, checked without rhyme or reason, arbitrarily chased out of my cabin, suddenly called into it, sent flying out of his pantry on incomprehensible errands, that accounted for the growing wretchedness of his expression" (128).

8. For additional discussion of the captain-narrator's oddness, see Kerr.

9. Harry White and Irving L. Finston have offered a very different interpretation that supports Leggatt and draws on the case of the killing on the *Cutty Sark*. To do so, they uncritically accept every claim made by Leggatt, fabricate a highly speculative account of the events on the *Sephora* which contradicts Archbold's affirmation that he gave the order to set the reefed topsail, postulates that he couldn't see the topsail and didn't remember (!) that it was already reefed (59). They only briefly mention and then entirely discount the testimony of the seamen, claiming that the men were repeating the captain's story rather than narrating what they had seen themselves (66).

10. Jakob Lothe, for example, simply states: "Although the narrator's vivid imagination and extreme egocentricity make him less than reliable, his unreliability is delimited by the absence from the text of firmer indications of authorial authority" (70–71). Other critics who pay close attention to issues of narration, perspective, and interpretation (Said, Daleski, Watts, Bonney, Facknitz) do not fundamentally question the essential credibility of the captain.

11. Murphy notes that he is building on an earlier article by J. D. O'Hara, whose position is somewhat tamer than Murphy's, as well as that of

Robert D. Wyatt, who is in many respects more thoroughgoing. Some of their points are also taken up by Daniel R. Schwarz, who however prefers to call the narrator "imperceptive" rather than unreliable ("History" 70).

12. Mark Ellis Thomas observes, "Conrad's doubles fasten onto similarity as the salient factor in their doubling relationships and so ignore the more important differences" (223).

Chapter 2

The Fate of Reading in the Work of Joyce: Illusion, Demystification, Sexuality

Reading and misreading are central and ubiquitous in Joyce's narratives; often, they are connected to some form of sexual desire. This dialectic begins with the stories in *Dubliners* and extends throughout Joyce's career. R. B. Kershner has drawn attention to the great surge of popular literature in Ireland during the second half of the nineteenth century that included numerous Wild West tales, Edward Bulwer-Lytton's novels, *The Count of Monte Cristo*, and other such works. He goes on to observe that "as a result the characters of Joyce's fiction are all *bovaristes*, and Joyce provides the textual evidence of their possession by their reading" (*Bakhtin* 301). This is certainly the case for a large number of the uncritical readers portrayed within *Dubliners*. A somewhat expanded Bovary-type model often prevails, as characters regularly misapply the conclusions of nonrealist fiction to situations in the actual world.

A paradigmatic example is found in "An Encounter," where some boys' passionate reading of Westerns engenders thoughts of freedom: the narrator, like the other boys, hungers "for wild sensations, for the escape which those chronicles of disorder alone seemed to offer" (21). They decide to skip school for a day and seek out excitement. Their truancy eventually turns into a very different kind of adventure than the boys had imagined. The main incident is an encounter with a "queer old josser" (26) who asks them about the romantic fictions of Thomas Moore, Walter Scott, and Bulwer-Lytton. He attempts to establish a rapport with them by telling the young narrator, "I can see you are a bookworm like myself" (25); more discourse about books quickly leads to the subject of nice young girls and then to the topic of vigorously whipping young boys. It becomes evident that the man is a pederast and the boys flee.

Many subsequent stories include some mention of key books or resonant reading experiences. At the beginning of "Araby," we are given the seemingly pointless information that the young protagonist finds three books in the room of the dead priest: Scott's *The Abbot*, *The Devout Communicant*, and *The Memoirs of Vidocq*. Kevin Dettmar, in his study of the ways that pre-existing narratives circumscribe the social experience of the characters of Joyce, notes that "from this textual brew, into which were no doubt thrown a number of other pulp romances, the boy has constructed a narrative of love that will dictate the course of his romance with Mangan's sister" ("Plot" 24), a failed quest that will end in a decidedly unromantic manner. Each of the books mentioned represents a different though intersecting kind of illusion: historical romance, organized religion, and the fraudulent memoirs of a notorious criminal. These are fused with the young narrator's infatuation with a neighbor girl he hardly knows as he thinks of her "in places the most hostile to romance" and imagines that he bears his "chalice safely through a throng of foes" (31). The romantic intoxication of "Araby," the name of the bazaar where he hopes to buy her a gift, is added to this haze of illusion: "the syllables of the word *Araby* were called to me through the silence in which my soul luxuriated and cast an Eastern enchantment over me" (32). We see Joyce's simultaneous critique of literature, popular culture, religion, Orientalist fantasy, and boyish infatuation together in the service of the demystification of romantic and idealistic illusions.

"Evelyn's" titular character is presented with a choice straight out of the romantic fiction of the period—running off with a sailor to Argentina—as scholars from Hugh Kenner to Margot Norris (*Suspicious* 55–67) have pointed out; Kenner comments dismissively that "penny romances are the liturgy of the innocent. The reader believes such stuff" (*Voices* 81).[1] Little Chandler has romantic aspirations of being a writer in "A Little Cloud," and his feelings of melancholy and enjoyment of Byron's more somber poetry induce him to think that he has the soul of a poet. He does not work at actually trying to write ("if he could get back into that mood" (84)); instead, his imagination only produces imaginary reviews of books he will never complete and which, if penned, would be expressed in an all too predictable idiom: "A wistful sadness pervades these poems . . . The Celtic note" (74, Joyce's ellipsis). In some of the later stories, Joyce extends his explorations of characters who read. In "A Painful Case," Mr. Duffy, little by little, "entangled his thoughts with" those of Mrs. Sinico, a married woman he meets at a concert. "He lent her books, provided her with ideas, shared his intellectual life with her" (110). They grow together in many ways, but Duffy cannot shake

54   *The Reader in Modernist Fiction*

off Victorian attitudes and mores and follow the injunctions of the Nietzsche he has on his shelf. After she raises his hand to her cheek, he rejects her; four years later, she dies tragically due to her despair. Margot Norris observes that "'A Painful Case' is about a *story* that is painful for its readers: a newspaper article of the same title that gives Mr. Duffy a disturbing shock when he reads of Mrs. Sinico's death"; this shock is staged for the reader of *Dubliners* to experience as well (*Suspicious* 158). Interpretive acts are central in this story: it is Mrs. Sinico's "interpretation of his words" that "disillusioned" Mr. Duffy; later, the reader must scrupulously interpret the meaning of the newspaper account to determine the full import of the story. Furthermore, as Cóilín Owens has suggested, the very contents of Duffy's bookshelves display the trajectory of his intellectual life as he moves from the stable instruction of the *Maynooth Catechism* through Wordsworth's providential pantheism to the later addition of Nietzsche's cynical metaphysics (114–15).

As several Joyce critics have pointed out, the sardonic concluding meaning of "Grace" is entirely built around an egregious public interpretive blunder that no character in the story is aware of. The culmination of the other businessmen's attempt to save Bob Kernan from drink occurs during a sermon delivered at a retreat. It concludes as the commerce-friendly Jesuit, Father Purdon, explicates the meaning of Luke 16:8–9, which teaches that one cannot serve both God and Mammon. "It is one of the most difficult texts in all the scriptures, [Purdon] said, to interpret properly" (173). In his gloss, however, the satiric lines "make unto yourselves friends out of the mammon of iniquity so that when you die they will receive you into everlasting dwellings" are interpreted straightforwardly; the Jesuit assures his audience that Jesus was not a hard taskmaster and was "setting before them as exemplars in the religious life those very worshipers of Mammon who were of all men the least solicitous in religious matters" (174). No one in the story (including the narrator) offers any hint of objection to this exegesis, though of course it is entirely wrongheaded, and can only be held if one ignores the context and misses the obvious irony in the Biblical passage. Thus, readers are placed in a position where they must experience the same passage and commentary as the characters do. The reader too must either accept or reject the construction set forth by the priest. The correct construal of the story's resolution hinges on a perception of the characters' collective misinterpretation and their casual hypocrisy, which is its precondition. The sharp irony (and consequent ideological critique) appears only as the reader discerns

The Fate of Reading in the Work of Joyce   55

that which the characters never suspect. This description is as good as any statement to depict a major vector of the modernist drama of misreading we see repeatedly re-enacted throughout the twentieth century.

"The Dead," though it does not involve much literal reading, nevertheless fully participates in the same dynamic of interpretation and misinterpretation as it presents a series of verbal performances before audiences and questionable interpretations of others' narratives. I suggest that "The Dead" is a subtle but relentless tour-de-force of misreading, misinterpretation, and misattribution. Gabriel Conroy is an insistent and egregious misinterpreter, consistently misconstruing those around him, his general situation, his wife and marriage, and even the narrative of his own life.[2] Books and images of reading frame this text. In the Morkans' house, where the dinner takes place, a photograph of Gabriel's mother is prominently displayed; she is depicted holding "an open book on her knees and was pointing out something in it to Constantine," Gabriel's brother (186). Gabriel finds something exceedingly, even sensually satisfying about physical volumes: "The books he received for review were almost more welcome than the paltry cheque. He loved to feel the covers and turn over the pages of newly printed books" (188). Twice he derives comfort from quoting to himself lines that he has written (192, 214).

But his passion for words does not help his poor interpretive abilities in social situations; most of Conroy's pronouncements and deductions will turn out to be erroneous, whether applied to himself or, more egregiously, when he is reading the semiotic signs produced by the three women he verbally blunders into during the course of the evening. Lily, the caretaker's daughter, rebuffs his awkward question about a possible upcoming marriage by stating, "The men that is now is only all palaver and what they can get out of you" (178). Molly Ivors reads through his vain attempt to obscure his identity by signing his reviews with his initials and can easily supply the missing letters that follow his published "G" and "C." Finally, Gabriel does not at first recognize his wife when he sees her listening to distant music and consistently misreads her behavior, attitudes, and intentions during the rest of the evening. He believes a woman listening to distant music was a symbol of something but can't determine what she might symbolize. He alludes to the three Graces but, as Hugh Kenner points out, he mixes up the mythological references: he "staggers from cliché to cliché into exegetical disaster. [There is a] confusion between the Three Graces and the three goddesses in the story of the Judgment of Paris" (*Voices* 39). More significantly for

56   *The Reader in Modernist Fiction*

our purposes, he cannot realize that he is an actor in a different mythological drama, one involving the Furies.

He learns of the young man, Michael Furey, who, many years before, sang beneath her window in the cold rain while he was very ill. Gabriel had not been able to imagine that Gretta could have her own narrative and that it could be such an affectionate one. This in turn causes him to question his own reading of her, of their marriage, and of his adult existence: he believes that she "had had that romance in her life: a man had died for her sake" (*D* 222). As Gretta sleeps, he assumes he must have played a poor part in her life and wonders whether there isn't something more to her story (*D* 222). But as Anne Fogarty points out, her story is "punctuated by gaps and ellipses and circular repetitions" and is "indeterminate, incomplete, and elusive" (58). Margot Norris further observes that "it is Gabriel who turns her story into a love story" (Norris and Pecora 369). Melissa Free questions why Gabriel uncritically accepts Gretta's claim that Furey died for her, and wonders whether "the young man's death was inevitable" (294). The skeptical reading I am proposing in this book would push this reasoning still further—it is equally plausible that Furey sang for Gretta *because* he knew he would soon be dead; it is, then, not the song that causes his death, but the impending death that produces the song. The dismal conclusions Gabriel draws about his own life may well be one more misinterpretation, a misinterpretation that many readers have felt invited to make as well.

The drama of reading is intensified by the way the material is narrated. As Vicki Mahaffey observes, Joyce and other modernists "trap readers into incomprehension" (*Modernist* 73). She explains, "a reader cannot learn anything meaningful from *Dubliners* by approaching it in the usual [conventional] way; if we try, we unconsciously replicate the habits of characters we dismiss as 'paralyzed' or not fully alive" (89); we need to resist sympathetic identification with narrators and characters, and approach each with a sensibility that is more critical in thought and flexible in feeling (106).

If an expanded concept of Bovarism is the dominant trope for the uncritical acts of reading undertaken by many of the characters in the earlier stories of *Dubliners*, the model is substantially altered by the time we come to *A Portrait of the Artist as a Young Man*.[3] Reading and interpretation figure prominently in this text; its opening pages show Stephen trying to comprehend the various signs around him. Books have a formative influence; they help him recognize and orient his experience. Tracing the changing pattern of their effects, we can see a partial recapitulation of the trajectory of some modern attitudes

The Fate of Reading in the Work of Joyce   **57**

towards reading as well as new developments of these positions. At Clongowes, Stephen feels "it was nice and warm to see the lights in the castle. It was like something in a book . . . And there were nice sentences in Doctor Cornwell's Spelling Book" (10). He enjoys "a book in the library about Holland. There were lovely foreign names in it and pictures of strangelooking cities and ships. It made you feel so happy" (26). Such emotions will reappear later as Stephen's feelings are assuaged by reading Shelley's verse (96).

The comfort derived from reading is often accompanied by an urge to act; such actions, however, prove to be more ambiguous. They can provide successful models that produce favorable results as when, inspired by Peter Parley's tales of heroic Greece and Rome, Stephen is moved to protest his innocence to the rector (55). At other points, the models will lead nowhere. Stephen's fascination with *The Count of Monte Cristo* allows him to live in his imagination "through a long train of adventures, marvelous as those in the book itself" (63). Insofar as this propels Stephen into the maze of romanticism it will produce nothing but illusion or "a strange unrest" (64)—the kind that doomed so many uncritical readers in earlier works by Joyce. Like Shelley questing for his epipsychidion, Stephen longs for his own Mercédès: "He wanted to meet in the real world the unsubstantial image which his soul constantly beheld" (65). At this point in the text, such a desire is mere wish fulfillment—and acknowledged to be such: "He would fade into something impalpable under her eyes and then, in a moment, he would be transfigured. Weakness and timidity and inexperience would fall from him in that magic moment" (65). Moving beyond the unfortunate model of Edmond Dantes's theatrical bravado and renunciation, Stephen proves able to communicate desire effectively with E----- C----- : "His heart danced upon her movements like a cork upon a tide. He heard what her eyes said to him from beneath their cowl and knew that in some dim past, whether in life or in reverie, he had heard their tale before" (69).

These passages suggest two complementary dramas of reading that run through the text: the first is that of the solace that reading can provide, a theme that continues to be elaborated until its final incarnation in Stephen's walk to the university, where the rain-laden trees evoked in him, "as always, memories of the girls and women in the plays of Gerhart Hauptmann" (176). The space of his walk becomes a kind of inner library arranged by geography as he knows in advance precisely where he will think of the prose of Newman, the poetry of Cavalcanti and Ben Jonson, and the spirit of Ibsen. The romantic authors that buoyed him previously have now been

58   *The Reader in Modernist Fiction*

replaced by much more realistic writers (176). The final reference to a Romantic narrative allegorically places Walter Scott's novel, *The Bride of Lammermoor* (the operatic version of which had inflamed Emma Bovary), into the hands of a "dwarf" priest who is rumored to have been born of an incestuous union (228).

One of the most powerful (and powerfully suggestive) acts of reading occurs in the anatomy theatre at Queen's College in Cork, where Stephen helps his father look for the initials he carved there many years earlier. Simon Dedalus is having trouble reconnecting with or even learning about his old mates and he can't seem to find the boyish marker of his identity gouged into one of the desks. Looking among the desks, Stephen reads on one of them the word *Fœtus* cut several times into the wood. This "sudden legend startled his blood" as he immediately envisions the absent students carving and laughing (89–90). The word and the vision "caper" before him as he walks away and yield unexpectedly to memories of the "recent monstrous reveries" he had been experiencing; "they too had sprung before him, suddenly and furiously, out of mere words" (90). The word generates a narrative of past events and brings on intense consciousness of private sexual fantasies and activities. "The letters cut in the stained wood of the desk stared upon him, mocking his bodily weakness" and resonate long after he can see them; a bit later, the effect of the carved word makes him almost unable to read other written words: "His very brain was sick and powerless. He could scarcely interpret the letters of the signboards of the shops" (92). To recover his sense of identity he states his name, his paternity, and his precise spatial setting; this proves to be only partially effective. The flesh is powerful, or rather the words in which the flesh is written are. About to visit a prostitute, the cry he had suppressed for so long finally issued from his lips: "a cry which was but the echo of an obscene scrawl which he had read on the oozing wall of the urinal" (100).

By contrast, other sets of letters that represent home and religion lack this kind of power. Place also becomes less compelling, as "the letters of the name of Dublin lay heavily upon his mind, pushing one another surlily hither and thither with slow boorish insistence" (111). The director of the school, inviting Stephen to consider joining the priesthood, explains that the sacrament of Holy Orders is one that can be received only once because "it imprints on the soul an indelible spiritual mark which can never be effaced" (160). Stephen does not find this mark anywhere near as compelling as the letters that signify the sexual.

The knowledge of human behavior that can be derived from literature turns out to be severely limited: "All the descriptions of fierce love and hatred which he had met in books seemed to him . . . unreal" (82); later in the text, it is again observed that "he had heard the names of the passions of love and hate pronounced solemnly on the stage and in the pulpit, had found them set forth solemnly in books, and had wondered why his soul was unable to harbour them for any time or to force his lips to utter their names with conviction" (149). His experience fails to corroborate his reading; life does not follow the patterns depicted in the novels of Dumas. One must observe, however, that given the miserable fates of so many modernist characters who believe the illusions found in books, Joyce lets Stephen off very easily. In a similar vein we learn that literature fails to prepare him adequately for his first experience of the touch of a woman: "It had shocked him too when he felt for the first time beneath his tremoulous fingers the brittle texture of a woman's stocking for, retaining nothing of all he read save that which seemed to him an echo or a prophecy of his own state, it was only amid softworded phrases or within rosesoft stuffs that he dared to conceive of the soul or body of a woman moving with tender life" (142).

The trajectory that is traced through the novel suggests that books can provide substantial solace, though they often prove to be inadequate or illusory. Other words, forbidden or obscene, written or carved by furtive hands, provide instead a searingly powerful vision as they articulate the unspeakable. In *A Portrait*, we have a different drama of reading from that presented elsewhere by Joyce. Romantic reading and books are not castigated and denounced, but merely outgrown; Stephen is no Emma Bovary or Lord Jim. Reading provides consolations and writing comes at the price of a retreat from social and sexual interaction. The deepest reading experiences remain the furtive but powerful glimpses of forbidden sexual words scrawled or gouged into obscure surfaces. By the end of the text, the drama of reading ceases, though it does not end: Stephen's mother says that he has "a queer mind and ha[s] read too much" (248). "Not true," Stephen rejoins, "I have read little and understood less" (248). Joyce's dramatization of the fate of reading will produce new variations and significant transformations in *Ulysses*.

Ulysses provides a considerably more extended investigation of reading, interpretation, and misreading. Spoken language is frequently played off against the conventions of spelling and typography. Stephen had imagined writing books titled only by a single letter ("have you read his F? O yes, but I prefer Q" [3.139–40]) and he acknowledges

60   *The Reader in Modernist Fiction*

his debt to George Russell in an alphabetic manner: "A. E. I. O. U." (9.213). Reading can be blatant, as when letters on the five tall hats of men wearing sandwichboards literally parade through the street (H.E.L.Y.'S [8.123–27]—though the "Y" lags a bit behind). Reading can even be literally turned around, as Bloom notes as he observes the typesetter proofreading: "Reads it backwards first ... mangiD kcirtaP" (7.205–6); this thought in turn reminds him of his father reading Hebrew from right to left and anticipates the line of "bitched type" he will encounter when reading the printed paper: ".)eatondph 1/8 ador dorador douradora" (16.1257–58). When the characters think, they sometimes think in letters: Bloom imagines telling a wealthy diner, "Do ptake some ptarmigan" (8.887), restoring in advance the silent "p" that Molly leaves off "neumonia" in her unspoken monologue (18.727). The reader may assume that she suspects that she is misspelling it in her mind since the lines that follow refer to her habitual misspelling of "symphathy": "I always make that mistake and newphew with 2 double yous" (18.730–31). Here we see her thinking typographically, reading the visual representations of her words as she subvocally articulates their sound in the dark. Bloom is more aware of the idiosyncrasies of the written word and recalls Martin Cunningham's spelling test: "It is amusing to view the unpar one ar alleled embarra two ars is it? [Bloom is correct] double ess ment of a harassed pedlar while gauging au the symmetry with a y of a peeled pear under a cemetery wall" (7.166–69). In this work there is no space, inner or outer, devoid of the reading of a text composed of letters.

We are at times provided with a phenomenology of reading as we observe characters going over written texts. We read over his shoulder (or rather, through his eyes) as Stephen skims Deasy's letter: "The doctrine of *laissez faire* which so often in our history. Our cattle trade. The way of our old industries. Liverpool ring which jockeyed the Galway harbour scheme. European conflagration" (2.324–27). We receive only the phrases that register on Stephen's consciousness though this mental editing does not cause any loss of meaning—we can fill in many of these gaps. And as Thomas Jackson Rice points out, "in one of the wittier moments in this chapter, Joyce allows Deasy to interrupt Stephen's skimming to remark, 'I don't mince words, do I?' Through the next paragraph Stephen continues to skim, continues in fact to mince Deasy's words through the balance of the letter" ("Mince" 144).

An especially salient instance of shared critical skimming is Bloom's consumption of Philip Beaufoy's *Tit-Bits* story, "Matcham's Masterstroke," which he reads while sitting in the outhouse. "Quietly he

The Fate of Reading in the Work of Joyce   61

read, restraining himself, the first column and, yielding but resisting, began the second. Midway, his last resistance yielding, he allowed his bowels to ease themselves quietly as he read, reading still patiently that slight constipation of yesterday quite gone" (4.506–09). John Lurz shrewdly observes that "the syntactical construction of the sentences explicitly interweaves the actions of reading and moving one's bowels. The 'restraining' and 'yielding' in the first sentence initially seem to refer to reading itself before the second sentence clarifies the object of those actions, as if the controlled and steady pace at which Bloom encounters the words of the newspaper is commensurate with the rhythms of his bowel movement" (70; see also Osteen, 86–87). Bloom's running commentary on Beaufoy's pages continues polysemically: "It did not move or touch him but it was quick and neat. Print anything now. Silly season. He read on, seated above his own rising smell. Neat certainly. *Matcham often thinks of the masterstroke by which he won the laughing witch who now.* Begins and ends morally. *Hand in hand.* Smart" (4.511–15). Bloom's analytical prowess is quite sound: he sees the story's overall trajectory, general formula, aesthetic slightness, and the workmanlike competence of the author. It is not to be retained and reread but rather to be consumed quickly, jettisoned, and then replaced by a different version of the same formula. As Patrick McCarthy observes in his chapter on reading in *Ulysses*, "'Matcham's Masterstroke' is the literary antithesis of *Ulysses*: Beaufoy's brief story begins conventionally and ends happily, Joyce's long novel begins somewhat unconventionally and ends ambiguously; the story Bloom reads is 'neat certainly' and makes few demands on its reader (who picked it up precisely because it was 'something new and easy'—4.501/68)," while the book we are reading is an often baffling and always challenging one (*Portals* 105). At a more general level it would appear that Bloom performs a decisive piece of criticism bodily when he tears the page in two and wipes himself with it.

His response to other kinds of formulaic writing is equally dismissive. He is not keen on the soft-core pornography Molly enjoys; in "Ithaca," *Sweets of Sin* is said to be "of inferior literary style" (17.733). Concerning the stories of murders, he observes: "The murderer's image in the eye of the murdered. They love reading about it. Man's head found in a garden. Her clothing consisted of. How she met her death. Recent outrage. The weapon used. Murderer still at large. Clues" (6.478–81). Bloom here reproduces clichéd phrases that may appear equally in murder mysteries or in sensationalistic newspaper stories. Concerning the weekly press, he notes "It's the ads and side features sell a weekly, not the stale news in the official

62   *The Reader in Modernist Fiction*

gazette. Queen Anne is dead" (7.89–90); the side features he imagines are slight indeed: "Cartoons. Phil Blake's weekly Pat and Bull story. Uncle Toby's page for tiny tots. Country bumpkin's queries" (7.94–95). What I wish to underscore is not Bloom's disdain for these types of discourse but his perception of the deeper functional, psychological, or economic base that lies within the seeming light diversion of the prose. In this regard he is an early version of what would later be called a "symptomatic" reader.

Bloom's reading discloses how readers create meaning out of incomplete material, whether it appears in the form of "POST 110 PILLS" which we read as "POST NO BILLS" (8.101) or, peering into the crown of his hat, "Plasto's high grade ha" (4.69–70), the final letter of which we invariably add. At the same time, Bloom is implicated, knowingly and not, in creating false impressions in print to influence other readers. He asks the editor of *The Daily Telegraph* for a "puff" or advertisement masquerading as a news item in return for paying for a two-month run of an ad (7.971–78). That evening's edition of the *Telegraph* will turn out to contain misleading information involving Bloom as seen in the published list of mourners who attended Dignam's funeral that includes Stephen Dedalus, C. P. M'Coy, L. Boom, and M'Intosh (16.1259–61). The first two were not present and the latter pair are misidentified. Hence the propriety of the punning designation of the paper, "tell a graphic lie" (16.1232). This is part of a larger critique of contemporary journalism made by many of the modernists, as noted in the introduction.

Most resonantly, Joyce regularly presents reading as a furtive act in *Ulysses*. Molly quickly and silently reads Boylan's card before hiding it under her pillow; Bloom finds an isolated spot where he can perform a close reading of his letter from Martha unobserved. "Wandering Rocks" is to some degree a chapter of secretive readings. Miss Dunne hides her copy of *The Woman in White* while she is at work (10.368–70). We learn that Maggie Dedalus sells Stephen's books without his knowledge to buy food for the family, though Dilly, perhaps with money from such a sale, also buys a French primer which she shows to Stephen. At this point Stephen has been flipping through a volume of esoterica: "Thumbed pages. Read and read. Who has passed here before me? . . . How to win a woman's love. For me this" (10.845–47). He hides the book that he is holding so Dilly won't make certain unfavorable judgments about him. Earlier, Stephen recalls trying to pawn a volume lifted from the theosophists: "Yogibogeybox in Dawson chambers. *Isis Unveiled.* Their Pali book we tried to pawn" (9.279–80). Bloom will later obscure the cover of

The Fate of Reading in the Work of Joyce   **63**

The Sweets of Sin, the book he bought for Molly moments before Stephen was hiding his book from Dilly, by turning it upside down so Stephen does not see the title (17.731–36).

Skimming *The Sweets of Sin* at the bookstall produces contradictory responses in Bloom. The work itself is utterly straightforward and entirely clichéd: "Her mouth glued on his in a luscious voluptuous kiss while his hands felt for the opulent curves inside her deshabille" (194). Laura Frost observes that reading these lines "signals a moment of reflection in which the distance between the reader of *Ulysses* and Joyce's character is temporarily collapsed as they share a common text of pleasure" (58). As he reads these and other lines, Bloom is moved by different emotions:

> Warmth showered gently over him, cowing his flesh. Flesh yielded amply amid rumpled clothes: whites of eyes swooning up. His nostrils arched themselves for prey. Melting breast ointments (*for him! for Raoul!*). Armpits oniony sweat. Fishgluey slime (*her heaving embonpoint!*) Feel! Press! Cherished! Sulphur dung of lions!
> Young! Young! 10.619–24

Jean-Michel Rabaté comments: "Bloom is highly sensitive to the sensual, and indeed sexual, impact of words; here, language is indeed made of flesh, a flesh that combines his own eroticized body and the female forms he hallucinates, along with a whole torrid scene triggered by a few words" (124). His skin becomes hot and he imagines not just arousing visuals but also viscous touch and a series of compelling scents. Bloom's emotions as reader fuse with his desire as a (frustrated) lover and potential voyeur, as the object of imagined desire glides from Raoul to Molly to Molly reading *Sweets of Sin* to Boylan enacting the role of Raoul to the imagined titillation of all involved.

Molly's sexual imagination is fueled by her reading and she is also adept at observing hidden (and presumably amorous) words: in "Penelope" she recalls Bloom "scribbling something a letter when I came into the front room to show him Dignams death in the paper as if something told me and he covered it up with the blottingpaper pretending to be thinking about business so very probably that it was to somebody who thinks she has a softy in him" (18.47–50). That is, she observes him writing to Martha just as he has observed her reading Boylan's note. It was just such a furtive note that had excited Molly over Mulvey: "I never thought hed write making an appointment I had it inside my petticoat bodice all day reading it up in every hole

64 *The Reader in Modernist Fiction*

and corner" (18.764–66). In this context we might note that the ad that Bloom once suggested to Hely consists of women writing words that cannot be discerned by casual onlookers: "a transparent show-cart with two smart girls sitting inside writing letters, copybooks, envelopes, blottingpaper. I bet that would have caught on. Smart girls writing something catch the eye at once. Everyone dying to know what she's writing" (8.131–35). This may not have produced additional sales of stationery, but it nicely exemplifies the logic of reading, stealth, and desire in *Ulysses*.

The novel continuously and unobtrusively chronicles the obscured circulation of written words that pass between characters like ships in the night, or more literally, like the crumpled flyer for the coming of Elijah, as it gradually wends its way to the ocean. Typically, these movements are in some manner illicit and often sexually charged; the quest for essential, hidden knowledge that is regularly dramatized by modernism includes, in the case of Joyce, the desire for carnal and criminal varieties. In "Circe," Bloom claims to have written a collection of prize stories, only to be immediately confronted by Phillip Beaufoy, who accuses him of plagiarism (15.801–45). He is soon humiliated by the disclosure of secret sexual letters he is accused of writing to women (15.1014–24, 1045–56, 1078–79).

Sexualized reading and reception permeates the episode set in the National Library, a site that might ordinarily be thought of as hostile to romance. Early on it is established that in Renaissance London, lovers are readers, and readers of Shakespeare: *Venus and Adonis* "lay in the bedchamber of every light-of-love in London" (9.249–50). In a discussion of Hyde's poems, Russell warns that "people do not know how dangerous lovesongs can be" and goes on to refer to Mallarmé's verse as the "flower of corruption" (9.103–10). It is repeatedly suggested that writing is motivated by the desire for sexual gratification. Sexual exegesis is also prominent as *Hamlet* and many of the other major plays are plumbed in order to yield intimate details of Shakespeare's marital life and are interpreted to suggest a personal drama of love, sexual betrayal, and reconciliation. The final, unlikely superimposition of sex and books appears in Buck Mulligan's onanistic playlet that is read out loud in the library.

In light of these passages, it is difficult not to think of the many years during which *Ulysses* itself would be banned; it had to be smuggled into Great Britain or the United States, frequently hidden within the dustjacket of another book. Much of the reason for the disguised nature of the characters' readings (as well as its prohibition by censors)

The Fate of Reading in the Work of Joyce   65

is, as has been indicated, sex: *Ulysses*'s readers thus came to mimic the furtive characters who disguise their perusings within the novel. Joyce not only represents sexuality but also sexualizes the act of reading. The underlying code of human communication is often erotically tinged, as is the sexualized human body that partly orders the last fifteen episodes of the book.

Misreading is also common in this book. The newspaper Bloom offers to Bantam Lyons as a "throwaway" will be incorrectly perceived as a sly tip to bet on the horse of that name. Glancing at an evangelistic flyer, Bloom mistakes Christ for himself as he thinks at first that its letters spell out his name: "Bloo . . . Me? No. Blood of the Lamb" (8.8– 9). What is a mistake at the literal level is, however, more accurate as a textual reincarnation, where "Elijah is coming" is enacted as Bloom becomes transfigured into the prophet at the end of the "Cyclops" episode: "they beheld Him even Him, ben Bloom Elijah, amid clouds of angels ascend to the glory of the brightness at an angle of fortyfive degrees over Donohoe's" (12.1915–18). The reader of *Ulysses* will also be challenged when, in the deceptive "Wandering Rocks," "Mr Bloom's dental windows" are mentioned (10.1115). Here, the "dental windows" are not an oddly mixed metaphor but a reference to a different Dubliner, Marcus J. Bloom, a dentist, who is unrelated (except alphabetically) to Leopold Bloom. There are other misprisions. Bloom remembers lines from a song Milly mentions in her letter: "*Your head it simply swirls*" (4.438). The phrase "simply swirls" (or, as it is once more rendered seemingly more phonetically, "simply swurls" [6.784]), will run through his head at several points during the day. However, the phrase is misremembered; the actual words are "Your head it simply whirls" (Gifford, 76–77; see also Conley).

Though Bloom is a perspicuous reader of Beaufoy, he is less adequate when dealing with Shakespeare, as we see in the fleeting hypothesis that perhaps Ophelia killed herself because she discovered that Hamlet was really a woman (5.195–97). On the other hand, his lack of extensive erudition does not prevent him from seeing through mystical poets like Æ: "Those literary ethereal people they all are. Dreamy, cloudy, symbolistic. Esthetes they are. I wouldn't be surprised if it was that kind of food you see produces the like waves of the brain the poetical" (8.543–45). Otherworldly poetry is here reduced to the effects of a gaseous vegetarian diet, a criticism that Joyce may well have felt to be metaphorically correct, if not exactly physiologically sound. Bloom's attempts to apply Shakespeare's words for the solution of difficult problems in life also proves faulty: "In spite of careful and repeated reading of certain classical passages,

66 *The Reader in Modernist Fiction*

aided by a glossary, he had imperfect conviction from the text, the answers not bearing on all points" (17.389–91).

Fritz Senn is especially compelling at identifying the layers of error in *Ulysses*. He notes that it is both annoying and highly appropriate that Joyce's text is rife with "derailment[s], deviation[s], dislocation[s], omissions, chance delays, and collisions," and argues that these divagations are intrinsic to the programmed malfunction of the work (161). As Colleen Lamos further explains, *Ulysses* "both thematizes and performs the work of erring; not only do its characters continually make mistakes and try to mend them, but their interpretive mishaps and corrections are mimed by the readers of *Ulysses*" (120). The "epistemological fumblings" are nevertheless guided by corrective urges that aim toward knowledge (see also McCarthy "Errors").

Bloom often misremembers material he has read. Walking in the sunlight in his mourning clothes, he ruminates: "Black conducts, reflects, (refracts is it?) the heat" (4.79–80). He is wrong in all three attempts: black absorbs the heat. Such "Bloomisms" appear throughout the book; as Cheryl Herr notes: "this modern Odysseus has merely blundered about in his culture's encyclopedia of texts and has emerged from his brief schooling with his facts awry" (66). Such factual errors are by no means confined to Bloom. As Don Gifford has documented, nearly all the historical statements made by Mr. Deasy in "Nestor" are false or misleading. I strongly suspect that most of the general statements that are made about the world in this book are false, often patently false. The conclusion I draw from this is that Joyce recognizes that most people's beliefs are full of inaccuracies and his own characters reflect that position; most live largely in and by fictions.

But if Bloom's memory of specific facts is extremely fallible, his general perception of the world and how it works is quite sound and largely demystified. Early on, he imagines traveling in the East: "Wander through awned streets. Turbaned faces going by. Dark caves of carpet shops, big man, Turko the terrible, seated crosslegged, smoking a coiled pipe" (4.88–90). After more such imaginings, Bloom reflects further, "Probably not a bit like it really. Kind of stuff you read: in the track of the sun" (4.99–100). In fact, by the end of the novel, we learn that he does have a copy of a book called *In the Track of the Sun* in his library. Bloom is smart enough to know when to be skeptical about conventional beliefs, however they are disseminated. The Orientalist discourse that thoroughly seduces the boy in "Araby" (and Marlow in "Youth") is seen through by

Bloom. Similarly, he is not deceived by the claims of religion: looking at the officiating priest, he can't puzzle out what the letters INRI on the cross stand for ("Iron nails ran in" is his humorous conjecture [5.374]); nevertheless, he knows well how organized religion works, "Wonderful organization certainly, goes like clockwork. Confession. Everyone wants to. Then I will tell you all. Great weapon in their hands ... Squareheaded chaps they must be in Rome: they work the whole show. And don't they rake in the money too?" (5.424–26; 434–35).

In this he resembles Stephen, the other major demystified and demystifying reader in the text. Stephen excels in rooting out theoretical contradictions, factual errors, and crucial elisions, as we see in his deflation of the excessive veneration of Shakespeare in the library and both his spoken and private ripostes to Mr. Deasy. Bloom, however, is especially keen at understanding the specific material and economic motivations behind the perpetration and even the acceptance of specific illusions. This difference is effectively dramatized when Stephen asks Bloom a basic practical question. "One thing I never understood," Stephen wonders, "Why they put the tables upside down at night, I mean chairs, on the tables in cafes" (16.1708–10). Bloom responds immediately with the obvious answer, "To sweep the floor in the morning" (16.1714). Even if Bloom is, once again, slightly off (the floors would normally be swept after the cafes close at night), he knows the general logic of the way things work in the everyday world, something Stephen cannot imagine. Stephen must acquire all that Bloom knows about the functioning of a city before he will be able to write a book like *Ulysses*.

Many of the other Dubliners by contrast are uncritically bound by statements, opinions, and worldviews propagated by the Church, the state, Edwardian conventions, and popular fiction. John Conmee, S.J. cannot rise above the most tired platitude. The mind of Gerty MacDowell is largely constructed by popular romantic fiction, as the depiction of her assessment of Bloom indicates: "Whitehot passion was in that face, passion silent as the grave, and it had made her his ... she knew he could be trusted to the death, steadfast, a sterling man, a man of inflexible honour to his fingertips" (299). Thomas Richards postulates that "she is an encompassing experiential record of a turn-of-the-century Irish common reader. She is part of Joyce's recognition, developed during the writing of *Ulysses*, that common readers, so far as they are shaped by the developing forms of consumer culture, have acclimated themselves to a world of goods to such an extent that they have become generalized and impoverished"

68 *The Reader in Modernist Fiction*

(755). Marian Eide offers a more generous reading of Gerty, writing that "rather than eschewing pulp fiction altogether as beneath his aesthetic notice, Joyce worked creatively within the constraints of the genre" and goes on to add: "Interested in how a young woman with few cultural or financial privileges might understand her own context, Joyce drew on the reading materials available to women of her class and experience to create Gerty's voice" (108). We observe that while her amorous sensibility is articulated in a sublimating and prophylactic prose, it is unable to restrain the physical passion it is intended to elicit and control: her words are as unobjectionable as her actions are illicit.

Critics have often taken Molly to task for her deficiencies in taste and knowledge; she doesn't know how to read Rabelais (18.488–92) and dislikes Defoe: "I dont like books with a Molly in them like that one he brought me about the one from Flanders a whore always shoplifting" (18.657–58). Bloom has tried many strategies to get Molly to read: "By leaving in a conspicuous place a certain book open at a certain page: by assuming in her, when alluding explanatorily, latent knowledge: by open ridicule in her presence of some absent other's ignorant lapse" (17.694–97). None of these attempts produce the intended results. We finally do learn what will do the trick: drawing together the twinned themes of sex and reading, she tells herself that if Stephen "comes out Ill read and study all I can find or learn a bit off by heart if I knew who he likes" (18.1361–62). She is entranced by the idea of being his lover and muse and having their story appear "with our 2 photographs in all the papers when he becomes famous" (18.1365–66); that is, she will read in order to be read about. In other areas Molly is largely immune to the lure of cultural capital; she is content simply to like what she likes. This does not mean she lacks any capacity for critical, skeptical reading; she is easily able to sift through layers of falsification fueled by male desire and generic convention: "Fair Tyrants he brought me that twice . . . the part about where she hangs him up out of a hook with a cord flagellate sure theres nothing for a woman in that all invention made up about he drinking the champagne out of her slipper after the ball was over" (18.493–96).

In part because of her comments on her reading, we get a fuller picture of Joyce's revolutionary depiction of Molly's sexuality, one that has been seriously misunderstood by much early criticism. In *Sexuality in Europe: A Twentieth-Century History*, Dagmar Herzog observes that one of the great dramas of the early twentieth century was "the effort to eroticize marriage itself and the related effort

The Fate of Reading in the Work of Joyce   69

to make women's sexual agency and experience be understood as a positive good, rather than a source of shame or dishonor. This meant openly defending premarital sexual experience also for women, as well as arguing for a sexual ethics that was based on the moral value of mutual consent rather than marital status" (17–18). Such historical contextualization helps us better appreciate just how significant Joyce's representation of Molly would turn out to be.

David Spurr has discussed the heterogeneity of reading in *Ulysses*, observing that characters who read in his novel "consume and are consumed by banal advertisements, pompous editorials, sensational headlines, ladies' magazines, physical exercise manuals, exotic postcards, pornographic novels, obscene letters, suicide notes, and throwaway flyers announcing the coming of Elijah" (97). He also points out that these scenes are freely combined with an immense group of texts that represent the entire range of Western and much Eastern literature and culture. The effect of this fusion of high and low cultural artifacts, Spurr concludes, "is not the debasement of the canon but rather a universalization of reading as a hermeneutic devoted to the forms of modern culture" (97). This is no doubt true, but the crucial point is not the heterogeneity of reading so much as the presence or absence of an informed, critical sensibility concerning what is read, whatever may be read. We observe Father Conmee reading his breviary and know he can explicate ecclesiastical practice and Catholic doctrine; though Bloom gets many of his facts wrong, he, unlike Conmee, understands the larger picture extremely well. On virtually every page of this text, the reader is confronted by dubious acts of interpretation that stem from material read in books. I suggest that the two great dramas of *Ulysses* are the intimately interrelated ones of how we interpret the text and how we interpret narratives in the world they purport to depict.

Stephen is always concerned with the correct interpretation of his words. In *A Portrait*, he imagines sending the villanelle he has composed to E----- C-----, and worries about its reception: "If he sent her the verses? They would be read out at breakfast amid the tapping of eggshells. Folly indeed! Her brothers would laugh and try to wrest the page from each other with their strong hard fingers. The suave priest, her uncle, seated in his armchair, would hold the page at arm's length, read it smiling, and approve of the literary form" (197). He quickly realizes, however, that she would never show his poetry to others. In *Ulysses*, hypothetical misreading continues to attract his attention. Stephen is concerned about how both his life and his work will be read. In Paris, he used to carry punched tickets in order to

70 The Reader in Modernist Fiction

prove an alibi in case he ever happened to be arrested (3.179–80) and might be falsely implicated in a criminal narrative. He had left instructions that, in case of his death, copies of his epiphanies be sent to all the great libraries of the world and then went on to imagine their reception a few thousand years later: "When one reads these strange pages of one long gone one feels . . ." (3.144–46). In this scene, Stephen's thoughts continue to flow in several directions, and he writes some lines of a poem. Soon he wonders, "Who ever anywhere will read these written words?" (3.414–15). With this sentence, the act of reading takes a decisively reflexive turn. Insofar as the character is addressing himself, the question is a perfectly legitimate one; at the same time, readers physically holding the book in their hands know that they are ones who literally read those words. At the level of represented events, Stephen is right to wonder; at the level of the presentation of those events, the reader is invited to share in Joyce's jest.

This polysemy is continued and developed throughout the book until it takes on a life of its own. In an episode surtitled "YOU CAN DO IT!" Myles Crawford, editor of the *Daily Telegraph*, urges Stephen to "Give them something with a bite in it. Put us all into it, damn its soul. Father, Son and Holy Ghost and Jakes M'Carthy" (7.621–22). At the level of the representation, this is rather unlikely; "As Stephen repeatedly acknowledges to himself, *Ulysses* offers even less evidence than *Portrait* of his creative or vital powers at work," Alan Friedman observes (75). Again, there is an obvious self-reflexive component: insofar as Stephen is an image of Joyce as a young man, he does do it, he puts them all into it, as we see by the very fact of reading the passage that performs this act. Other passages have a similar dual resonance. The "Scylla and Charybdis" episode is based on an actual conversation Joyce had with the men who are re-presented in the novel. John Nash notes that "the temporal disjunction between the setting of the scene in 1904 and the writing of it over a decade later is written into the text: Stephen tells himself: 'See this. Remember . . . Listen' (9.294, 9.300): a form of mental note-taking for future writing" (82). The continuation of this line of thought is still more self-reflexive: "In the future, the sister of the past, I may see myself as I sit now but by reflection from that which I will then be" (9.383–85). By the very fact of reading this passage, we corroborate its accuracy. In the hospital, Vincent states, "All desire to see you bring forth the work you meditate, to acclaim you Stephaneforos. I heartily wish you may not fail them" (14.1120–22); here again, the material book is the demonstration of the success of its author as a

The Fate of Reading in the Work of Joyce   71

no longer young man; Joyce elides once more the normally imperme-able barrier between author and character and between narratee and actual audience.

We may now take up a particularly vexing question of Joyce criti-cism: who is the intended reader of *Ulysses*? Not surprisingly, extreme positions abound on this point. Colin McCabe has suggested that the book is addressed to Joyce himself as a solitary individual (156–57); Richard Ellmann and others propose that Joyce's ideal audience lies in the future and it is one that Joyce's texts are working to create: "We are still learning to be Joyce's contemporaries" (Ellmann 3). Mark Wollaeger argues that Joyce's project is "the invention of a cosmopolitan subject that incorporates without fully assimilating the colligated subject-positions of the Irish colonial subject" ("Read-ing" 146); this position is an attractive one. John Nash, who briefly discusses these and other stances critics have taken on the intended reader of *Ulysses*, postulates instead that Joyce refused to embrace a future or ideal audience, but affirms instead "the inevitable fact of partial reading" (1–27, esp. 4–7); "for Joyce, there can be no model of an audience, but there must of necessity be readers" (4).[4] Sophie Corser identifies the paradox that "the manner in which we read *Ulysses* provokes attitudes towards the author which are seem-ingly incompatible: that the ways we learn to read *Ulysses* re-enact a Barthesian concept of 'authorless' reading, while the same textual intricacies that prompt such ways of reading simultaneously affirm the activity and control of an author" (139).

Turning to the reader response theorist who has most thoroughly analyzed the textual dynamics of *Ulysses*, however, we find him backing away from the position of determinate reader response when dealing with Joyce. Wolfgang Iser notes that "the reader is virtually free to choose his own direction, but he will not be able to work his way through every possible perspective, for the number of these is far beyond the capacity of any one man's naturally selective perception . . . Each 'picture' composed out of each pattern repre-sents one possible meaning of the text concerned, but the reader will not be content to accept each 'picture' as an end in itself. He will search for a complete picture of everyday life, and this is precisely what the novel withholds from him" (*Implied* 231–32).

My own sense is that Joyce is addressing a number of differ-ent audiences that at times merge, diverge, oppose each other, and fuse again into different alliances. Most important is the interpre-tive drama that is staged page after page. He repeatedly sets forth a number of positions on different social and cultural issues, both

72 The Reader in Modernist Fiction

major and minor, and invites the reader to adjudicate among them. Garret Deasy, representing the clichéd positions of the Anglo-Irish ruling class, makes a number of claims concerning recent Irish history and history in general; these are countered by Stephen's words and thoughts. In this instance, there is not much of a battle: Deasy is wrong on all counts and Stephen's position does much more justice to the facts. This kind of interpretive agon is frequently enacted on every topic that an encyclopedic novel can be expected to address: religion, philosophy, politics, ethics, sex, the self, the arts, relations between the sexes, and so forth. Readers are constantly invited to adjudicate among rival positions, one of which is often shown to be correct (though naturally in other cases, the evidence for any particular position is inconclusive). As Iser states, "Instead of providing an illusory coherence of the reality it presents, this novel offers only a potential presentation, the working out of which has to be done actively by the reader. He is not led into a ready-made world of meaning, but is made to search for this world" (*Implied* 232). Joyce does not validate all possible answers, and he does (at times obliquely) articulate multiple positions on some of the questions he raises.

For the most part, traditional reader response criticism has been divided between a monistic approach that postulates a single, fixed, ideal or model reader (Booth, Iser, Eco, Rabinowitz) and a position that resists all determinate readings (Holland, Bleich, Fish, Hillis Miller). *Ulysses* seems to be able to support both positions: its textual logic continues to encourage the refutation of inaccurate statements and interpretations and suggests that many of the book's puzzles can be conclusively solved; at the same time it keeps opening up new aspects of itself to new critical approaches. Even though we will probably never know the real identity of the man in the mackintosh, we can all agree that the figure of the milkwoman in the first episode is realistic parody of the Shan Van Vocht persona which identifies an old Irish peasant woman with the spirit of Ireland and functions as a demystification of the literary uses to which this figure was put by Celtic revivalists such as Yeats and Lady Gregory, who embodied this identification in their play *Cathleen ni Houlihan* and elsewhere.

The novel also seems resistant to the opposition of "symptomatic" versus "surface" readings. Symptomatic readings are usually directed to other kinds of text; those that attempt to take on *Ulysses* often seem trivial, irrelevant, or strangely beside the point; the conceptual binaries that wrack other works typically come deconstructed in advance in *Ulysses*. A "surface" reading of the novel

The Fate of Reading in the Work of Joyce   **73**

is, at best, a paradoxical endeavor: despite the various stories of, say, the Irish sailor who loved reading it while onboard a ship, it is a book whose surfaces immediately impel the reader to numerous depths. Every surface feature, including the letters themselves starting from the first oversized "S," point insistently to an elaborate subterranean network of intercalated meanings and associations; the surface of this text is the surface of a maelstrom. In this regard, it is the quintessential modernist text: it invites us to explore the depths it has itself created.

Concerning Joyce's implied reader, my own position is somewhat mixed, or, more accurately stated, multiple. Above all, Joyce's implied reader is a skeptical, critical reader—perhaps the most extreme of the many critical readers implicitly inscribed within modernist narratives. Going further, we may specify that its implied reader would have to understand several languages; know all the major and many minor works of Western literature, philosophy, music, Catholic theology, and history; have an intimate knowledge of Dublin's geography, history, and society; understand and appreciate the Flaubertian aesthetic of modernist authors; resent imperial domination; be familiar with popular culture in British Isles at the turn of the century; be tolerant of non-Victorian sexual preferences; and know key details of Joyce's life. One fact readily emerges as obvious (and has no doubt colored the many different responses to the question of Joyce's audience): the distance between *Ulysses*'s ideal and actual audiences is perhaps greater than that for any book ever written. Whatever we imagine such an ideal reader to be, there is no doubt that there are very few individuals in the world who might begin to approximate such a figure.

The other most salient feature of the ideal reader of *Ulysses* is that it seems to undergo a transformation as the novel changes. A Flaubertian aesthetic governs the first nine episodes, utilizing what Karen Lawrence calls the work's "initial style." But after the ninth episode, the book's aesthetic alters, becoming more Rabelaisian and avant-garde—expansive, unruly, and, by the time we reach "Eumaeus," the sixteenth episode, even self-negating. Karen Lawrence writes that in the dead prose of this chapter, "Joyce chooses the 'wrong' word as scrupulously as he chooses the right one in the earlier chapters" (*Odyssey* 167).[5] Rather than posit a single ideal reader who can switch at will from one aesthetic to its negation, we may be on better grounds to think of the work as inviting two distinct implied readers, a primary Flaubertian one and a secondary, more Rabelaisian figure, as I have argued elsewhere (*Unnatural* 120–21). To a large extent,

74 *The Reader in Modernist Fiction*

such a judgment is primarily a matter of interpretation: those who view the novel more formalistically as an organic totality will infer a single implied author and a single implied reader, however difficult it may be to fabricate these unified entities. Poststructuralists who see *Ulysses* as more decentered, fragmented, and heterogeneous will have no trouble constructing more than one implied author and reader.

To summarize the positions I have affirmed in this chapter, in *Dubliners* Joyce pursues a sustained critique of naïve readers of romantic, adventure, or idealistic texts largely in the spirit of *Madame Bovary*. In the *Portrait*, we see reading, even the reading of romantic texts, provide consolation and, eventually, knowledge, even as books compete with hidden, illicit words for Stephen's sensibility. In *Ulysses*, we find by contrast a sustained drama of misreading and of skeptical reading. There are numerous acts of misreading throughout the text and a great many misinterpreters: Haines, Deasy, Father Conmee, the Citizen, and several others. The verbal aspects of the mind of Gerty MacDowell are almost entirely constructed by the popular romances she consumes, though her actions show her to be able to elude the constraints of their coy discourse. In the same episode, Bloom is shown to see through the signs of religion: "Mass seems to be over. Could hear them all at it. Pray for us. And pray for us. And pray for us. Good idea the repetition. Same thing with ads. Buy from us. And buy from us" (13.1122–24). Printed words are repeatedly set forth as potentially or typically deceptive signs that critical readers are urged to see through; Bloom, Stephen, and Molly repeatedly perform such demystifications. At the same time, reading and sex are regularly coupled: Bloom and Molly are excited by the words in the letters they receive and the books they encounter; Molly will read more in order to make herself more sexually attractive to Stephen; Stephen reads and writes of love; Gerty's magazines and novelettes, though their language is chaste, lubricate her passion as the euphemized sensuality of her reading becomes embodied in a physical desire that it was presumably intended to sublimate. Kevin Birmingham correctly perceives this connection when he observes that Joyce "wanted people to read novels as carefully, as ardently and as sleeplessly as they would read dirty letters sent from abroad. It was one of modernism's great insights. James Joyce treated readers as if they were lovers" (143).

At a larger level, I suggest that the numerous hermetic texts, uses of code, furtive acts reading, and self-referential jokes about meaning are all miniature allegories of critical, modernist reading. When Stephen affirms: "Signatures of all thing I am here to read . . . Snotgreen,

The Fate of Reading in the Work of Joyce   75

bluesilver, rust: colored signs" (3.2–4, my ellipsis), he is both alluding to the Swedenborgian doctrine of the symbolic nature of the physical world and articulating the general task of the reader of *Ulysses*: to perceive the hidden patterns, salient correspondences, and obscured facts that permeate this book. It is also analogous to correspondences established to elude political censorship: a newspaper image provided the extemporaneous map that revealed the details of the Phoenix Park murders despite imperial attempts to suppress this information from being communicated. As Bloom remarks a little later, "Good system for criminals. Code." (8.325). The same is true for revolutionaries and for modernist authors.

It has been claimed that Bloom would never be able to read the novel that was written about him. We might instead view Bloom's skeptical analyses of the discourses around him as exemplary acts of the kind of critical reading that modernism intended to foster; this is certainly true of the way he quickly sees through "Murphy" in the "Eumaeus" episode. With a little training, Bloom could learn to read *Ulysses* very well indeed. Finally, the ultimate testimony to a work is that it continues to be read; the most lasting gift a writer can bestow is to ensure that his friend or lover is granted immortality by being encountered in print over centuries, an idea well known to Dante, Shakespeare, Joyce, and others. We still know about Beatrice Portinari and Edward King because of the literary tributes paid to them by Dante and Milton ("Lycidas"). In fact, the ancient Greek raiding party that attacked cities to the east is remembered only because we continue to read about it in Homer's narrative. And Homer's oral epic survives because it was written down. If for Mallarmé everything exists to end up in a book, for Joyce we might say the supreme goal for an author (and the individuals represented by him) is for their book to be read; there is no other immortality.

Notes

1. Norris observes, "The reader obliged to make dubious inferences, to be suspicious, to speculate with fragmented and incomplete information, to create scenarios that are unverified and unverifiable occupies a position very similar to Evelyn's own" (*Suspicious* 56).
2. I develop this interpretation in "Misreadings, Self-Misconstruals, and Fabricated Resolutions in Joyce's 'The Dead.'"
3. For a compelling account of the differences between oral and silent reading in this and other works of Joyce, see Patrick McCarthy, "Joyce's Silent Readers."

76   *The Reader in Modernist Fiction*

4. Brian Caraher provides a richly suggestive account of several classic postulations of the protocols of reading *Ulysses*.

5. I discuss the anti-aesthetic elements of the later parts of *Ulysses* in my article, "Bad Joyce"; I argue for the usefulness of positing multiple implied authors and readers for that text in *Unnatural Voices*, 81–86 and 120–21.

Chapter 3

"Books Were Not in Their Line": The Use and Abuse of Reading in Katherine Mansfield and Virginia Woolf

Katherine Mansfield and Virginia Woolf knew each other well and admired each other's work. Hermione Lee writes that "their friendship was intimate but guarded, mutually inspiring but competitive" (381). The Woolfs' Hogarth Press was the first to publish Mansfield's "Prelude." More pertinently for our purposes, they both were keenly interested in reading and misreading, good and bad interpreters, unfortunate allusions, and the importance of a perceptive, critical sensibility. They both expand the range of materials that had previously been used in dramas of misreading, extending this probing into larger issues of interpretation in the case of Mansfield and into the materiality and affordances of physical books in Woolf. Both include issues of power in dramatizing their interpretive challenges, focusing on women's perceptions, class positionality, and the sensibilities of children. Both also foreground hermeneutical dilemmas produced by characters who cannot be confined to cisgender or binary sexualities. And they both featured suggestive scenes of failed discussions of literature at dinner parties.

Katherine Mansfield

Mansfield is one of English literature's keenest observers of the act of perception and the circuits of misunderstanding. Many of her stories dramatize the inability of the upper classes to imagine the inner life of those beneath them socially ("Revelation"), or worse, how the upper classes learn to become blind to the suffering of the working class ("The Garden Party") and others in less fortunate circumstances ("Her First Ball"). Not surprisingly, theatrical scenes, allusions, and

78   *The Reader in Modernist Fiction*

metaphors frequently appear; one story, "Miss Brill" (1920) unfolds as an unwitting public performance. The protagonist is a single, elderly tutor who visits a public park each Sunday and looks forward to observing the people who reappear each week. At one point she discovers the source of her enjoyment: "How she loved sitting here, watching it all! It was like a play. It was exactly like a play. Who could believe the sky at the back wasn't painted?" (*Collected* II, 253). Further reflection on this theme leads to additional revelations: "They weren't only the audience, not only looking on; they were acting. Even she had a part and came every Sunday"; imagining a sense of her own modest importance to the social spectacle, she continues: "No doubt somebody would have noticed if she hadn't been there; she was a part of the performance after all" (*Collected* II, 253). As she happily feels herself belonging to a larger community, she notices a young man and woman approach. "The hero and heroine, of course," she overgenerously designates them. Then she hears them refer to her as "a stupid old thing" and wonder too loudly, "Why doesn't she keep her silly old mug at home?" (*Collected* II, 254). She is noticed, but not wanted; the others are performing in a very different drama from the one she has been imagining.

Several of Mansfield's stories foreground the motifs of reading and misinterpretation and dramatize the disjunctions between life as presented in literature and that experienced by the character— usually a woman—who reads it. "The Tiredness of Rosabel," one of her first works (1908), begins with an observed scene of reading as the protagonist sits beside a young woman her own age who is reading raptly. Rosabel cannot see the volume clearly but she does observe that "it was something about a hot, voluptuous night, a band playing, and girl with lovely, white shoulders" (*Collected* I, 133). The book turns out to be *Anna Lombard,* an exotic middlebrow novel that centers on an illicit and unconventional love triangle in India that concludes with a preposterous though "moral" ending. The edition she observes is a cheap paperback whose pages have been "tear-splattered" by the rain (*Collected* I, 133). Rosabel is disgusted by the reader, who mouths the words as she reads them and licks her finger as she turns the pages on the crowded bus. The quality of the text, the physical condition of the book, and the particular circumstances of its consumption all suggest the common, even the vulgar. Back in her cold, rented room, Rosabel goes over the events of the working day, and her mind fixes on a dashing, wealthy young couple she had waited on. She fantasizes that she could change places with the woman and that she is engaged to the man. The fantasy

The Use and Abuse of Reading in Mansfield and Woolf   79

continues, becoming more elaborate and detailed, until it comes to "a voluptuous night, a band playing, and *her* lovely white shoulders" (*Collected* I, 136, Mansfield's emphasis). She goes to sleep, and wakes to another cold dawn. Mansfield is at once critiquing the mass-produced visions afforded by middle-brow, escapist tales of passion, and showing how they insinuate themselves into the minds of even those who scorn to read them in printed form. This literature can produce illusions without even being read. As Kate Fullbrook points out, "the fact that Katherine Mansfield used these clichés to populate her character's mind is as much her comment on the power of entrenched imaginative forms to control the contents of consciousness as it is an attack on the final cruelty of such images as drugs for the minds of oppressed women" (380). Fullbrook affirms that the young Mansfield recognized the function of escapist romances for women which invite "dreams of being the perfect beneficiaries of the sexual system that in fact victimizes them" (380).

The modernist drama of mistakenly applying social trajectories found in fiction to situations found in life is dramatized in "A Cup of Tea" (1922). Rosemary Fell is rich, as well as "young, brilliant, extremely modern, exquisitely well-dressed," and she is also "amazingly well read in the newest of the new books" (*Collected* II, 461). Standing outside a shop on a winter day, she is approached by a poor woman who asks for money to buy a cup of tea; the woman is penniless and near fainting. "How extraordinary!" Rosemary says, thinking that the encounter suddenly seems to be an adventure. "It was like something out of a novel by Dostoevsky" (*Collected* II, 463). She considers taking the woman home with her; it would be "one of those things she was always reading about or seeing on the stage" (*Collected* II, 463). Once she imagines narrating the story to her friends, she cannot stop herself and brings the woman to her house, quickly envisaging a confused though utopian scene which would demonstrate that "wonderful things did happen in life, that—fairy godmothers were real, that—rich people had hearts, and that women *were* sisters" (*Collected* II, 463–64). As the cups of tea are served, Rosemary learns that her unfortunate guest is contemplating suicide. At this point her husband, Philip, discovers them together and calls her into the library to discuss what he feels to be her inappropriate behavior. Rosemary's defense is a literary one: "one's always reading about these things" (*Collected* II, 466). This however has no effect on her husband; for him, such things simply are not done. Philip also indicates that the young woman is extremely pretty; this annoys Rosemary since earlier in the story she is described as "not

80   *The Reader in Modernist Fiction*

exactly beautiful" (*Collected* II, 461). Shortly afterward, she sends the unusual guest away with three pound notes as the experiment in equality ends abruptly. The wealthy husband rewards his wife by buying her a costly little trinket as the web of affiliation created by capital is shown to quickly trump any bonding enabled by literature. Rich people, it seems, don't have hearts after all, and the fiction of Dostoyevsky proves to be a poor pretext for self-congratulatory dramas staged by the bourgeoisie.

There is a possible intertextual connection here as well. Rosemary is regularly claimed to be modeled on Elizabeth von Arnim, Mansfield's cousin once removed, whose book, *The Enchanted April* (1922), likewise includes a fallible reader figure. This character, Mrs. Fisher, is an older, aloof woman, the daughter of a famous critic, and someone who has personally known many celebrated Victorian writers. She is often seen holding a book, but rarely reading one. Her grip on literature seems faint. Concerning Carlyle, a frequent house guest whom her father had called immortal, she reflects: "She had read him; she had certainly read him. Of course she had read him. There was Teufelsdröck—she quite well remembered a tailor called Teufelsdröck. So like Carlyle to call him that. Yes, she must have read him, though naturally details escaped her" (101). Her time in Italy enjoying the spring flora invigorates her, expands her emotions, and allows her to empathize with others instead of hiding scornfully behind a book. This is another version of the romantic association of reading (and culture, more generally) with emotional stultification and physical decay; it is a mild version of the position of Somerset Maugham, D. H. Lawrence, and others of the period who were mentioned in the introduction. It is certainly not a stance that Mansfield would share. Both works were written quickly in the spring of 1922 and published the same year; it is not evident that one influenced the other. From a certain angle, this makes the conjunction all the more fascinating as it shows how prevalent and insistent dramas of reading were during the early years of modernism. On the other hand, the two cousins may well have discussed the subject—at the time she wrote the story, Mansfield was staying in Switzerland half an hour away from von Arnim, who visited her frequently during this period. In this case, Mansfield's story, which is entirely consistent with her other works on the limitations of the powers of reading, would be an especially appropriate riposte to her cousin's treatment of the theme.

Other stories by Mansfield are more oblique or more general in their interpretive struggles. "The Little Governess" (1915) portrays the dangers of the inability to read social signs, and critiques the

The Use and Abuse of Reading in Mansfield and Woolf   81

belief that ideas derived from books can be applied simply and successfully to life. As the story begins, a young and very inexperienced governess is about to take a train to Munich where she is to meet the family she will be working for. She is warned that it is better to mistrust people at first rather than trust them, and that it is safer to suspect people of evil intentions rather than good ones. In the station, she is approached by a man in a black leather cap who asks her where she is headed. Once she responds, the man takes her bag and walks quickly toward her train. She insists she does not want or need a porter, but the man ignores her. Beside the train, he waits for his "fare," which he now announces to be a franc. He is shocked that she only gives him four sous and he scornfully gives the coins right back. He then exacts his revenge by assisting an older gentleman into the car and removing the "Women Only" sign, thus enabling the man to sit close to her.

She is at first unsure how to read her fellow passenger, but his class status seems relatively high and he acts pleasantly enough. As she eats the strawberries he buys for her, she reflects, "What a perfect grandfather he would make! Just like one out of a book!" (*Collected* I, 429). In modernist narratives, such a judgment regularly leads to misfortune. Another misreading occurs once he gives her his card: seeing the title, "Herr Regierungsrat" ("Government Councillor") on it, she falsely deduces that since he had a title he "was *bound* to be all right!" (*Collected* I, 429): her literary naïveté is paired with a faulty social inference. Later, he lures her into his apartment and forcibly holds and kisses her. The description of the scene of the unwanted kiss is ominous: "he held her against the wall, pressed against her his hard old body and his twitching knee and, though she shook her head from side to side, distracted, kissed her on the mouth" (*Collected* I, 432). Afterwards, she runs into the street, crying, "pressing her hands to her mouth" (*Collected* I, 432) in a way that makes onlookers think she has had a painful experience at the dentist's. Returning to the hotel, she finds that the family she was to work for will not accept her services due to the intervention of the waiter, another working-class individual whom she had refused to tip and had spoken rudely to. The class drama, a variant of which we find elsewhere in Mansfield's work, is now complete: workers are not to be treated as indifferent lackeys, and the bourgeoisie is much more mendacious than is usually represented in fiction.

And there may well be yet another drama of mis- or incomplete reading in this text. The description of the scene of the unwanted kiss is very brutal; it is followed by an ominous set of elliptical

82   *The Reader in Modernist Fiction*

dots. We must wonder whether the "kiss" was not, in fact, a worse violation, something that Mansfield could gesture toward but not publish in 1915. Even as one laments the young woman's inability to read the codes that regulate behavior among different classes and cultures, she certainly cannot be faulted for not being more suspicious. Unlike many of Mansfield's later protagonists, she is less a victim of naïve misreading than of inexperience, deception, and predation. And, in fact, of never having read the kind of story Mansfield provides here.

"Marriage à la Mode" (1921) contains a miniature drama of reading and writing that both frames and triggers the events of the text and reveals the ethics they embody. William works in London and supports his wife and children in their new house in the country. On his weekly train trip back to visit his family, he attempts to read some business correspondence; Mansfield lets us into his mind to observe his reading (or at least, skimming): "Our client moreover is positive . . . We are inclined to reconsider . . . in the event of—" (*Collected* II, 331). But William cannot focus on the papers: he "hung on to that sentence, but it was no good; it snapped in the middle, and the fields, the sky, the sailing bird, the water, all said, 'Isabel'" (*Collected* II, 331); he cannot read, he can only think of his wife. She meets him at the station but brings a crowd of her new friends with her, a group of shallow, selfish aesthetes. They constitute a kind of second-rate salon and make themselves at home with Isabel, who feeds them and pays some of their bills. Reaching into the edge of an armchair, William finds, instead of one of his children's misplaced toys, "another paper-covered book of smudged-looking poems" (*Collected* II, 335).

William is utterly lost amid the constant posing and chatter about art; he also realizes that his wife's affection for him has diminished considerably. He tries to read again but falls asleep instead. While at home, he never sees his children, who are either sleeping or out with their nanny; nor is he able to have private time with his wife. On returning to London, he writes her a long letter, explaining that he does not wish to be a drag on her happiness. Upon receiving it, she reads the letter aloud to the guests, and all roar with laughter at its simplicity and sentiment. The final cruelty is marked by a writer's request for the missive: "You must let me have it just as it is, entire, for my new book . . . I shall give it a whole chapter!" (*Collected* II, 337). A moment later, Isabel crumples the letter up and goes to her room. For a few minutes she is filled with remorse; she decides to write back to her husband. Then the guests call to her, she reflects that writing is too difficult and, laughing in her new way, goes off

The Use and Abuse of Reading in Mansfield and Woolf   83

to join them. William's letter, a handwritten object of pathos in life, may, without a word being changed, become a source of satire for a work of fiction. The effects of its reading change wildly with different readers and listeners, eliciting antithetical aesthetic, emotional, and ethical responses.

"Bliss" (1918) provides a deeper investigation into the social dynamics of reading, interpretation, and allusion. Bertha Young, an immature, middle-class housewife with pretensions to high culture, is filled with a feeling of joy for her life, including her friends— "modern, thrilling friends, writers and painters and poets or people keen on social questions" (*Collected* II, 145). That day she is hosting an evening party for guests that include Norman Knight, a man who plans to start a new theater; his wife, a modern interior decorator; Eddie Warren, who has just published a small book of poems; and Pearl Fulton, a beautiful woman "who had something strange about" her (*Collected* II, 144) and whose connection to modern culture is both unquestioned and unspecified. As the evening begins, the reader quickly perceives the guests to be poseurs and mediocrities rather than serious artists or thinkers. Bertha, for her part, simply looks over at them and thinks "how delightful they were, and what a decorative group they made, how they seemed to set one another off and how they reminded her of a play by Tchekof!" (*Collected* II, 148). The last comparison is of course most unfortunate, since Chekhov's characters typically live lives of futility, failed ambition, marital disappointment, and sexual frustration. Unknown to Bertha, this mistaken allusion will in fact turn out to be particularly apposite for the drama of blindness, discovery, and betrayal about to unfold before her.

Like the principal characters in "The Secret Sharer," "The Dead," and *To the Lighthouse*, Bertha also believes she detects a significant symbolic correspondence; thinking of the pear tree in her garden, she envisaged it "with its wide open blossoms as a symbol of her own life" (*Collected* II, 145). This is true, though not in the ways that Bertha can express or conceive it: one meaning that Bertha cannot comprehend at this point is the sexual awakening that it portends. Bertha is infatuated with Miss Fulton and believes they have much in common. She finds it "miraculous" that she has guessed the other woman's mood "so exactly and so instantly" (*Collected* II, 148–49), and hopes that Miss Fulton will at some point "give a sign" (*Collected* II, 149), thereby recognizing their shared feelings. The sign comes quickly: Miss Fulton asks, in a "cool, sleepy voice," whether they have a garden (*Collected* II, 152). The two step over to the window and admire the

84 The Reader in Modernist Fiction

pear tree, now bathed in moonlight. Enveloped by the unearthly light, both understand each other perfectly, Bertha thinks; she also realizes that, for the first time, she physically desires her husband. This too is a misreading, as it is evident that it is Miss Fulton whom she desires, though she cannot consciously acknowledge that feeling. Soon, the guests begin to depart, but before leaving, Eddie wants to show Bertha a new poem. As they move across the room to get the book, Bertha suddenly sees her husband and Miss Fulton caressing each other and making an assignation for the next day. The story ends in a genuinely Chekhovian situation and is even articulated in language typical of the Russian writer as Bertha utters the words, "Oh, what is going to happen now?" (*Collected* II, 152), a kind of variant of the indeterminate thoughts expressed in the final sentences of Chekhov's "The Lady with the Lapdog," the unresolved ending of which Woolf would go on to praise in her essay, "The Russian Point of View" (*Common* 175–76).

Overall, we see in Mansfield's stories a sustained account of the difficulty of the reading of social signs, a failure to respond to them appropriately, a skepticism about useful knowledge being derived from books, a satire on many who claim to represent modern literature and art, a middle class that cannot or will not read working-class signals, and a depiction of the prevalence of unexamined stereotypes that mislead even those who dismiss their more obvious manifestations. Reading is less likely to save than to harm her characters. Ethically, the positions of the protagonists vary greatly: Rosabel is unwittingly interpolated into the social narratives she scorns when they appear in popular novels; Rosemary Fell simplistically believes in easy solutions to social problems; the governess is young and inexperienced; Isabel is insensitive and selfish; and Bertha is naïve and rather childlike. All suffer due to their insufficiently critical belief in the written word and the larger social narratives expressed by that discourse.

Virginia Woolf

Reading is a subject Virginia Woolf regularly reflected on in her critical work and dramatized in her fiction in evolving ways, some of which have provoked opposed critical readings. Anne E. Fernald observes, "From her girlhood in her father's study to the end of her life, Virginia Woolf read widely and with passion" (1). Woolf wrote on the subject during most periods of her career and regularly included exemplary scenes of reading and misreading in her novels. Julia Briggs affirms that "in their various ways, all Woolf's

The Use and Abuse of Reading in Mansfield and Woolf   85

work—novels, short stories and essays—contribute to an ongoing debate" about the nature of reading (63). Woolf also had a "thoroughgoing physical relation to books: their heft, their appearance, even their smell got her attention" (65), Theodore Leinwand observes; he goes on to quote a diary entry in which sight, smell, and touch are all invoked: "I went in and found the table all laden with books. I looked in & sniffed them all. I could not resist carrying this one off & broaching it" (*Diary*, August 24, 1933; 5.173). Woolf's fiction often represents the varied effects of reading; her critiques, though subtle, can go deeper than her critical writing on the subject does.

Her first published novel, *The Voyage Out* (1915), contains numerous ambivalent depictions of reading. Christine Froula observes that in this text everyone is always reading a book (148–59), and Susan Stanford Friedman states that the novel is a "parable about reading" (64). The results of the reading are ambivalent, even contradictory. Briggs notes that protagonist Rachel Vinrace, "struggling to come to terms with life, is using books to help her do so. The men and women around her encourage her by presenting her with different books, from Jane Austen's *Persuasion* to Gibbon's *Decline and Fall of the Roman Empire*—books that reflect their hopes for her, rather than her own" (67). Rachel discovers some books that "promise greater self-determination," including proto-feminist works like Meredith's *Diana of the Crossways* and Ibsen's *A Doll's House*; she is also haunted "by a cheap novel of social criticism" that depicts the terrible fate of a woman whom poverty has forced into prostitution (67).

Froula sees the book's depictions of reading as representing a dialectic of nature and culture, where Rachel rejects being objectified as passive in nature and instead positions herself as a full participant in and potential producer of culture. Her reading of Edward Gibbon "creates a highly complex and self-reflexive representation of female initiation, for it compounds the chrysalis metaphor of female initiation with the image of Rachel *reading*, and not only reading but, in her not-reading, potentially *writing* into history what Gibbon . . . has left out: among other things, women's history" (151). Other scholars offer darker views of reading in the novel. Kate Flint argues that in this work, "literature can only be a partial guide to life. For when Rachel begins to feel a certain amount of first-hand interest in men, she finds the experience perplexing, and 'none of the books she read, from *Wuthering Heights* to *Man and Superman*, and the plays of Ibsen, suggested from their analysis of love that what their heroines felt was what she was

86 *The Reader in Modernist Fiction*

feeling now" (*Woman* 272). Friedman goes further, concluding her study of representations of reading in the novel:

> As the privileged reader whose development ends in death, Rachel Vinrace serves as both [a] positive and negative model of reading. Against the foil of all the other characters who read, Rachel's mode of reading is generally favored, but because her reading leads toward her death—whether causally or not matters little—her method remains suspect, a dire warning about the dangers of reading to one's psychological and physical health. (64)

Friedman articulates a dangerous parable implicit in Vinrace's reading experiences and in her final end, though she notes the absence of a clear causal connection between reading and suffering, the kind that we found in Conrad, Joyce, and Ford.

In *Jacob's Room* (1922) the scenes of reading are fewer but more consistent. After a faculty wife states that she doesn't know the truth of anything until she has read Shaw and Wells, Jacob tells a companion: "such a thing to believe in—Shaw and Wells and the sixpenny weeklies! What were they after, scrubbing and demolishing, these elderly people? Had they never read Homer, Shakespeare, the Elizabethans?" (35). The point here seems to be not that reading is wrong, but that limited reading produces limited knowledge. The novel also contains a passionate account of a letter protesting censorship that ironically is not allowed to be published in the literary journals and therefore goes unread (70). The difficulties of a common reader, that is, of reading properly without a formal education, are also noted, as Fanny Elmer reads *Tom Jones* on the advice of Jacob and reflects that there is something "about books which if I had been educated I would have liked" (122). There is also a poignant scene announcing the gilding of the final "Y" in "Macaulay," the last name inscribed on the dome of the British Museum. Hundreds of feet below, numerous readers sat "copying from printed books into manuscript books" (105). The feminist Julia Hedge, waiting for her books, notes the final letters in Macaulay's name and exclaims, "Oh damn," as she wonders, "Why didn't they leave room for an Eliot or a Brontë?" (106). Even though women were allowed in the British Museum, their bodies were literally circumscribed by the names of eminent men.

While *Jacob's Room* stresses the inequality of women's educational possibilities and points out the limitations of an incomplete course of reading, *Mrs. Dalloway* (1925) focuses on flagrant acts of misreading. Septimus Smith, as noted in the introduction, finds nonexistent patterns seemingly written in the world around him. Noticing the mostly indecipherable writing in the sky, Rezia tells her husband to observe it: "So, thought Septimus, looking up, they are signaling to me. Not indeed in actual words; that is, he could not read the language yet; but it was plain enough, this beauty, this exquisite beauty, and tears filled his eyes as he looked at the smoke words languishing and melting in the sky" (22). In part, he resembles an "incomplete" reader, described as "one of those half-educated, self-educated men whose education is all learnt from books borrowed from public libraries, read in the evening after the day's work, on the advice of well-known authors consulted by letter" (84). Of course, Septimus's situation is far more grave; tellingly, his wild misinterpretations parallel the fatal misreading of his condition made by his autocratic doctor.

Woolf's most sustained examination of reading and nonreading appears in *To the Lighthouse* (1927); it reiterates, extends, varies, and greatly augments the model of reading and misconstrual that we have been following in the work of Conrad and Joyce and, like Katherine Mansfield's stories, moves out into other, adjacent territories of reception, interpersonal interpretation, and the status of the material book. The opening paragraphs of the novel set forth some of the work's central concerns involving audience response: James Ramsay is sitting on the floor next to his mother, cutting pictures out of a catalogue, investing the images he is looking at with the joy produced by his mother's hopeful comment that they would indeed go to the lighthouse the next day if the weather is good. In a flagrant case of what New Criticism would later (and vainly) castigate as the affective fallacy, James "endowed the picture of a refrigerator, as his mother spoke, with heavenly bliss . . . The wheel barrow, the lawnmower, the sound of poplar trees . . . all these were so coloured and distinct in his mind that he had already his private code, his secret language, though he appeared the image of stark and uncompromising severity" (3–4). In these lines we have a depiction of an ordinary image accidentally endowed with bliss, suggesting the adventitious and often fleeting associations that are part of the reception experience of any audience. The emotional turmoil of his mind in contrast to his stoical appearance parallels the same pattern in the behavior of his father, as well as that of official Victorian society that the older Ramsay both belongs to and stands for. Finally, the reference to the child's private code or secret language is an image of the submerged cluster of meanings present in the modernist text, which can be appreciated by a critical, engaged audience but is easily missed by

88 *The Reader in Modernist Fiction*

a more hurried or indifferent observer whose interpretive practices do not exceed the limits of conventional Victorian reading habits.

It is only appropriate that one of the most central scenes and tropes of *To the Lighthouse* is the act of reading, or more accurately, the scene of apparent reading, since it is often the case that actual reading does not occur, or that reading is largely a pretext for the person holding open the covers of a book. The power and multiform nature of the scene of reading are evident from the transformations played upon its first appearance in the text, Mrs. Ramsay's reading a fairy tale to James. As Mr. Ramsay strolls up and observes this tableau, he finds the image iconic and compelling; in short order, he moves over and stands in front of them, displaying his need of sympathy, jealous of the attention given to his son. James, in his turn, tries to use the book to divert the man it had just summoned: "By looking fixedly at the page, he hoped to make him move on; by pointing his finger at a word, he hoped to recall his mother's attention, which, he knew angrily, wavered instantly his father stopped" (37).

But the scene of reading has more power to attract than to repel. James's stratagem fails, as he feared it would; Mrs. Ramsay ignores him to satisfy her husband's needs. The tropes used to depict this interaction are revealing: after listening to his wife's words of encouragement, Ramsay is described as being "filled with her words, as a child who drops off satisfied" (38). For Mrs. Ramsay, this is a much more arduous task than anyone realizes: "the whole fabric fell in exhaustion upon itself, so that she had only strength enough to move her finger, in exquisite abandonment to exhaustion, along the page of Grimm's fairy story" (38). The act of reading she returns to does not hold her attention at all, though the act of discerning and satisfying her husband's unspoken need before returning to do the same for her son fills her with "the rapture of successful creation" (38). Hidden within this account of absent-minded reading, that is, lies a foreshadowing of the weariness that prefigures Mrs. Ramsay's sudden death later in the novel as well as the difficult though successful acts of creation that connect her psychologically and thematically to Lily Briscoe, an artist.

As this scene is taking place, William Bankes asks Briscoe what was indicated by a triangular purple shape on her canvas. That, she explains, is a depiction of "Mrs. Ramsay reading to James" (52). Both are uncomfortable: Bankes for being unable to decipher what the patch of color represents, Lily at the scientist's narrowly representational sensibility. Though he is the proud owner of a pleasant painting of the cherry trees on the banks of the Kennet, he has no understanding of modern painting, and the aesthetic questions of "the relations of masses, of lights and shadows" are issues he had never considered (53). In short, he cannot fully appreciate traditional, representational art, and he cannot read a modern painting at all. This statement of ignorance is another figure, a *mise en abyme*, of the reading of the novel itself: a resolutely conventional sensibility will have trouble comprehending many of its aspects, from its temporality to its characterizations to its unusual plotting. Thus, Lily's desire "to connect this mass on the right with that on the left" (53), perhaps by bringing the line of the branch across, is a visual metaphor for Woolf's own bridging of the book's two main parts by way of the narratively slender stretch contained within "Time Passes"—and one equally liable to misinterpretation by a traditional reader.

And what is the story being read to James? It is a misogynistic fairy tale, "The Fisherman and his Wife." The precise nature and function of this seemingly odd choice of inner text has occasioned considerable speculation and contradictory responses in the critical literature. It is all the more vexing since, as Mark Hussey notes, Woolf chose it to replace other, less offensive fairy tales ("The Three Dwarfs," "The Three Bears") in earlier manuscript versions ("Introduction," 220–21). The story relates the fate of a poor fisherman who one day catches an enchanted flounder. The fish speaks and asks to be set free; the fisherman is happy to comply and returns it to the water. That evening in their hovel the fisherman's wife tells him to go back to the sea and ask the fish to provide them with a cottage. He does, and his wish is granted. Some ten days later, however, the wife is again dissatisfied, and she tells her husband to find the fish again and request a castle. He does, and the wish is granted. Later she demands to be made first king, then emperor, and finally, pope; all this too is achieved. At last she insists on having the power to make the sun and moon rise at her command. The flounder returns them to their original hovel where, the text concludes, they are still living to this very day.

What are we to make of this blatantly sexist parable of "woman's insatiable desire for power," as Jane Marcus calls it (*Patriarchy* 154)? Howard Harper believes the tale is providing "a brilliant analogue for the Ramsays. Like the fisherman's wife, Mrs. Ramsay is utterly dominant—in the excitement of the story we don't anticipate her inevitable fall" (141). Maria DiBattista likewise affirms this association, stating that "in the fairy tale, the final wish of the fisherman's wife is to be God. Certainly, such is the unconscious, implied wish of Mrs. Ramsay in her solipsistic reveries when she dreams of ruling

90 *The Reader in Modernist Fiction*

and reforming a world she feels to be unjust and much mismanaged" (81). Beth Rigel Daugherty views Mrs. Ramsay as one who has been destroyed by the narratives of the patriarchy; her fate is that which Lily must struggle to avoid: "through her use of the fairy tale and the Angel of the house, Woolf shows the implication of patriarchal myths for women—they kill" (302). Deborah Wilson identifies aspects of the fable's demanding wife with both Mr. and Mrs. Ramsay; she argues that "the tyranny of both Ramsays becomes a central obstacle the artist, Lily Briscoe, must overcome in this novel . . . as the fairy tale wife is deposed by the fish, they are in a sense deposed by [Lily's] determination to pursue an elusive vision" (122). Despite numerous points of divergence, differences in emphasis, and alternative contextualizations, most of these accounts postulate a significant identification between the fishwife and Mrs. Ramsay. This is an obvious reading, though it remains a very problematic one, while accounts that offer alternative conceptions are not that compelling and seem to reach too hard to explain away this intertextual conundrum.[1]

The repeated staging of key dramas of misreading that helped construct modernism and its reader that I have traced throughout this study suggests a differently configured oppositional interpretation. Like Conrad's Leggatt, Joyce's Gabriel Conroy, and Mansfield's Bertha Young, Mrs. Ramsay fails to correctly apply the narrative she invokes: as she reads the story to her son, she is in fact reciting a version of her own life that cannot be recognized as such by any of those who hear it. She is not, however, the insatiable wife: one must invert the gender of the central actants to appreciate the identity of the protagonists. She is, rather, a victim of repeated demands by males who are never satisfied; she assumes the position of the enchanted fish, though she unfortunately lacks its supernatural powers. It is then not surprising that she finds comfort in imagining herself drowning and finally finding "rest on the floor of the sea" (84).[2] The narrative of Mrs. Ramsay thus functions as a critical rewriting of the sexist fairy tale from the perspective of the oppressed, and the misogynistic slander is thus refuted by the very acts that surround its dissemination.

This view of the function of "The Fisherman and His Wife" is consonant with Woolf's practice of allusion elsewhere in the text. The unidentified lines of verse that Mrs. Ramsay finds so satisfying and so restful as she sits reading with her husband—"*Steer, hither steer, your winged pines, all beaten Mariners*"—come from William Browne's "The Inner Temple Masque" (121). This work, as Alice Fox has pointed out, "deliberately suppresses the sirens' motive for destruction, and would perhaps have attracted Woolf by its

The Use and Abuse of Reading in Mansfield and Woolf   91

elimination of the misogyny implicit in Homer's tale" (45).[3] This reading also meshes well with the ironic vision that animated Woolf as she conceived of the novel: "father's character, sitting in a boat, reciting We perished, each alone, while he crushes a dying mackerel" (*Diaries* 3, 18–19, entry for May 14, 1925): he rests comfortably as he imagines experiencing death while his hands are actually inflicting death on another creature.

The fact that Mrs. Ramsay does not herself identify the correspondences I have just suggested only shows that misogyny is so widespread as to be literally unremarkable: it is the function of patriarchy to make audiences ready to identify any woman with the demanding fishwife. To be sure, Mrs. Ramsay is not concentrating fully on the story; the partially phenomenological depiction of her reading nevertheless shows how closely the reading is woven into the events occurring around her:

> "'Well, what does she want then?' said the Flounder." And where were they now? Mrs. Ramsay wondered, reading and thinking, quite easily, both at the same time; for the story of the Fisherman and his Wife was like the bass gently accompanying a tune, which now and then ran unexpectedly into the melody. And when should she be told? If nothing happened, she would have to speak seriously to Minta. (56)

The last two sentences here refer to Mrs. Ramsay's plan to give marital advice to Minta Doyle in the near future; tellingly, that marriage has been brought about thanks in part to her maneuverings, but it turns out to be, like all the marriages in the book, unsatisfactory.[4] The contrapuntal imagery of the passage suggests still closer connections between Mrs. Ramsay's reading and her life. After all, she is plotting to arrange a marriage even as she reads about an utterly failed union. The fairy tale and the first part of the novel mirror each other much more closely than has been suggested in the critical literature; one need only bear in mind that a mirror reverses the relations that it reflects.

Mrs. Ramsay, it must be admitted, is not much of a reader. She doesn't pay much attention to the story she is reading to James; at one point, her reading is compared to sleeping (121). Neither does she peruse the volumes she owns: "She never had time to read them. Alas! Even the books that had been given her and inscribed by the hand of the poet himself" (27). Ramsay "liked to think his wife was not clever, not book-learned"; he even doubts whether his wife understands what she is reading (121). Ironically, he is partially correct

92   *The Reader in Modernist Fiction*

in this, though not for the reasons he assumes. Tansley's relation to reading is quite different; he is remembered by Lily as "always carrying a book under his arm—a purple book" (159). For him, books serve as an escape from people: he finds conversation inane: "He was not going to talk the sort of rot these people wanted him to talk . . . He had been reading in his room, and now he came down and it all seemed to him silly, superficial, flimsy" (85).

Most of the other characters are inadequate readers. Paul Rayley claims that the books one read as a boy truly last, and praises a novel by Tolstoy he knows he will always remember, though he cannot at first recall its title. That subject of conversation does "not take them very far. Books were not in their line" (108). Minta Doyle carelessly leaves the last volume of *Middlemarch* behind in the train and therefore never learns how the novel ends (98). Even Lily feels ashamed she had not read Carlyle since she was at school (46). It should be pointed out that these details differ sharply from Woolf's accounts of her own passionate experience as a reader, as Hermione Lee has documented (403–05); likewise, though she advocates a number of acceptable answers to the question, "How Should One Read a Book?" in her essay of that title, these do not include the forgetful or slovenly modes displayed by the characters in her novel. Moving on to Mr. Ramsay, we may note that he does indeed read, but he reads Walter Scott, who proves to be a thoroughly dated and generally unfortunate favorite, since even Ramsay's disciple Tansley affirms that people don't read Scott any more (118).

In this narrative, books serve many functions other than that of being read, and Woolf dramatizes several of their different affordances; many of these center on the physical volume itself. Books are said to grow of themselves (27). They may be offered along with stamps and tobacco as a gesture of politeness (41), banged on the floor to express frustration (116), or considered awkward objects to be "clawed up" from the grass (191). To fetch "up from oblivion all the Waverley novels" does not mean restoring the prominence of their author but rather cleaning mold from the spines of several tomes (139). Rather insidiously, books can produce a material transformation never intended by their authors: in the closed-up room there are "long rows of books, black as ravens once, now white-stained, breeding pale mushrooms and secreting furtive spiders" (140).[5] Leah Price states that, for the Victorians, "books function both as trophies and as tools . . . their use engages bodies as well as minds, and . . . printed matter connects readers not just with authors but with other owners and handlers" (2); we see all these functions at work in *To the Lighthouse.*

The Use and Abuse of Reading in Mansfield and Woolf   93

Equally suggestively, a book may provide a physical medium for the perception that someone has drawn near: "A shadow was on the page; she looked up" (39). This is an image pregnant with numerous other associations. In the case at hand, it is relatively benign, indicating merely that Mr. Carmichael is shuffling past, but it can easily stretch to include the various men whose shadows disturb the creative work of women, both in the novel and elsewhere in Woolf's corpus, as it does in another incarnation of the trope in *A Room of One's Own*. In this text, after reading a chapter or two of a well-regarded male novelist, Woolf observes that "a shadow seemed to lie across the page"; it was the dominating "I" of the novelist which entirely obscured any landscape or woman that might lie behind it (103–04).

The act of being read, that is of one's sensibility continuing to produce responses in the minds of others, is a major concern in the novel. It is most clearly present in the mind of Mr. Ramsay, who figuratively measures his intellectual achievement with the sequence of the letters of the alphabet, and obsessively wonders "how long will he be read" (107), a query that causes him considerable anguish, since (as he accurately surmises) his works are going out of fashion and are no longer influential. As William Bankes observes, "Ramsay is one of those men who do their best work before they are forty" (23). Ramsay has had trouble with reception all along. Loudly reciting Tennyson as he strode outside, he was embarrassed by the unexpected presence of unwilling listeners. Thinking of those whose work will last two thousand years, the name of Shakespeare presents itself (35). Soon, he grows angry at Shakespeare, without realizing why (43).

At the supper table, a literary dispute breaks out between William Bankes, who praises the Waverley novels, and Charles Tansley, who denounces them (106–07). This scene in turn produces characteristic responses from those assembled around the table: Mrs. Ramsay sees Charles's words merely as another of his transparent acts of self-assertion that really has nothing to do with "poor Sir Walter, or perhaps it was Jane Austen" (106). Bankes attaches no importance to such changes in fashion (though, as we have seen, he still rues them), and Minta Doyle says she does not believe that anyone really enjoys reading Shakespeare. Ramsay, however, thinks primarily of himself during this conversation: any discussion of the endurance of authors over time makes him irritable since he knows, despite the cheery reassurances he demands of his wife, that his works are increasingly being left unread. Later that night, he takes up a volume of Scott's

94   *The Reader in Modernist Fiction*

and goes over it carefully, critically, to determine whether Tansley's attack is at all justifiable. He then proceeds to enact the moving solecism that if he still reads Scott, who is said to be out of fashion, others will then read his own books, which appear to be equally passé.

Mrs. Ramsay also shares in her own way the desire to live on in some form after death that so obsessively drives her husband; she is sure that Minta and Paul Rayley, whom she had brought together, would, "however long they lived, come back to this night; this moon; this house: and to her too. It flattered her, where she was most susceptible of flattery, to think how, wound about in their hearts, however long they lived she would be woven" (113). Given what seems to be the final, casual state of their marriage, it is doubtful that they ever conceive that particular thought. Others, however, do. In the end, she is the one whose (spoken) words and (good) works endure long after her actual demise. Lily Briscoe acknowledges Mrs. Ramsay's power and draws strength from her example as she tries to emulate her, recalling "Mrs. Ramsay making of the moment something permanent (as in another sphere Lily herself tried to make of the moment something permanent)" (161).

Intriguingly, Lily seems far less concerned about the ultimate fate of her composition: "it would never be seen; never be hung even" (48); she paints to achieve her moment of vision more than to live on in posterity. In the end she recognizes that words and paint do endure; even if her canvas is "rolled up and flung under a sofa" the picture itself is still true, enduring though unseen; indeed in some sense it "remained forever" (179). This entire drama of the persistence of the works of an individual after death can be seen as the development of Mrs. Ramsay's comically vague depiction of the topic of a dissertation: "It was about the influence of somebody upon something" (66). This is, in the end, the only genuine form of immortality available to humans; ironically, Ramsay's intellectual influence ends before his life does, while his wife continues to live in memory and inspiration long after she has been buried. And while the public fate of Lily's works is left unrecorded, her private triumph is unquestionable.

It is by no means obvious which theories of reception best fit the numerous dramas of the act of reading in this text. To be sure, most of them, from James's first investing of the pictures in the catalogue with bliss to his father's embarrassing declamation of melodramatic lines by Tennyson and Cowper, with which he identifies much too closely, correspond best with subjectivist accounts set forth by Norman Holland and David Bleich. A radical and somewhat reductive idea of reading communities can be deduced from a comment in

The Use and Abuse of Reading in Mansfield and Woolf   95

Mrs. Ramsay's flow of consciousness indicating that, at the dinner, she readily imagined herself "saying she liked the Waverley novels or had not read them" (107); that is, she is so willing to provide the response that will best create the greatest harmony among her guests that the general aesthetic value of the author in question is hardly relevant: indeed actually having read the books (and remembering one has read them) would appear to be unnecessary.

Another serious option that is also presented at crucial points in the text is that of a deep or fundamental uninterpretability. This is most clearly presented in Mrs. Ramsay's attempts to communicate with Cam: "The words seemed to be dropped into a well, where, if the waters were clear, they were also so extraordinarily distorting that, even as they descended, one saw them twisting about to make Heaven knows what pattern on the floor of the child's mind" (54). Lily also tries out such notions as she imagines the mind and heart of Mrs. Ramsay in terms of "treasures in the tombs of kings, tablets bearing sacred inscriptions, which if one could spell them out, would teach one everything, but they would never be offered openly, never made public" (51).

This is a particularly rich trope that links together the hidden patterns that govern a mind with an archeological reconstruction, which as noted in the introduction was a comparison Freud himself made on occasion.[6] Typically, Woolf places this within a specific social context (Lily is physically touching the woman she is trying to understand) and dramatizes the entire situation: at this point in the text, it is by no means clear that understanding will be achieved, that opaque characters will be able to be deciphered. Here too we find a miniature version of the drama of interpretation and misinterpretation that runs throughout this work and so many other modernist texts of the period: there is a crucially important covert meaning, if one could only spell it out. It recurs again in the "Time Passes" section as the personification of divine goodness is said to cover his treasures in a drench of hail, "and so confuses them that it seems impossible that their calm should ever return or that we should ever compose from their fragments a perfect whole or read in their littered pieces the clear words of truth" (128). This kind of arduous reading is that which is staged by the novel and required of the reader; in this we may note the fundamental consonance of Woolf's project with the comparable dramas of reading enacted by Conrad, Joyce, Ford, and Mansfield.

Lily too has moments of extremely creative response: though she has never read a line of Mr. Carmichael's poetry, she feels she knows

96   *The Reader in Modernist Fiction*

its rhythms and subjects: "It was seasoned and mellow. It was about the desert and the camel ... It was extremely impersonal; it said something about death" (195). While we get a compelling description of the physical appearance of the volume that so engrosses Mr. Ramsay as the family, after ten years, finally makes the excursion to the lighthouse ("a little shiny book with covers mottled like a plover's egg" [183]), we never learn its author or title; it is clear that in most key respects, these particulars don't matter. Here again, the scene of reading is paramount; it restages earlier such episodes that James was reluctantly thrust into: "James felt that each page was turned with a peculiar gesture aimed at him: now assertively, now commandingly; now with the intention of making people pity him; and all the time ... James kept dreading the moment when he would look up and speak to him sharply" (183). This too would seem to support the theoretical position of epistemological indeterminacy: no matter what signs his father displays, James will always give them the same reading—even as his sister is infused by the opposite response while she observes the identical act of reading.

The issues of social distinction manifested by judgements of taste examined by Pierre Bourdieu are also evident here: Tansley performs his high seriousness by "always carrying a book under his arm" (159). Minta does come off as a philistine because she admits she doesn't appreciate Shakespeare; Lily can't imagine her actually reading books, but only "dragging them about the garden, sticking in leaves to mark the place" (170). Likewise, Ramsay's unchanging affection for Scott causes him to lose cultural capital as times and sensibilities alter. On the other hand, two of the lines that recur at various points in the text point to a hidden but retrievable interpretation that a critical reader is expected to discover. The line that begins the final part of the novel following immediately after the highly unusual "Time Passes" section asks: "What does it mean then, what can it all mean?" (145). A number of questions nest within this one (including, unavoidably, the meaning of the innovative book as a whole). The implication of this is that some of these questions do indeed have appropriate if only incomplete or provisional answers, and that it is our task to look closely for them.

Another recurring line, "Someone had blundered," from Tennyson's poem, gestures toward Ramsay's persistent miscalculation of the responses of his various audiences. It may also point back to the relevant sets of historical events that produced the carnage on the battlefield that the poet elegizes: during the Battle of Balaclava, Lord Raglan, from his position on the heights, observed the Russian troops removing guns from captured British artillery posts and ordered the Light Brigade to attack. Because of their limited visual perspective far below in the valley, Lord Cardigan misunderstood the command, and instead of attacking the isolated Russians on the heights, led his troops though the exposed valley between the heights; nearly half the men were slaughtered because of the misinterpretation.

Finally, theories that foreground the relation between reading and gender find ample material in this text. Lily Briscoe is certainly a kind of "resisting reader" (Fetterley) to the androcentric cultural discourse that surrounds her. Insofar as Woolf uses the life of Mrs. Ramsay to rewrite sexist fairy tales such as "The Fisherman and His Wife," she is the kind of revisionary "disobedient writer" celebrated by Nancy A. Walker.[7] The earlier history of the reception of Woolf's works confirms the kind of feminist theory of reading set forth by Patrocinio Schweickart. This position accepts the possibility of accurate readings (otherwise, there could be no misreadings) and is attuned to the subject position(s) of the work's implied reader.[8] French feminism has also provided a useful lens for reading Woolf; Patricia Laurence's account of the reading of silence in her fiction (89–96) is one of many examples that might be adduced. It should be noted however that there is no agreement on precisely how far these theories usefully can be applied to Woolf. Jane Marcus has set forth an interesting theory of gendered reading regarding *To the Lighthouse* in her essay, "Other People's I's (Eyes)," which offers a dichotomous account of reading experiences that reflects the polarization of the sexes in Victorian marriages. She finds that Mr. Ramsay's "readings of people and books are aggressive, intrusive male actions" (55), a logical progression along the alphabet. By contrast, "Mrs. Ramsay's readings go out of the self into the mind of the author"; her reading is a "privileged way of being" (55). In short, his reading is analytical, hers is experiential. Though this is a convincing account of certain aspects of their reading experiences, I believe this dualistic (if not in fact Manichean) opposition is deconstructed by the end of the first and third part of the text as their different modes of reading begin to merge, as I will describe below.

If actual reading is much more rare than one might normally expect, the effects it produces are commensurately more impressive. At different points in the text, both Mr. and Mrs. Ramsay identify reading with a placid sense of relaxed familiarity: "It was like reading a good book again, for she knew the end to that story" (93; see also 33). The end of the first part of the novel provides both an alternative scene of reading to those we have encountered up to this

98 *The Reader in Modernist Fiction*

point and a kind of coda to the theme of reading. Both Mr. and Mrs. Ramsay take up books, different yet characteristic volumes: Ramsay, his favorite novelist, Scott; and Mrs. Ramsay, some lines of poetry by an unnamed author (whom Alice Fox has identified as William Browne). There are obvious differences in genre, of motivations, and the way that each begins: Ramsay seeks out a specific passage, while Mrs. Ramsay opens her book at random. Gradually, however, they yield to an experience that is both parallel and shared. Though each dives into the middle of a book, both are soon reading in a linear fashion: Ramsay is "tossing the pages over" (118) while Mrs. Ramsay is following successive lines of verse, "Swinging herself, zigzagging this way and that, from one line to another as from one branch to another" (119). Sitting apart and reading different works, both become entirely engrossed in their reading; they now steep themselves in their books, as Woolf recommended, and begin to merge with the words they hold, thus fulfilling another piece of advice of Woolf's: "Do not dictate to your author; try to become him" (*Second Common* 235). Ramsay does this almost too well: "He was acting it—perhaps he was thinking himself the person in the book," his wife observes (118).[9] Both seek a form of completeness, though Mr. Ramsay concludes he will have to read the novel again to regain "the whole shape of the thing" (120). Mrs. Ramsay, however, finds a distilled totality in a poem: "And then there it was, suddenly entire; she held it in her hands, beautiful and reasonable, clear and complete, the essence sucked out of life and held rounded here—the sonnet" (121); in this passage, Mrs. Ramsay's "evening of companionable reading results in a revelation," Abbie Garrington observes (135).[10]

Intriguingly, these private acts of identification with others bring them closer together. Ramsay in particular ceases to be so compulsively driven and finds a release from the issues that hounded him earlier. He forgets the perceived slights, uneasiness, and feeling of boredom; most significantly, he abandons the sequential teleology that has so obsessed him during the day: "it didn't matter a damn who reached Z (if thought ran like an alphabet from A to Z). Somebody would reach it—if not he, then another" (120). His vast, noisy, overbearing ego starts to dissolve as he merges with the book he is absorbed by. This nicely anticipates Lily's reflections on the dissolution of the artist in the act of creation: "she lost consciousness of outer things, and her name and her personality and her appearance, and whether Mr. Carmichael was there or not" (159). The self, with all its cumbersome baggage, is temporarily shed as the reader (or in Lily's case, the painter) becomes one with the work. As she reads,

The Use and Abuse of Reading in Mansfield and Woolf   99

Mrs. Ramsay feels she is ascending "on to the top, on to the summit. How satisfying!" (121). This time, Ramsay's response to seeing his wife reading is more generous; he stifles his desire to complain about the waning reputation of his books: "he was determined; he would not bother her again" (121). Instead, he admires her silently, and goes on to apostrophize her mutely: "Go on reading. You don't look sad now" (121). Reading here creates an ethical effect, and seems to turn some of the characters into better people.

This effect is produced again much later in the text. Near the end of the book a symmetrical scene of reading appears. Cam watches her father onboard the boat to the lighthouse, thinking that he reads "as if he were guiding something, or wheedling a large flock of sheep, or pushing his way up and up a single narrow path; and sometimes he went fast and straight, and broke his way through the bramble, and sometimes it seemed a branch struck him, a bramble blinded him, but he was not going to let himself be beaten by that; on he went, tossing over page after page" (190). Jane Goldman notes that Ramsay's "mastery over pastoral imagery seems gradually to slip"; she concludes that Cam's admiration for her father's learning "is mixed with indications of its decline" (Stevenson and Goldman 184). We might add that this perception brings to mind both the depiction of Mrs. Ramsay's brachiating style of reading and the rough physicality of Ramsay "tossing over" the pages of his book in the earlier depiction of him consuming Scott (118). Watching him read, Cam cannot maintain her compact with James to resist their father's tyranny. Instead, she recalls her habit of walking into his study, taking a book from the shelf, and pretending to read as she watched him write (189). For his part, Ramsay was always pleasant to her in this setting. On the boat, finishing his reading, Mr. Ramsay is unusually muted; he does not declaim aloud the lines of verse his children had come to expect with loathing. Instead he is relaxed, at peace with himself and those around him, and even gives his son a rare (though greatly appreciated) word of praise, as the family's rough emotional journey comes to a tranquil pause.

There is no sex in the book, other than Lily's brief reflections on the Rayleys' unusual yet successful domestic arrangement. Instead, the deepest communion often comes from acts of reading; the joint reading of Mr. and Mrs. Ramsay can be viewed as a kind of surrogate sexual interaction. This also corresponds to some of the metaphors Woolf uses to describe reading in her essays. In the "Patron and the Crocus," she depicts the desired patron in suggestive terms: "He must make us feel that a single crocus, if it be a real crocus, is enough for

100 *The Reader in Modernist Fiction*

him; that he does not want to be lectured, elevated, instructed, or improved . . . that he is now ready to efface himself or assert himself as his writers require; that he is bound to them by a more than maternal tie; that they are [Siamese] twins indeed, one dying if the other dies, one flourishing if the other flourishes; that the fate of literature depends upon their happy alliance" (*Common First* 209–10).[11] Again we see reading, love, and sublimated sexuality flowing together in the passage. It might be added that in her private correspondence, Woolf forewent the sublimation: "Sometimes I think heaven must be one continuous unexhausted reading. It is a disembodied trance-like intense rapture that used to seize me as a girl, and comes back now and again down here, with a violence that lays me low. Did I say I was flying? How then can I be low? Because, my dear Ethel, the state of reading consists in the complete elimination of the ego; and it is the ego that erects itself like another part of the body I don't dare to name." (letter to Ethel Smyth, 29 July 1934, L 5:319).[12]

The multiple facets of the book come together through parallel and interpenetrating acts of reading and creation. Lily's completion of her painting occurs at the same time as the completion of the trip to the lighthouse, which takes place as Ramsay finishes reading his book, which involves, one must assume, the merging of the reader with the author that Woolf recommended. This act of reading precedes and, once again, seems to have produced a pleasing transformation in the interactions of the family; likewise, the entire scene can be assumed to affect those of us who literally hold the book in our hands. This final identification is made stronger by seeing our own reading experience reflected back at us in the text. The children watch their father with his book: "Mr. Ramsay had almost done reading . . . He was reading very quickly, as if he were eager to get to the end" (202–03); these descriptions are equally applicable to most readers of *To the Lighthouse* as well; Woolf generously enhances our merging with her text by having us experience the response it depicts.

When Mr. Ramsay obsesses over how long his books will be read, he fails to take note of a different kind of reading of himself: how the events that make up his life are narrativized by those around him. This, it turns out, is not the reception he imagines. His best work is long behind him; professionally he has in fact been in a slow but steady decline since his first book appeared when he was twenty-five. It is also thought that his marriage has contributed to his demise. He has no idea how predictable or offensive his various outbursts are to his family, and he is partly oblivious of the preposterous figure he cuts while striding across the landscape declaiming sentimental verse. By

The Use and Abuse of Reading in Mansfield and Woolf   101

contrast, Mrs. Ramsay's warmth and generosity continue to inspire others long after her death. Her giving shape to chaos, making of the moment something permanent (161), endows her life with a narrative pattern far more substantial than the typical Victorian social pattern she had imagined for herself. Both central characters thus misread their own lives, and each does so in a characteristic manner.

We may use this opposition as a way into Woolf's treatment of the Other as interpreter in this work. While the educated males are the unquestioned masters of complex written texts (though they often differ on the significance of many of these), the women are nearly always the superior readers of social relations and interactions. Though Ramsay knows much more about philosophy and literature, he knows much less about his wife than she knows about him; she is quite astute at a wider range of social knowledge than any of the others imagine. The other most epistemologically privileged observer in the book is certainly Lily, a New Woman, a rare female painter, one with a hint of the Sapphic, who lives outside the conventional realm of heterosexual, childbearing arrangements. It is only right that she has by far the most perspicacity concerning art; once again, knowledge is centered at the margins of power.

And what is the final status of Lily's painting of Mrs. Ramsay reading to James? Even though her vision is presented as having endured intact over a decade, the final depiction of the picture contains a significant transformation: its subject now seems to be Mrs. Ramsay writing letters (160). Mrs. Ramsay, that is, goes from being a reader of others' words to an author of her own, a fitting revision for the canvas that Lily is able to complete as she is inspired by her memories of Mrs. Ramsay. This movement from reading to writing is paralleled near the end of the book in a depiction of a reciprocal scene of reading. Watching her father read produces affection for him, as it had for her mother. Next she tells herself a story about escaping from a sinking ship; once again, reading engenders a creative act.

We may now summarize the trajectory that the drama of reading takes as it is played out in *To the Lighthouse*. Reading is first presented as a facade, something people largely pretend to do and an activity which they are happy to have interrupted. The very possibility of genuine communication, whether through high literature or ordinary conversation, is repeatedly called into question, as is the possibility of one's books persisting over time—for every Shakespeare that endures, there must be several Scotts who fall permanently out of fashion. In many aspects, this novel represents a move beyond the

102   *The Reader in Modernist Fiction*

modernist model we have been tracing in this study as it explores a wide range of attitudes towards and responses to reading: here, even casual or compulsive reading can be helpful, even producing ethical responses. However, we also noted the central scene depicting Mrs. Ramsay uncritically reading a sexist fairy tale to James and failing to note that, if the gender of the principals is inverted, the relation mirrors her own familial situation. A critical assessment of this scene would have benefitted Mrs. Ramsay. Woolf's representation of reading incorporates and extends many of the approaches outlined in this study: enlightenment (Wells), aesthetic (James), skeptical (Conrad, Joyce), and social semiotic (Mansfield). In addition, she adds an ethical component and stages scenes of interpretation for the reader to re-enact. In many respects, this work presents a culmination of writing about reading to this point.

We also note that a number of approaches to reading that would later emerge in theoretical formulations are assayed within the novel, though it finally affirms the value of a committed, passionate reading experience in which author and reader merge. The act of engaging with books can make the readers (and often those who observe the readers) better people, more generous and less self-absorbed. In a new technique of the representation of reading, inscrutable signs give way to moments of understanding, and the scene of reading leads to the act of writing. Finally, our reading of the end of this text merges with both Ramsay's reading his text and his children's observing him read, and it fuses as well with Lily's completing of her painting. At the end, we have all had our vision.

Taken together, we see in the works of Mansfield and Woolf a fascination with the theme of reading, the often unexpected consequences of reading, and repeated presentations of characters in the act of reading. Books can be and often are the sources of illusion. In many of the situations depicted in the texts, the act of reading is itself dubious or dangerous for the protagonist. In particular, uncritical reading is chastised and a more wary, skeptical reader is implicitly called for. Allusions to narratives, both literary and popular, can be misleading and are rarely applied correctly by the characters who are often the unwitting analogues of the personae they invoke. It is evident that for Mansfield and Woolf a critical perspective is essential to reading, whether of specific texts, semiotic codes, or gender relations and other ideological constructs. Both employ imagery from other arts (especially, respectively, theater and painting) to underscore issues of reading in their texts. The two also give attention to the physical book, whether the cheap, rain-splattered paperback edition

The Use and Abuse of Reading in Mansfield and Woolf   103

of *Anna Lombard* described by Mansfield or the books banged on the floor, lying in the grass, carried as a kind of talisman, or exuding mildew and spiders in *To the Lighthouse*.

Notes

1. A similar stance is set forth by Jane Marcus, who suggests that Mrs. Ramsay is helping her son through his Oedipal struggle by "teaching him to identify with the hated father and to see his nurturing mother as rejecting and cold, and, through the story, that women are greedy and power mad" (*Patriarchy* 154). Marcus sees in the submarine imaginings of Cam, however, a significant counterpoise to this male myth. Jane Goldman also states that the story "serves as a warning against uxorial ambition, and implicitly recommends the containment of feminine desire" (*Feminist* 176). She goes on, however, to suggest that the novel does seem to rework the story for feminism through "its color deployment [which] feeds into Woolf's gendered allegoric vocabulary" (176).
2. See Beth Rigel Daugherty for a full discussion of Mrs. Ramsay's situation.
3. For an additional, extended discussion of Browne's text and Woolf's, see Kelly Anspaugh.
4. This is true of most of the marriages in Woolf's work, beginning with the betrothal of the protagonist that leads to her death in *The Voyage Out*. As Rachel Blau DuPlessis points out, "After the first two novels, heterosexual romance is displaced from a controlling and privileged place in her work. It will never again appear as the unique center of narrative concern; it will never again appear assumed or unquestioned" (47–48).
5. It is just possible that this line is itself an ironic commentary on Milton's claim in the *Aereogaptica* that books are like dragons' teeth, and can bring forth armed warriors.
6. Building on the work of Julia Kristeva, Patricia Laurence suggests another interesting possibility by seeing this passage as a feminist attempt to elude the masculine connotations of the alphabet, so vividly apparent in Ramsay's attempt to get to the letter "Q" and beyond. "In order to escape the alphabet, Woolf has used images relating the 'deciphering of pictographs' or 'decoding of hieroglyphs' in relation to the reading of women's dreams, delirium, hysteria: all states of 'absence' of the conscious mind and the 'presence' of the unconscious" (139).
7. See Walker's chapter "Twice Upon a Time," which analyses women authors' rewriting of fairy tales in *The Disobedient Writer: Women and Narrative Tradition* (45–83).
8. Schweickart emphasizes that reader response criticism cannot take refuge "in the idea that a gender-neutral criticism is possible" (39); at the same time she asserts that subjectivist and relativist accounts are no

help to oppositional readers: "feminists insist that the androcentricity of the text and its damaging effects on women readers are not figments of their imagination. Those are implicit in the 'schematized aspects' of the text" (49).

9. Kate Flint's comment on her earlier novel is equally pertinent to *To the Lighthouse*: "Acknowledgement of the degree to which the individual can get absorbed by fiction is coupled in *The Voyage Out* with a recognition (which the reader is expected to share) that such habits of identification, of slipping into the skin and mind of a fictional character, can go hand in hand with a self-awareness of the process which is taking place" ("Reading" 272).

10. Helen Tyson notes that "there is a movement in Woolf's writing from the description of the phenomenological, sensory and perceptual qualities of reading (reading as hallucination, almost) to the evocation of psychic, emotional and ontological engagement and disturbance" (1451). We see this occurring in the depiction of Mrs. Ramsay reading.

11. As Jeanne Dubino notes in her analysis of Woolf's "common reader": by the end of "The Patron and the Crocus," the relationship "is one of equality . . . with the reader and the writer becoming increasingly highly intimate equals: more than mother and child, they are Siamese twins, . . . and sexual partners" (133). For a general overview, see Cuddy-Keane (59–114).

12. For additional examples of association of reading with sexual pleasure, see Lee 403–04.

Chapter 4

The Dangers of Reading from Edith Wharton to Ralph Ellison

Many writers of the period deployed the trope of the book and staged dramas of reading and misreading. In this chapter I will cast my net more widely and try to provide a sense of what other modernist authors from the 1920s and 1930s and beyond were doing. The effect of reading was a powerful and nearly ubiquitous trope; it was used to continue and extend modernist practices as well as, in some cases, to indicate difference from them. The work of Conrad, Joyce, Mansfield, Ford, and Woolf can thus serve as a kind of touchstone by which we can better perceive related, analogous, and alternative hermeneutical dramas. Most of these works continue and extend the modernists' critique of uncritical reading of literary works and of social codes. Here, reading and misreading figure centrally in the sexual entanglements the characters get themselves into. Edith Wharton narrates a drama of differential misreading, as her protagonist's fascination with the new European culture that he learns of through his books does nothing to help him read or act within the social world that ensnares him. Faulkner chronicles different types of misreading in his works as well as offering a kind of hermeneutics of the reading of deliberately obscured writings involving slavery, rape, and death. In "Old Mortality," Katherine Anne Porter presents us with a combined personal and cultural drama of misreading, as romantic authors both exemplify and fuel the repressive illusions of the Old South. Elizabeth Bowen shows us a different fate for a different kind of reading, as the insights of a diary are contrasted with other, less effective forms. Graham Greene reanimates ideas and scenes strongly reminiscent of Conrad in his exploration of the fate of reading in a colonial context. Ralph Ellison discloses the material effects of reading and being read in *Invisible Man*, laying particular stress on the writing of history and the documentation of those who are usually written out of its pages. Lastly, I will briefly consider the many references to books and reading in Tayeb Salih's *Season of Migration to the North*, his rewriting

106   *The Reader in Modernist Fiction*

of "Heart of Darkness," to point to a different, paradoxical struggle over books and their reading by the colonized, and observe how this leads away from the modernist model I have been describing.

Edith Wharton

Like the other authors discussed in this study, Edith Wharton repeatedly created stories of personal and social reading and misreading; early in her career (1903), she also published an essay entitled "The Vice of Reading" in which she denigrates what she calls the "mechanical reader." This mechanical reader reads for duty rather than pleasure, can tell exactly how many hours he has spent reading, mimics the opinions of others, mistrusts and dislikes all works he cannot understand, is compulsively linear, must necessarily "miss all the by paths and cross-cuts of his subject" and cannot know "the delights of intellectual vagrancy, of the improvised chase after a fleeting allusion" (101). Worst of all, this kind of reader encourages the mechanical author. This essay, which anticipates some of Nabokov's later denunciations of passive middle-brow readers, uses the tropes of industrial capitalism to identify the hollow reader who is unable to have an organic, integrated, or "natural" relation to reading. These concerns will figure substantially in her fiction.

Agnès Berbinau-Dezalay writes that in Wharton's short stories

> reading appears as one of the defining features of a character—it is part of the social image he or she projects. But various factors—and above all gender—affect that image. There are male readers and female readers, and they are not perceived in the same way by their social environment. In Wharton's narratives, reading is usually a subversive activity for women and a conformist one for men. Indeed, unsupervised reading was considered as a threat to a young girl's morality in the upper-class society in which Wharton was raised and most of her short stories are set. New York society in the 1860s was characterized by the wariness of all forms of intellectualism. In that context, women who read were usually marginalized. (para 17)

Wharton's most sustained examination of reading and interpretation appears in *The Age of Innocence* (1920), a novel that chronicles the tragedy of two readers, each of whom is in their own way deficient in comprehending social signs. Both Newland Archer and Ellen Olenska are alienated from New York society by their genuine love

The novel opens with Archer arriving fashionably late to the

of reading, desire for knowledge, and their disdain for the hypocrisy and pretense that society demands. That is, most of the associations made by Mansfield are here inverted; in this work contemporary high culture represents moral and intellectual enlightenment. Significantly, this work is set in the 1870s as the latest advances of the social sciences and the arts were shockingly, even scandalously new (anthropology is prominently featured) and threatened to upset conventional social and aesthetic norms if allowed to continue.

The novel opens with Archer arriving fashionably late to the opera, only because it "was not the thing" to arrive earlier, and "what was 'not the thing' played a part as important to Newland Archer's New York as the inscrutable totem terrors that had ruled the destinies of his forefathers thousands of years ago" (842). And what this revealed, as the livery-stableman discerned, was that "Americans want to get away from amusement even more quickly than they want to get to it" (841), even if that "amusement" was diva Christine Nilsson singing in Gounod's *Faust*. Still, to a large extent Archer defines himself and his worth by his reading: "In matters intellectual and artistic Newland Archer felt himself distinctly the superior of these chosen specimens of old New York gentility; he had probably read more, thought more, and even seen a good deal more of the world" than any of his metropolitan peers (844–45).

His vision of marital happiness is based in part on the reading and literary conversations he expects to have later with his fiancée, May Welland: imagining reading *Faust* with her beside the Italian lakes, he hazily conflates "the scene of his projected honey-moon with the masterpieces of literature which it would be his manly privilege to reveal to his bride" (844). This rapidly proves to be a greater challenge than he had anticipated once he contemplates "that terrifying product of the social custom system he belonged to and believed in, the young girl who knew nothing and expected everything" and who "looked back at him like a stranger through May Welland's features" (873). A little later, she will remind him of the "Kentucky cave-fish, which had ceased to develop eyes because they had no use for them. What if," he wonders in horror, "when he had bidden May to open hers, they could only look out blankly at blankness?" (905). She rejects his more daring suggestions by saying that "we can't behave like people in novels" (906), when it is just this freedom that Archer craves.[1] As things turn out, after they are married he will no longer read literature to her: "she had spent her poetry and romance on their short courting: the function was exhausted because the need was past" (1074).

108   *The Reader in Modernist Fiction*

As he gets to know the newly arrived Ellen Olenska, a different vision appears. She shares his desire for new and dangerous knowledge and is considerably ahead of him in its discovery. "Poetry and art are the breath of life to her" (965). The many books scattered around her drawing room "whetted Archer's interest with such new names as those of Paul Bourget, Huysmans, and the Goncourt brothers. Ruminating on these things as he approached her door" we learn in a revealing aside, "he was once more conscious of the way in which she reversed his values" (922). This is not entirely accurate: she does not reverse them exactly, but rather forces him to see the contradictions between his beliefs and desires on the one hand and the inalterable codes of society behavior on the other. The fact that these authors were less inhibited in depicting matters of sexual embraces than their coevals in Britain or America no doubt adds to their fascination for Archer just as it increases the wariness by which they are scrutinized by the more stolid New Yorkers who, if they read at all, prefer *The Marble Faun*, Ouida's picturesque novels, and "Good Words" magazine (865–66).

Even when they read the same authors, the particular titles chosen by Archer and Olenska differ. As Emily J. Orlando has noted in her study of gender, art, and representation in *The Age of Innocence*, "Archer, like Ellen Olenska, reads the work of French authors" including those linked to naturalism, but he does not read their more tragic or naturalist texts, "opting instead for their more romantic stories" (175). Thus, he enjoys Alphonse Daudet's tales featuring the quixotic rather than his novels of passion and anguish. We might even say that Wharton's novel traces the fortunes of three different libraries and their readers: though he eschews the staid, lightweight works preferred by New York society, Archer cannot fully enter into the world represented by and depicted within Ellen's more radical and risqué volumes but hovers somewhere in between with his own personal cache. And sexuality is part of the mix: Archer regularly shocks his family by looking forward to the day in which women will be more free and judged by the same standards as men are; his desire for artistic and intellectual pleasure spills over into a desire for justice for women and an openness to sensuality. This is clear as he attempts "to picture the society in which the Countess Olenska had lived and suffered, and also—perhaps—tasted mysterious joys" (922). As Elizabeth Ammons has observed, old New York "distrusts passion, intellectual and artistic no less than physical" (145).

A new division is emerging in America, one between those with money and those with taste. In a slightly earlier era, the most celebrated

The novel's major literary allusions underscore these points. The book opens on (and later returns to) the scene in Gounod's *Faust* in which Margaret is wondering whether Faust loves her, an appropriate image of the misperceptions of the unfortunate pair later in the novel, though of course Archer's problem is not a lack of knowledge but rather insufficient will. More interesting is the scene in Boucicault's melodrama *The Shaughraun* in which the male protagonist, before leaving, kisses the back of the velvet ribbon on the neck of the heroine without her knowledge. Intriguingly, watching this scene reminds Archer of his leave taking of Madame Olenska several days earlier—though he cannot understand why (930–31). It is in fact a scene of romantic renunciation that he will approximate again at two points later in the narrative, once when he decides not to approach her in the summer house in Newport as she, in the distance, looks away at the water before her; here, Archer actually remembers the scene in the

writers had all been "gentlemen" (921); now, however, things were different: beyond the world of the wealthy "lay the almost unmapped quarter inhabited by artists, musicians, and 'people who wrote.' These scattered fragments of humanity had never shown any desire to be amalgamated with the social structure" (920). Ellen Olenska lives (both metaphorically and literally) in this Bohemian neighborhood. Unlike their European analogues, such pockets will unfortunately never be able to thrive on this side of the Atlantic: "the New York of literary clubs and exotic restaurants, though a first shake made it seem more of a kaleidoscope, turned out, in the end, to be a smaller box, with a more monotonous pattern, than the assembled atoms of Fifth Avenue" (939). Increasingly, the place he seeks is reduced to the mental space he shares with Ellen, "a kind of sanctuary in which she throned among his secret thoughts and longings. Little by little it became the scene of his real life, of his only rational activities; thither he brought the books he read, the ideas and feelings which nourished him, his judgments and his visions" (1048). Just how utopian this desired space is becomes clear twenty pages later as Archer adumbrates to Ellen his wish to be with her. When she asks directly whether he wants her to be his mistress, Archer responds, "I want somehow to get away with you into a world where words like that—categories like that—won't exist." Ellen wonders rhetorically where such a country might be, and coolly observes that she has known "so many who've tried to find it; and believe me, they all got out by mistake at wayside stations: at places like Boulogne, or Pisa, or Monte Carlo—and it wasn't at all different from the old world they'd left, but only smaller and dingier and more promiscuous" (1069).

110   *The Reader in Modernist Fiction*

play as he is in the process of reenacting it (1010). The other is when he refuses to go up to her apartment in Paris at the end of the book, but sits alone outside on a bench instead.[2]

Parallel to and intersecting with the story of the devoted though frustrated readers is another interpretive drama of reading (and unwittingly communicating) social codes; this drama is expressed in images of linguistic and semiotic systems, and these are often fused with tropes of isolation, imprisonment, or acting out a script. Early on, it is noted that the New York upper crust "all lived in a kind of hieroglyphic world, where the real thing was never said or done or even thought, but only represented by a set of arbitrary signs" (874). It is a language that Ellen freely admits she imperfectly understands: New York is much more a social labyrinth than she had suspected (900), where no one will speak or hear the truth (901). "There are only two people here who make me feel as if they understood what I mean": Beaufort and Archer. Ellen is once again imperfectly comprehending her situation: though "Beaufort understood every turn of her dialect, and spoke it fluently" (949), his attentions will harm her in society, which will read them as predatory. When Archer, acting as her attorney, tries to discuss Ellen's situation with her, he quickly realizes "how little practice he had in dealing with unusual situations! Their very vocabulary was unfamiliar to him, and seemed to belong to fiction and the stage" (926). In their first serious disagreement Ellen expresses her frustration by saying, "I don't speak your language!"—a retort that "smote him like a blow" (944), since he knew "that in some respects this was true" (949). Later, reflecting on this scene, he "could not bear the thought that a barrier of words should drop between them again" (972).

By contrast, the other New Yorkers (including his wife) are masters at communicating without having to be explicit. The most extreme such exchange occurs between Newland and May just as Newland mentions he will soon be leaving to spend a few days in Washington. Ellen is now living in that city, and Newland had invented a specious business trip in order to have a chance to visit her. May simply smiles, looks him straight in the eyes, and tells him to be sure to visit Ellen while he is there. The narrator explains: "It was the only word that passed between them on the subject; but in the code in which they had both been trained it meant: 'Of course you understand that I know all that people have been saying about Ellen, and heartily sympathize with my family in their effort to get her to return to her husband. I also know that, for some reason you have not chosen to tell me, you have advised her against this course'" (1051). This impressive,

The Dangers of Reading from Wharton to Ellison   111

unspoken "pseudo-dialogue" continues for several sentences, containing many turns and disclosing several nuances, as nearly a full page is devoted to revealing May's unspoken but unmistakable discourse. This unusual scene furthermore prefigures Archer's final revelation at the end of the novel and underscores Orlando's observation that "Archer is not a close reader, and Wharton's women continually expose him as such. Ellen Olenska and May Welland succeed in collapsing his readings of them and, what is more, they read him more accurately than he reads himself"[3] (174).

Allusions to theatrical performance are used to express Archer's alienation from his wife and the stultifying society she so perfectly represents. Just as Ellen often feels as if she "were in the convent again—or on the stage, before a dreadfully polite audience that never applauds" (945), Archer finds his own wedding "like a first night at the opera" (982) and reflects that "the things that had filled his days seemed now like a nursery parody of life, or the wrangles of mediaeval schoolmen over terms that nobody had ever understood" (983). In a most revealing phrase, Archer feels it "hateful to find himself the prisoner of this hackneyed vocabulary" (1085). This harks back to an earlier use of the trope of imprisonment which was also combined with an image of spectacle: following a round of family visits after their engagement is announced, Archer "parted from his betrothed with the feeling that he had been shown off like a wild animal cunningly trapped" (893).

The culmination of these images is the moment in which some of them are literally instantiated in a key scene at the end of the novel. Without her husband's prior agreement, May has arranged to give a party in honor of Ellen's impending move to Paris. As he looks around the dining table, he suddenly perceives "all the harmless-looking people engaged upon May's canvas-backs as a band of dumb conspirators, and himself and the pale woman on his right as the center of their conspiracy." To all of them he and Madame Olenska are lovers, "lovers in the extreme sense peculiar to 'foreign' vocabularies" (1106). He realizes that he has been closely observed by them for months, and that Ellen's removal has been carefully orchestrated by those sitting with him. Furthermore, the talk around him of Beaufort's demise and his family's expulsion from their social world is an elaborate, carefully enacted spectacle designed "'to show me,' he thought, 'what would happen to *me*—' and a deathly sense of the superiority of implication and analogy over direct action, and silence over rash words, closed in on him like the doors of the family vault" (1106–07). The entire time he had been dismissively using images of

112 *The Reader in Modernist Fiction*

theater and anthropology to describe the behavior of those around him, they had been framing his actions within their own expectations and staging their own drama for his gradual edification. The irony is all the greater since the two lovers never did have the physical contact that all the others had naturally assumed to have taken place, and the hypocrisy is all the more flagrant since society cares exclusively about appearances as opposed to actual deeds (1109). Despite a determination to break free and travel to Ellen in Europe, Archer is finally frustrated by May's strategic though premature announcement of her pregnancy. He is defeated. Even after his wife dies years later, Archer cannot bring himself to leave.

The conclusion of this work is a somber one. Even though set in a period firmly rooted in the older epistemology that equated the activity of reading with the acquisition of knowledge and even the ethical imperative to eschew an unexamined life, we see that sophisticated cultural discernment is of no help to the protagonists in reading the social messages that are being circulated all around them. Archer is not a good enough interpreter in the end. Neither is he able to act on the knowledge that he does possess: learning that he is "a prisoner of this hackneyed vocabulary" and the socio-economic constraints it articulates does not allow him to escape them; instead, it only deepens his frustration and makes him aware of his weakness. Finally, Wharton suggests (as Mansfield was demonstrating and others like Bowen would later show) that the literary and artistic sophistication of Europe may snugly coexist with moral vileness, as exemplified in the figure of the count, Ellen's cultured but cruel ex-husband. And there is at least a suggestion that the new, freer generation may very well be socially careless and aesthetically vapid: Archer's son and daughter-in-law might well feel rather at home at one of Mansfield's soirees or garden parties, though of course they would be too well behaved to say anything hurtful. The potential of reading, set forth in its fullest promise, proves in the end to be sadly deficient at most levels and in many spaces.

William Faulkner

Like Ford, Woolf, and Graham Greene, William Faulkner was a devoted reader of Conrad. Faulkner would provide some of the most interesting and elaborate incarnations of bad readers and their unfortunate destinies. The tall convict, the anonymous protagonist of "Old Man" (1939), obsessively reads cheap paperbacks about

The Dangers of Reading from Wharton to Ellison   113

the exploits of outlaws, "the paper novels—the Diamond Dicks and Jesse Jameses and such" (*Novels 1936–40* 509). Eventually, having "laid his plans in advance, he had followed his printed (and false) authority to the letter; he had saved the paper-backs for two years, reading and rereading them, memorizing them, comparing and weighing story and method against story and method" (*Novels 1936–40* 509–10), he attempts to rob a train, having bought a pistol with money he has made by selling subscriptions to the *Detectives' Gazette*. He fails utterly, he is caught immediately, and sentenced to fifteen years hard labor.[4] In prison, he continues to read such texts surreptitiously. Other prisoners are more skeptical of what they read. When the newspaper announces, in large print which "even the illiterate should be able to read," "*Crest Now Below Memphis. 22,000 Refugees Safe at Vicksburg. Army Engineers Say Levees Will Hold,*" another convict accurately responds: "I reckon that means it will bust tonight" (*Novels 1936–1940* 513). It does, and the tall convict winds up in a skiff floating down the flooded Mississippi to Louisiana. When he returns to the prison to turn himself in, he creates a dilemma for the warden and deputy since there was a written report that he had died. Trapped by those printed words, the men decide to say the prisoner had been caught trying to escape, and ten more years are added to his sentence. Finally, it is worth noting that the tall, lean convict is paired in jail with a shorter, plump prisoner who has a more realistic sensibility. Together, the two bear a physical resemblance to Don Quixote and Sancho Panza.

In *Light in August* (1932), Gail Hightower, a disgraced pastor, is a man who "read a great deal" (451); in particular, he is a compulsive reader of Tennyson, whose words in the dog-eared volume are called "the gutless swooning full of sapless trees and dehydrated lusts" (634). A thorough romantic, Hightower cannot "get religion and that galloping cavalry and his dead grandfather shot from the galloping horse untangled from each other, even in the pulpit" (443). Still worse, "he could not untangle them in his private life, at home either" (443): his wife keeps running off and is eventually found dead, having fallen or jumped from a Memphis hotel room that she had checked into under an assumed name with a man. Near the end of the text Hightower concludes "how false the most profound book turns out to be when applied to life" (755). He would have been correct had he stated, "*uncritically* applied to life."

The central figure in this book, Joe Christmas, is an ordinary, linear, and at times compulsive reader. He prefers the type of reading material "whose covers bear either pictures of young women in

114   *The Reader in Modernist Fiction*

underclothes or pictures of men in the act of shooting one another with pistols" (479–80). Just before he kills Joanna Burden in *Light in August* (1932), he buys a magazine full of stories and starts to consume it in an obsessively linear manner: "He had previously read but one story: he began now upon the second one, reading the magazine straight through as though it were a novel" (480). When he reached the last story he stopped reading and counted the remaining pages. "Then he looked at the sun and read again. He read now like a man walking along a street might count cracks in the pavement, to the last and final page, to the last and final word" (481).

Several linear orders are here superimposed: sequential pagination, walking in one direction, the movement of the sun across the sky, and a sequential reading that always moves from left to right from the first page to the last. Christmas's reading is pure diversion, the consumption of story after story that leaves its reader entirely unchanged. This linear, unreflective reading discloses the pattern of his mind and the trajectory of his life: in the end, he cannot break free and create a new existence and is therefore doomed to return to Jefferson and be killed. Reading Joanna's written note requesting him to visit her, Christmas "was bound just as tightly by that square of still undivulging paper as though it were a lock and chain" (599–600). Gavin Stevens correctly affirms that Christmas was sent "against all reason and all reality, into the embrace of a chimera, a blind faith in something read in a printed Book" (731). Here too we see that uncritical reading leads to failure or disaster, as misreading becomes a trope for the misinterpretation of and the mistaken acquiescence in existing social codes. Christmas is said to be of African-American descent, though there is no convincing evidence to establish this supposition. Christmas lives, suffers, and dies under the designation "Negro," which is accepted without question both by himself and the community, and which may well be entirely fictitious.

Absalom, Absalom! (1936) offers a sustained investigation, at times almost an interrogation, of fragmented texts, recalcitrant signs, and a seemingly irretrievable history. This situation is explicitly commented on by Mr. Compson:

> It's just incredible. It just does not explain. Or perhaps that's it: they don't explain and we are not supposed to know. We have a few mouth-to-mouth tales; we exhume from old trunks and boxes and drawers letters without salutation or signature, in which men and women who once lived and breathed are merely initials or nicknames out of some now incomprehensible affection which sound to us like Sanskrit or Choctow . . . They are there, yet something is missing; they are like a chemical formula exhumed

The Dangers of Reading from Wharton to Ellison   115

along with the letters from that forgotten chest, carefully, the paper old and faded and falling to pieces, the writing faded, almost indecipherable, yet meaningful, familiar in shape and sense, the name and presence of volatile and sentient forces; you bring them together in the proportion called for, but nothing happens; you re-read, tedious and intent, poring, making sure you have forgotten nothing, made no miscalculation; you bring them together again and again and nothing happens: just the words, the symbols, the shapes themselves, shadowy inscrutable and serene, against that turgid backdrop of a horrible and bloody mischancing of human affairs. (*Novels, 1936–1940* 83–84)

This description perfectly illustrates the late modernist figure of a very important meaning cached within unyielding material that nevertheless must be sifted through in a discerning manner and yet may remain undisclosed: "almost indecipherable, yet meaningful" could be the motto of the deeper reaches of modernist literary epistemology. And there is another layer as well: the dubious or inscrutable signs may be partially or temporarily obscuring cruel or horrific historical facts.

An extensive drama of reading and misreading centers on Charles Bon's letter in *Absalom, Absalom!* As David Krause remarks in his analysis of the text, "within the novel, we receive at least six perspectives on reading this problematic letter" (225). He argues that no single perspective produces a satisfactory reading of it. "The letter, however, does provoke in and through each of its several readers a series of sustained meditations on the problems of reading" (225). For Krause, this results in a writerly text; the free play of its signifiers cannot be arrested. Others, in the text itself and in the critical community, have a different view and believe that a compelling reading can be performed—Warwick Wadlington, for example, both offers such a reading (170–219) and defends its implicit theory of reading against theorists of the insistent indeterminacy it seems to approach (221–24).

"The Bear" (1942) is centrally concerned with a wide range of reading and interpretation: of animal tracks, the topography of the forest, likely behavior of men and beasts, and the larger trajectory of the history of the South. It likewise focuses on an act of interpretation of an obscure written text and can thus provide a kind of metacommentary on the interpretive issues surrounding Bon's letter; in fact, the very debate engaged by critics about Bon seems to be restaged within the pages of "The Bear." In the initial discussion about the status of reading, "Ike reads like Norman Holland and his cousin [McCaslin Edmonds] reads like E. D. Hirsch," writes David Wyatt (283).[5] The physical text itself is one that begs for interpretation: old

116 *The Reader in Modernist Fiction*

family ledgers, written in brown thin ink on yellowed pages, bound in scarred, cracked leather bindings. The material in the volumes is difficult to interpret, even, at times, to those who wrote it—Ike's father and uncle, who no longer have any oral intercourse but communicate to each other through the ledgers and wonder occasionally what the other's words mean. In the rather Vedantic passage below we see Ike McCaslin commenting on comments contained on those pages:

> *June 21 th 1833 Drownd herself*
> and the first:
> *23 Jun 1833 Who in hell ever heard of a niger drownding him self*
> and the second, unhurried, with complete finality; the two identical entries might have been made with a rubber stamp save for the date:
> *Aug 13 th 1833 Drownd herself*
> and he thought *But why? But why?* He was sixteen then. (*Go Down* 197–8)

We have, that is, a hermeneutic mystery between the brothers that is also puzzled over by their sons in a way that both mirrors and guides the work's readers' own responses. Though difficult and obscure, the text that all are fixated on gradually reveals itself; it "took substance and even a sort of shadowy life with their passions and complexities too as page followed page and year year" (196). Careful readers, both within and outside the narrative, finally learn that Ike's grandfather, Carothers McCaslin, raped his slave Eunice and had a child by her, and later raped that child and had a child by *her*. As Erik Dussere points out in his impressive study of the ledgers, they are in fact "the only historical documents to record the stories of the McCaslin slaves" (18). The chronicles of economic affairs can be read so as to disclose a powerful, hidden narrative history of the community, black and white.

Karl F. Zender has observed that "Faulkner's purpose is not to indict us for our inadequacies as readers but to liberate us from them. By allowing us to misread, he teaches us how to read" (97). Throughout his career, Faulkner demonstrates the dangers of uncritical reading as well as the searing knowledge that can come of an arduous, critical reading—the kind required to properly appreciate the novels he constructs. He extends the Flaubertian critique of the naïve reading of romantic literature to that of popular true crime narratives, and goes on to continue the paradigm of reading and misreading in *Light in August* and more spectacularly in "The Bear." These works raise the stakes considerably for both effective and ineffective acts of reading as racial identity and the cryptic markers of

The high modernist drama of reading and misreading is also developed in the work of Katherine Anne Porter. Porter's "Old Mortality" (1938) is an especially revealing examination of romance, interpretation, and sexual desire and can be seen as a case study of the dangers of reading in the context of the American South. The short novel centers on and is primarily focalized through the mind of the girl, Miranda; it chronicles the way she learns to interpret her obscured family history and the social world around her as she develops from an eight-year-old child to a young woman of eighteen. The story thematizes accurate interpretation as well: Miranda's father "had a disconcerting way of inquiring, 'How do you *know?*' when [the sisters] made dogmatic statements in his presence" (192). Such training would prove to be partially inadequate, despite Miranda's later determination to know the truth. Her world begins steeped in romanticism, idealism, and the suppression of unpleasant facts. The text starts with the description of the photograph of Miranda's audacious Aunt Amy and the tales that are told about this unusual woman. Her family "loved to tell stories, romantic and poetic, or comic with romantic humor" (182). Their imaginations were captivated by their past and their stories "were almost always love stories against a bright blank heavenly blue sky" (183). We are even given their method for interpreting partial or incomplete stories: "They listened, all ears and eager minds, picking here and there among the floating ends of narrative, patching together as well as they could fragments of tales that were like bits of poetry or music" (184).

It rapidly becomes apparent, even to an eight-year-old, that the narratives often fail to match the evidence they purport to represent. "Photographs, portraits by inept painters who meant earnestly to flatter . . . were disappointing when the little girls tried to fit them to the living beings created in their minds by the breathing words of their elders" (183). In particular, the actual photograph of Amy fails to corroborate the beauty all claim she possessed. The girls' lives are framed by an utterly romantic family tale: "Their Aunt Amy belonged to the world of poetry. The romance of Uncle Gabriel's

118   *The Reader in Modernist Fiction*

long, unrewarded love for her, her early death, was such a story as one found in old books" (186). These books include Dante's *Vita Nuova*, works by Spenser, and the poems of Edgar Allan Poe. Amy's story includes dancing at a costume ball, the threat of a duel, a shot fired at a dashing Creole who had danced with Amy, and Amy's brother hiding out in Mexico for a year until all the trouble blew over. And soon after the dance, Amy finally agrees to marry Gabriel after scorning him for many years. Several weeks later, however, she dies in New Orleans of an overdose of her medicine. As Miranda (and the reader) learn more details of this doomed romance, a very different picture begins to emerge. Far from being a soulful, tragic lover, Gabriel emerges as a spoiled, selfish, irresponsible alcoholic and compulsive gambler. Amy seems to be unaware of or indifferent to the mass of social narratives circling around her; nevertheless, she insists to her mother, "if I am to be the heroine of this novel, why shouldn't I make the most of it?" (197).

Many years later another relative, the clear-headed Cousin Eva, a suffragette who is not easily fooled by touching family stories, speculates on the circumstances surrounding Amy's death. Admitting that Amy was wild, indiscreet, and heartless, she nevertheless attests to Amy's virtue. "But you could hardly blame anyone for being mystified. The way she rose up suddenly from death's door to marry Gabriel Breaux, after refusing him and treating him like a dog for years, looked odd, to say the least" (221). Eva goes on to add that there was also "something very mysterious about her death, only six weeks after marriage" (221). One last bit of actual as opposed to genteel family history can reveal the genuine narrative of these events. "That fellow Raymond," who was "almost a stranger," persuaded Amy to elope with him; her brother then "had to run him down to earth and shoot him" (221). Miranda responds, "Aunt Eva, my father shot *at* him, don't you remember? He didn't hit him" (221). So powerful is the family story for Miranda that she presumes to "correct" someone who was there at the time instead of trying to learn the actual facts of the case. Despite the unassailable evidence supplied by Eva, Miranda cannot stop reproducing the incoherent romantic version. Eva can only respond grimly: "You poor baby . . . do you believe that? How old are you anyway?" (221). Eva goes on to urge Miranda to attain a more thorough demystification: "Knowledge can't hurt you. You mustn't live in a romantic haze about life" (221–22).

The family story becomes an interpretive contest both for characters within it and for literary critics attempting to analyze it. Suzette W.

The Dangers of Reading from Wharton to Ellison   119

Jones, for example, sides substantially with the family version: "Porter suggests that Amy uses marriage to Gabriel, a man she does not really love, as an escape from her family and a way to New Orleans for Mardi Gras and perhaps a meeting with her old beau Raymond" (285). She goes on to claim that the ending is an unhappy one: "vivacious Amy, constricted by a disappointing marriage, takes her life just six weeks after her wedding" (285). My own reading is more aligned with Cousin Eva's and goes considerably further. Utilizing the hermeneutical formula set forth in the text, we may reassemble the pieces of the story and deduce that Amy and Raymond ran off together, made love, and were tracked down by her brother, who shot Raymond and fled to Mexico (being the scion of a powerful local family, he wouldn't have had to hide out of the country for a full year if he had only shot at him). Amy soon discovered she was pregnant, married Gabriel right away, and went to New Orleans for reasons more consequential than observing Mardi Gras. All the other versions, details, and embellishments of this story are fabrications.

In the narrative, Eva deromanticizes Amy's illness: "to hear them tell it she faded like a lily. Well, she coughed blood, if that's romantic" (224); this story is no Dumas-style *La Dame aux Camélias*. Eva also demythologizes the romantic attractions of Amy and the other young women: "it was just sex," she states. "their minds dwelt on nothing else. They didn't call it that, it was smothered under pretty names, but that's all it was, sex" (255). Just beneath the surface of the romantic and chivalrous discourse was the subordination and sexual repression of women, and the concomitant denial of their access to contraception and abortion—the likely actual cause of Amy's death. An important objective of those like Eva who worked for the emancipation of women was to make both of these services available. I postulate that the main reason Amy insisted on going immediately to New Orleans was to have access to "medicine" that would produce an abortion (Amy, after all, had abruptly called off two earlier engagements—very possibly, it is easy to speculate, because her menstrual cycle had resumed). It might be further noted that early twentieth-century advertisements for often dangerous or at times deadly abortifacients were themselves written in a kind of code that had to be deciphered, such as "Dr. Vandenburgh's female renovating pills, from Germany, an effectual remedy for suppression, irregularity, and all cases where nature has stopped from any reason whatever" (Onion).

Though she does not seem to be able to fully incorporate Eva's information into her own construct of their family history, Miranda certainly appreciates its general thrust. In the final pages, we see that

120   *The Reader in Modernist Fiction*

she feels a strong resentment against those "who denied her the right to look at the world with her own eyes, who demanded that she accept their version of life and yet could not tell her the truth" (229). She refuses to accept "the legend of the past, other people's memory of the past, at which she had spent her life peering in wonder like a child at a magic-lantern show" (230). The tale's final sentence confirms how difficult this will be: "At least I can know the truth about what happens to me, she assured herself silently, making a promise to herself, in her hopefulness, in her ignorance" (231). As Jones concludes, in this work, "Porter demonstrates the difficulty of reading or writing a story rather than being read or written by it—the problem of unconsciously playing out old plots, even after one has become a feminist reader aware of their dangers" (295).

In "Old Mortality," Porter shows us a discursive world that is a composite of literary romance, Southern chivalry, and conversational propriety. The title of the novella refers ostensibly to Gabriel's poem that is engraved on Amy's tombstone; it also implicitly alludes to Walter Scott's narrative of the same title. This is a significant reference; Mark Twain once semi-jocularly blamed the Civil War on Scott's novels, which were extremely popular in the antebellum South, because of their "romantic sense of the chivalry of combat" and their insistence on the "nobility of serving sentimental causes that were probably doomed to fail," as Jerome Beaty notes (449). Miranda, having been trapped within this illusory discursive web, tries to free herself from it, though Porter indicates that such self-liberation is harder to attain than it may appear. Scott's novels, which were seen to be a distillation of romantic falsehoods and unreality by modernist authors, produced an even more dangerous effect in the Old South. This is an indictment that we will shortly see rearticulated and intensified by Ishmael Reed.

Elizabeth Bowen

Elizabeth Bowen's 1938 novel *The Death of the Heart* takes the drama of reading into new areas, areas that have hardly been touched on except in the work of Mansfield. This text also dramatizes the dangers of reading in a more subtle manner than we have seen in earlier works, and it is one which engages the reader to participate in the same hermeneutic dilemma that is presented to its protagonist. As the novel opens, sixteen-year-old Portia has come to live with her sister-in-law, Anna Quayne. The work's plot begins with Anna's surreptitious reading of Portia's diary, Anna's anger over what she has read, and Portia's feelings of outrage and betrayal upon her eventual discovery of this act. Normally, this might seem too slender a storyline to base a novel on, but Bowen uses it to frame a much larger drama of the ends and ethics of reading.

The other central figure in the novel is Eddie, a young man whose life is defined by the effects of reading: "When he came to London he got a job on a paper; in his spare time he worked off his sense of insult in a satirical novel which, when published, did him no good at all. Its readers, who were not many, were divided into those who saw no point in the book whatever, and those who did see the point, were profoundly offended, and made up their minds to take it out on Eddie" (62). He goes on to make more unfortunate decisions. He has an amorous intrigue with Mrs. Quayne, though exactly how far this extends physically is not entirely clear. Eddie was her "first troubadour" and he appeared to lend himself to "Anna's illusions about living. By his poetic appreciation he created a small world of art around her" (66). He also begins a flirtation with Portia. This too is fueled by literature: "The impetus under which he seemed to move made life fall, round him and her, into a new poetic order at once" (105).

This man, so concerned about his words' reception, makes one demand of her: she must promise she will never write about him in her diary. As he explains, "I hate writing; I hate art—there's always something else there. I won't have you choosing words about me. If you ever start that, your diary will become a horrible trap" (109). These remarks echo in part the words of other characters about the diary. Anna is very disturbed by reading the depiction of herself in its pages; she says there "does not seem to be a single thing that she misses, and there is certainly not a thing that she does not misconstruct" (12). As she reads it, she thinks, "Either the girl is mad, or I am" (10). The reader is eventually able to encounter several sections of the journal; it does not seem to contain any significant distortions. It becomes increasingly evident that one of the things that so upsets Anna is the verisimilitude of Portia's account.

It is precisely on this point that Anna's friend and confidant, the writer St Quentin Miller, seeks to reassure her. "You've got to allow for style, though," he cautions. "Nothing arrives on paper as it started, and so much arrives that never started at all. To write is always to rave a little" (10). Miller inverts this thesis when talking to Portia about diary-writing late in the book. "One's nature is to forget, and one ought to go by that," he advises (249); further, "if one didn't let oneself swallow a few lies, I don't know how one would ever carry the past" (249). The problem, it turns out, is

122   *The Reader in Modernist Fiction*

that the immediacy of daily writing leads to an ungovernable accuracy of impression which is doomed to be negative: "a diary would come much too near the mark. One ought to secrete for some time before one begins to look back at anything. Look how reconciled to everything reminiscences are" (249). It seems then that writing and reading are indeed powerful and revealing, and are rightly feared by those whose behavior will not stand up to scrutiny once it is fixed in the form of a continuous narrative. As Joseph Elkanah Rosenberg states, "Anna's fear is that the diary does not merely offer an account of Portia's inner thoughts, but acts . . . as an objective account of the Quayne household that catches in place what it observes, playing back the happenstance of the Quaynes' everyday life as a tale of Portia's own victimhood" (82). It is just this function that Miller seems to fear as well. He goes so far as to suggest that such diary-writing is unethical: "You're working on us, making us into something. Which is not fair—we are not on our guard with you"; continuing in this line, he goes on to conclude rather preposterously, "You set traps for us. You ruin our free will" (250). It is hard to imagine the diary of a sixteen-year-old, however vivid, having such formidable power; it is evident that Miller too fears the reading that the narrative of his actions would likely produce. As Rosenberg observes: "Anna's feelings of being imprisoned by (or, rather, in) Portia's diary are best expressed by her later accusation that Portia 'crowds me into an unreal position, till even St Quentin asks why do I over-act'" (246; Rosenberg 82); Anna states rather cruelly that the "only honest way left is to be harsh to them both, which I honestly am" (246).

When Portia stays with Mrs. Heccomb at her house on the coast while the Quaynes are visiting Capri, the old woman warns her against excessive reading and notes that, at one time, "Anna read too much" (130). Her daughter, Daphne, takes this advice rather too thoroughly: although she works at a library, she scorns reading and is contemptuous of those who seek out books. Portia realizes that "the tomb-like hush of Smoot's library, where she had to sit all day, dealing out hated books, was not only antipathetic but even dangerous to Daphne" (137). Curiously, the patrons of the library find this attitude oddly refreshing. "Her palpable wish never to read placed at a disadvantage those who had become dependent on the habit, and it was a disadvantage they seemed to enjoy . . . [F]or this clientele of discarded people her bloom and her nonchalance served, somehow, to place her above literature" (184). Such readers expected no more from life, and "just dared to look in books to see how much they had missed" (184).

In this text we see a wide-ranging encounter with numerous acts of reading that is somewhat reminiscent of Virginia Woolf's varied and unintegrated conglomeration of readers and nonreaders. In the case of Bowen, we see the raw power of direct, unmediated reading, especially as a clear window into the actual state of things and people. Interestingly, it is the diary form as written by an intelligent though unsophisticated young woman that is valorized over more polished works of published literature. Indeed, reading literature seems to be less important in this book than in earlier works I have discussed in preceding chapters; the power of the book appears to be declining somewhat at the center of the empire.

Graham Greene

The modernist drama of misreading continues in Graham Greene's *The Heart of the Matter* (1948), which is set in a West African colony during World War II. Intelligence agent Edward Wilson pretends to nearly everyone he meets that he does not like or read poetry; however, we learn that he does in fact enjoy poetry, but he "absorbed it secretly, like a drug. *The Golden Treasury* accompanied him where ever he went, but it was taken at night in small doses . . . His taste was romantic" (12). After the examples of Conrad and Ford, this is all we need to know in order to suspect that the trajectory of his actions will conclude in failure. Naturally enough, he falls in love with a woman, "Literary Louise" Scobie, who is similarly smitten by the written word. She is very unhappy in Africa, and is unable to share her love of reading with her husband or anyone else there. When she meets Wilson, her first question is, "Do you like reading?" (30). Her husband, the novel's protagonist, strolls off, knowing that his wife is now happy, and he feels an immense gratitude to the other man, who stops by later that night to borrow a book.

With a tip from a disgruntled steward, the intelligence officer Scobie intercepts a suspicious letter intended for an address in enemy Germany. Contrary to his orders, Scobie opens it and reads it carefully to determine whether it could be a missive in code. He finds that it is harmless, and deems the story he has heard of its transmission "sufficiently irrational to be true" (51). He then destroys the letter, an act that sets in motion an ever escalating series of problems. It is also the case that his ability to decipher the narratives of the colonized is gravely inadequate. He spends two and a half hours listening to witnesses in a case of petty larceny and does not believe a word

124   *The Reader in Modernist Fiction*

said by any of them (140). He feels that in Europe there were words that rang true and others that did not; narratives that sounded plausible and those that did not, and in a case of theft, one can assume that something had actually been stolen. But in Africa, there were no such assurances for the police officer.

Reading is carefully controlled in the colonies. As Scobie tries to find an interesting work to read to a sick boy, he is told that all the books are "safe": they "are censored by the committee before they come out . . . We are not teaching the children here in order that they read—well, novels" (127). Eluding the effects of fiction will prove harder than the authorities had imagined. Scobie selects one of the books, *A Bishop among the Bantus*, that does in fact reflect the ideology he publicly affirms, and he pretends to read it while instead inventing a swashbuckling story of pirates for the boy. The private, felonious narrative superimposed upon the serene public one is a fair image of the turn his own life has taken, as he gets more deeply involved with local criminals—the most powerful of whom is an ardent admirer of Shakespeare.

Wilson is deluded because of his reading; after showing her his just published poem, he tells Louise he loves her. As he utters this sentence, he feels helpless: "He thought: it's a lie, the word means nothing off the printed page. He waited for her laughter" (215). She doesn't laugh, but she can't take his affection seriously. She concludes their discussion of the subject by stating that "We don't *die* for love, Wilson—except, of course, in books" (215). Though she is also a reader, she is a much more skeptical one who is careful not to misapply literature to life. Her husband is not so fortunate. He becomes trapped by the public narratives around him to the point where he feels it is his duty to commit suicide. There is a problem, however, with the way he imagines the narrative of his life being interpreted in the manner he feels is acceptable. In fact, he cannot imagine his decision being properly comprehended except in a literary context: "She would understand, he thought, if I were in a book," he decides. This feeling of relief is quickly tempered as he goes on to wonder "would I understand her if she were just a character?" His response is negative; he goes on to conclude, "But I don't read that sort of book" (253). Needless to say, his suicide is not construed the way he hoped it would be: Louise comments acerbically, "And at the end this—horror . . . Oh, why, why did he have to make such a mess of things?" (271–72). This resounding affirmation of the incommensurability of life and fiction is a fitting conclusion to this analysis of the fate of misreading, the conjunction of reading and sex, and the price paid for the misunderstanding of the surrounding social world. Finally, she and Wilson do not form a couple after Scobie's death; she rejects his proposal and refuses to talk about love.

Ralph Ellison

Henry Louis Gates points out that "[m]isreading signs could be, and indeed often was, fatal. Reading, in this sense, was not play; it was an essential aspect of the literacy training of a child. This sort of metaphorical literacy, the learning to decipher complex codes, is just about the blackest aspect of the black tradition" (6). Reading is a significant act and theme in many African-American works. One of the most extended encounters appears in Ralph Ellison's *Invisible Man* (1952). At the end of the first chapter the narrator has a dream, one that he would remember and dream again in the years to come. In it, his grandfather tells him to open his new briefcase and read the letter inside. The envelope contains another envelope, which in turn encloses another. After opening thirty such envelopes ("Them's years," his grandfather elucidates), he opens the final one and is told to read aloud the engraved document inside: "To Whom It May Concern," the text states, "Keep This Nigger-Boy Running" (33). The narrator indicates that at the time of the first dream he had no insight into the meaning of these words; the rest of the novel chronicles his many attempts to survive and succeed in a racist America, a journey that will finally disclose the letter's meaning.

In this novel the reading of texts is often presented as unusual and is regularly depicted in oneiric terms. In a typical passage, the narrator describes a feeling of déjà-vu, and notes he couldn't determine if it was caused by "watching some similar scene in the movies, from books I'd read, or from some recurrent but deeply buried dream" (293). In the novel's final chapter, he falls down a manhole while fleeing a white mob; there is no light, and he looks for paper to make a torch to guide his movements in the darkness. The only papers he has are those that are inside his briefcase; he reads each one before setting it aflame. Doing so, he realizes that the author of the denunciatory letter that cost him his status in The Brotherhood, a communist-type organization, was also written by the same man who was his mentor in the group: "I knelt there, stunned, and watched the flames consume them. That he, or anyone at that late date, could have named me and sent me running with one and the same stroke of the pen was too

126   *The Reader in Modernist Fiction*

much" (555). He realizes that he had been manipulated and discarded by the very group that had promised to battle against such oppressive practices. In between these symmetrical acts of revelatory reading, a vast drama of interpretation and misinterpretation unfolds.

One major strand is the documentation and understanding of historical events. Dr. Bledsoe, the dean of the college he attends, explains: "You are a black educated fool, son. Those white folks have newspapers, magazines, radios, spokesmen to get their ideas across. If they want to tell the world a lie, they can tell it so well that it becomes the truth" (141). The narrator sees this media mastery in action at several points in the text, most clearly during the riot in Harlem. His sole recourse is to send an open letter to all the local presses in which he denounces them for distorting the events they pretend to depict and for "inflating minor incidents," thereby obscuring the genuine causes of the unrest (503). The novel's twentieth chapter contains a sustained meditation on the reading and writing of history which focuses on acts of depiction, transmission, and reception. This set of reflections follows the narrator's witnessing the death of Tod Clifton, a former member of the Brotherhood, who is shot and killed by a policeman on a street in Harlem. First, the narrator wonders why a man like Tod would decide to remove himself from the historical movement he had been helping to enable; why would he "give up his voice and leave the only organization offering him a chance to 'define' himself?" (428). As bits of paper whirl upward in the air, the narrator continues to reflect on the power of words and the void of silence: "Why did he choose to plunge into nothingness, into the void of . . . soundless voices, lying outside history?" (428). He looks at the situation from the perspective of the Marxist philosophy of history, an inexorably teleological narrative which he now glimpses "from a distance of words read in books, half-remembered. History records the patterns of men's lives, they say" (428), he begins.

Right away he modifies this thesis; noting that since history records "who won and who lived to lie about it afterwards" (429), the historical record is itself compromised, necessarily incomplete and, in fact, structured to be so. He continues to develop his historiographic critique: "All things, it is said, are duly recorded—all things of importance, that is. But not quite, for actually it is only the known, the seen, the heard and only the events that the recorder regards as important that are put down, those lies his keepers keep their power by" (429). But the police killing he has just witnessed will not be recorded as such in any public document. He goes on to wonder where the historians of today were, and how they would put it down (429). Historians' exclusive focus on events deemed important invariably neglects and thereby eliminates more marginal figures from authorized narratives of the past; they refuse to write the lives of those "birds of passage who were too obscure for learned classification, too silent for the most sensitive recorders of sound, of natures too ambiguous for the most ambiguous words, and too distant from the centers of historical decision to sign or even applaud the signers of historical documents. We who wrote no novels, histories or other books" (429). Such figures can never be read; they are mere blank spaces on the page. Neither will their absence even be surmised.

Other, popular narrative forms are able to partially record traces of these lives. While he is walking down the street, forgotten names sing through his head "like forgotten scenes in dreams" (433). Outside a record shop, he hears a loudspeaker blaring a languid blues song. "I stopped. Was this all that would be recorded? Was this the only true history of the times, a mood blasted by trumpets, trombones, saxophones, and drums," but in the end "a song with turgid, inadequate words" (433). Finally, this fragmentary, alternative history hardly fares much better in establishing a historical presence for those excluded from written texts.

Up to this point, the Brotherhood's reading of the pattern of history had seemed both intellectually satisfying and emotionally fulfilling: "The Brotherhood had both science and history under control"; it had "given the world a new shape, and me a vital role. We recognized no loose ends, everything could be controlled by our science. Life was all pattern and discipline" (373). Now, however, the narrator is able to move beyond the Marxist metanarrative of history, and starts to question its determinism, completeness, and inevitability: "What if Brother Jack were wrong? What if history were a gambler, instead of a force in a laboratory experiment . . . What if history were not a reasonable citizen, but a madman full of paranoid guile?" (431). The narrator ceases to believe in the narrative of history that he had been devoting his life to help create, and grows skeptical of the very texts that had earlier aroused his suspicion of other works. Valerie Smith points out that "when he decides to write his own story, he relinquishes the meaning generated by other ideologies in favor of one that is primarily self-generated. By designating a beginning and an end to his story, he converts events that threaten to be chaotic into ones that reveal form and significance" (209; see also Pioro).

Ellison's deployment of intertextuality is also relevant to the work's reception and self-situating. He engages in the tradition of

128 *The Reader in Modernist Fiction*

"signifyin'" to indicate his debt to and distance from antecedent works like Dostoyevsky's "Notes from the Underground" and Richard Wright's "The Man Who Lived Underground." His citation of African-American works of popular culture and allusion to James Joyce ("Stephen's problem, like ours, was not actually one of creating the uncreated conscience of his race, but of creating the *uncreated features of his face*," Ellison's emphasis, 345–46) indicate the fusion of the two cultures that will be necessary for the protagonist in his attempt to forge an effective sense of self, even as it announces Ellison's self-selection of his predecessors and articulates the standards he aspires to. Also important is the most insistent set of allusions in the text: those that point to Ralph Waldo Emerson and Booker T. Washington and their collective insistence on self-reliance. The narrator's experience provides a sustained critique of the naïveté of such notions when applied to black life in the first half of the twentieth century: there were too many barriers imposed by white supremacists for self-reliance to be anything but a cruel joke. Finally, we may point to the work's reflexivity; *Invisible Man*, like *Ulysses*, performs the very act that it calls out for: "Being invisible and without substance, a disembodied voice as it were, what else could I do? What else but try to tell you what was really happening when your eyes were looking through?" (568). The words on the pages of the book provide the representations that are missing from all other accounts.

The book's last sentence, directed to the white reader, clearly discloses the nature of the dual audience that Ellison is addressing. Such strategies are nearly ubiquitous in African-American literature before the 1960s. James Weldon Johnson wrote in 1928: "The Aframerican faces a special problem which the plain American author knows nothing about—the problem of the double audience. It is more than a double audience; it is a divided audience, an audience made up of two elements with differing and often opposite points of view" (477). Ellison is writing both to give voice to the experiences of Black Americans and to educate white Americans about those experiences.

African-American critics like Gates have identified the presence of a fixed (though often missed) meaning. The novel's last lines also point to a distinctive feature of African-American fiction. Robert Stepto has stressed the rhetorical and instructional component of much Black literature, noting that it is less concerned with unreliable narrators than unreliable *readers*: "In Afro-American storytelling texts especially, rhetoric and narrative strategy combine time and again to declare that the principal unreliable factor in the storytelling paradigm is the reader (white American readers, obviously, but

The Dangers of Reading from Wharton to Ellison

blacks as well), and that acts of creative communication are fully initiated not when the text is assaulted but when the reader gets 'told'—or 'told off'—in such a way that he or she finally begins to *hear*" (202–03). Ellison's text is clearly informed by such intentions.

Tayeb Salih

Tayeb Salih's novel, *Season of Migration to the North* (1967), an African rewriting of "Heart of Darkness," models the transition from the modernist paradigm to a postcolonial one. Though its poetics is entirely contained within high modernism, its treatment of the effects of reading is quite different. The work centers on the life of the Kurtz-like figure of Mustapha Sa'eed as told by a narrator. Sa'eed's life is constructed by and through books, though not in ways he can imagine, understand, or control. As a young boy in Sudan he is an outstanding student; his abilities finally land him in England. There his education continues; we learn later that he will go on to write several volumes of anticolonial political and economic theory. In the strange, cold, corrupt land of England his vices also proliferate; he repeatedly seduces Englishwomen who, with his collaboration, see him as an exotic, primitive, fascinating, hypersexual Other. Anne Hammond's response to him exudes Orientalist mythology: "unlike me, she yearned for tropical climes, cruel suns, purple horizons. In her eyes, I was a symbol of all her hankerings" (27). With Isabella Seymour, he plays the role she imagines for him even more extravagantly. Parodying Othello, he "related to her fabricated stories about deserts of golden sand and jungles where nonexistent animals called out to each other" (33). He tells her "the streets of my country teemed with elephants and lions and that during siesta time crocodiles crawled through it" (33). Soon, they would be in bed together: "she gazed hard and long at me as though seeing me as a symbol rather than reality' (33). His most desperate (and fatal) relation is with a woman who offers to give herself to him if he offers her a Wedgewood vase, a valuable Persian rug, and a rare Arabic manuscript. He agrees, only to see her smash the vase, burn the rug, and destroy the book: "Taking up the old, rare manuscript she tore it to bits, filling her mouth with pieces of paper which she chewed and spat out" (130). She then leaves the apartment. Soon after, they become deeply intertwined; some time later, Mustafa marries her. Not long after their marriage, he helps her end her life.

130   *The Reader in Modernist Fiction*

The narrator is both fascinated and repulsed by Mustafa's story, unable to integrate it into his worldview. The narrator had written a dissertation on an English Romantic poet; Mustafa mocked him for having chosen such an impractical subject. Once Mustafa vanishes, the narrator is named guardian of the other's family, but he proves unable to prevent another death, that of Mustafa's widow. After returning to the village, he finally unlocks the door to an unused room in Mustafa's house. There he finds, to his amazement, a vast library of English and European books:

> Books on economics, history and literature . . . Books bound in leather. Books in paper covers. Old tattered books. Books that looked as if they'd just come from the printers. Huge volumes the size of tombstones. Small books with gilt edges the size of playing cards. Words of dedication. Books in boxes. Books on the chairs. Books on the floor. (113–14)

But there are no books in Arabic. Mustafa's hidden library functions as an allegory of the dubiousness of knowledge provided by the colonizer: "the schools were started so as to teach us to say 'Yes' in their language" (79). The passionate, hateful, and self-destructive antagonism of his English wife likewise functions as an allegory of colonial occupation. In the end, neither books nor love is enough: careful, concerted action with others is essential. In the new postcolonial world, it is not possible to be an isolated intellectual.

There is another book in the walled-off library, a notebook with the title "My Life Story, by Mustafa Sa'eed" (125). Other than a dedication, the pages are all blank. The narrator wonders, "Did this too have significance or was it mere chance?" (125). The critical reader may confidently assert that it is indeed significant, though not perhaps in the way the narrator can imagine: Mustafa's life story is blank, not because it is yet to be written, or even lived, but because it has already been scripted for him by the web of circumstances that surround him, circumstances created by indigenous tradition and British occupation, which he is unable to elude. As the narrator increasingly comes to resemble Mustafa (at one point, he mistakes his own image in a mirror for that of the other), it becomes apparent that their fates will similarly converge.

Mustafa also leaves behind an unfinished poem in English; the narrator obligingly corrects and completes its final line. He discovers numerous scraps of paper filled with various phrases, and speculates that they were "like pieces in an arithmetical puzzle, which Mustapha Sa'eed wanted me to discover and to place side by side and so come out with a composite picture which would reflect favorably on him" (127). He resists doing this, but realizes he needs to complete the trajectory of his own life. Like the invisible man, whom he resembles in significant ways, he is finally able to survive by writing out his own story. More starkly than in *Invisible Man,* reading has contradictory effects: it is liberating and alienating, empowering and debilitating; it gives the narrator knowledge but leaves him isolated and irrelevant. The enlightenment paradigm here collapses in on itself, and being a skeptical reader is insufficient to ward off failure, though in this work, as in Conrad's "Youth" and Joyce's "Araby," the folly of uncritically accepting Orientalist discourse is demonstrated ("Her eyes brightened and she cried out ecstatically: 'The Nile'" 33). Postcolonial narratives, even when utilizing the tropes and strategies of high modernism, can require a very different explanatory model for their interrogation of reading.

Notes

1. After Archer proposes that they move up their wedding day, May "smiled dreamily upon the possibility; but it seemed that to dream of it sufficed her. It was like hearing him read aloud out of his poetry books the beautiful things that could not possibly happen in real life" (955). Here, reading expresses what May and her social set could never want to do and what Archer would actually never dare to do.
2. For additional salient allusions to poetry and painting, see Orlando (178–92).
3. Orlando ingeniously suggests that "Wharton shows us Ellen's bookshelves as a way of constructing a counterreading to Archer's 'fictions'" (186).
4. This is perhaps not as preposterous as it may seem to the law-abiding reader. After "Bunty," a notorious gangster in New Delhi, was shot to death in a pre-dawn raid, authorities found "true crime" magazines at his hideout, as well as clippings he kept about himself, English-language exercise books, a telephone directory written in code, and a cache of guns" (*International Herald Tribune,* August 28, 2008, p. 5).
5. In his essay, Wyatt discusses reading in *Sartoris* and *The Unvanquished* as well as "The Bear."

Chapter 5

Reading Ruins: From Modernism to the Illegible Texts of Postmodernism and Beyond

In the 1950s in the West, literacy was near universal and more books were published than at any time in history up to that point. In the United States and elsewhere, there were more college graduates than ever before. At universities, the formal study of modern literature grew rapidly; Nabokov taught modernist fiction at Cornell; many other colleges would hire professors in this field as modern literature became a legitimate object of academic study. Outside the academy, well-funded and well-stocked libraries were present in every community; bookstores were widespread. Paperback publishing was no longer a limited, rather tawdry aspect of book production, responsible for the type of reading material "whose covers bear either pictures of young women in underclothes or pictures of men in the act of shooting one another with pistols," as Faulkner expressed it in *Light in August* (*Novels 1930–1935* 479–80). There was a transformation in the quality of the titles printed, in the new, strong ties to mainstream publishing, and in the widespread distribution of the books (Luey 274–76). Sales rose dramatically: in 1947, 95 million paperbacks were sold; in 1952, sales reached 270 million.

A new suburban literary culture became entrenched, one that welcomed effective guides to help readers sort through the mass of volumes being printed. One of the distinguishing features of this culture was the mail order book club, an important component in petit bourgeois *Bildung*. As Molly Travis explains, "The emergence of the twentieth-century middlebrow book club signaled a transition from production to consumption in America. Culture and practical knowledge were conflated so that culture became *news*. A reader of the reports written by the Book-of-the-Month Club's selection committee gained advance knowledge of the books before publication. Supplied with a steady stream of book reports rather than critical reviews, book club members found they did not actually need to read a book to be familiar with

Reading Ruins: Postmodernism   **133**

it" (22). Not only was critical reading largely absent in this scenario; reading itself could be superfluous. Despite all the writing, the number of accessible books, and extensive forums of instruction, the general level of US literary culture did not increase; if anything, the period was often marked by intellectual timidity. Producing, disseminating, and analyzing modernist classics and other great books was not enough to produce great readers. Many readers, resisting New Critical calls for close reading, preferred to be what Merve Emre has dubbed "bad readers" in a "paraliterary" culture (1–7). Along with the rise of television and the increase in movie theaters, the cultural precondition for the development of postmodernism was fully in place.

From Modernism to Postmodernism

Nabokov has played with readers his entire career; to take only one of several prominent examples, in *The Real Life of Sebastian Knight* (1938), the narrator, V., journeys in search of the details of the life of his brother, Sebastian, who had died before V. was able to know him in any depth. Much of his information about his brother's mature sensibility comes from reading Sebastian's novels. Without realizing it, V. goes on to experience all the events that Sebastian had written about in his fiction; Nabokov thereby produces a cunning puzzle for the reader and a compelling allegory of the way a text creates its audience. The book is constructed to reward the reader who is able to see all that the narrator fails to perceive, and realize that the descriptions of fictional books are also present in the larger work that contains them.

As noted in the introduction, "Signs and Symbols" is about a boy whose madness lies in his belief that the natural world reflects his personality and situation. Of course, in modernist fiction, details of the external world do reflect the protagonist's situation: the dying bird in the puddle is in fact an apt image of the unlucky boy. But this is something that only readers are supposed to be able to discern, not the characters themselves, so Nabokov is playing a game here, uncomfortably fusing the represented event with the act of its representation. Some Nabokovians read yet additional meanings into this text. Others find in it an ambiguous allegory of interpretation. And since the story is set a few years after the Nazis killed many of the family's friends and relatives, the idea of an irrational malignant world is not a paranoid delusion, but a historical fact.

The last lines of the story simply state that the phone rings again after midnight; the logic of the narrative demands that it provide a

134   *The Reader in Modernist Fiction*

resolution to the situation, specifically that the boy is dead. David Richter remarks that the "process of symbol hunting," which is essential for the successful interpretation of the text, has no natural stopping point; every detail is potentially symbolic. The text therefore "assimilates us readers to the schizophrenic son himself, whose disease is described as 'referential mania'" (428). Michael Wood presses on this paradox, stating that "the strength of the story is that what seems to be the 'right' reading, the banal, accidental wrong number, is simultaneously the sanest and the hardest to settle for" (72). The text has trained us to believe in pain but not in chance accidents. "Referential mania is one of the ways in which we find the author in the text" (73). Without knowing what the phone call will divulge, we have to assume it is tragic, he concludes. Another way to look at this dilemma is that if the phone call announces their son's death, it violates our sense of probability: this is not a likely event in our experience of the world. On the other hand, if the call does not announce the death, then the story fails as a story, and we are left with important issues unresolved for no good reason, artistic or otherwise. Nabokov takes this basic opposition—essentially, that between artifice and actuality—and self-consciously makes it the hermeneutical hinge on which the text revolves. The reader must choose between them.

"The Vane Sisters" (1951) can be thought of as a kind of revenge by the deranged boy on the "normal" world. In this text, the drama of interpretation is simultaneously alphabetical and cosmological. At the beginning of the story, the narrator is attracted by images of melting icicles and observes them with keen fascination. Oddly, the large, vivid drops of water seem to have no shadow. Just then he meets a colleague who informs him that the narrator's former lover, Cynthia Vane, has died. We are told the story of the narrator's involvement with the two Vane sisters (the other was named, most appropriately, Sybil) and we learn of Cynthia's belief that the dead can visit the living and communicate with them in various obscure ways—a belief mocked by the rational narrator as particularly silly. He remembers a "novel or short story (by some contemporary writer, I believe) in which, unknown to the author, the first letters of the words in its last paragraph formed, as deciphered by Cynthia, a message from his dead mother" (*Stories* 622). The distraught narrator, afraid that he will see some evidence of Cynthia's postmortem presence, has difficulty falling asleep. Once he finally nods off, he has a dream, but it is a very inconclusive one that he cannot decipher: "I set myself to reread my dream—backward, diagonally, up, down—trying hard to unravel something Cynthia-like in it, something strange and suggestive that must be there," he notes. Unsuccessful in this attempt at interpretation, he concludes: "I could isolate, consciously, little. Everything seemed blurred, yellow-clouded, yielding nothing tangible. Her inept acrostics, maudlin evasions, theopathies—every recollection formed ripples of mysterious meaning. Everything seemed yellowly blurred, illusive, lost" (*Stories* 631). These words do however obliquely yield the correct reading and disclose the preternatural act of communication: the first letters of the story's last five sentences form an acrostic that does resolve the plot in a way the narrator can never comprehend. Understandably, Nabokov suggested that such a plot device could only be used once every thousand years.

Lolita (1953) explicitly thematizes and probingly explores the subject of reading relations. It parodies a number of familiar types of narratee, castigates inappropriate expectations and responses to the events, provides a running commentary on the values of several authors and genres, and shows how individuals variously attempt to gain cultural capital or enhance their social position through the books they read or claim to read. The work is also a sustained drama of reading and misreading, though we will see that it finally veers away from the modernist pattern that I have been tracing throughout this study. *Lolita* is filled with codes, disguised words, and hidden messages, as well as language and behavior designed to produce systematic misinterpretations. Humbert invents "elaborate dreams, pure classics in style, in order to mock the psychoanalysts who attempt to interpret them" (*Annotated* 36).[1] His damning diary is written in a microscopic script that "only a loving wife could decipher" (44). Humbert constantly acts in a way to simultaneously disguise and satisfy his criminal desires, creating as it were a semiotic polysemy that allows him to be one thing while appearing another.

Charlotte Haze is depicted as a naïve reader who has "blind faith in the wisdom of her church and book club" (77–78), though the novels Humbert found lying around when he arrived are quickly replaced by illustrated catalogues and homemaking guides as their relationship progresses (80). Humbert knows exactly how to manipulate such an uncritical sensibility: while listening to accounts of Charlotte's past love life and inventing stories of his own, Humbert notes that the two sets were technically "congeneric since both were affected by the same stuff (soap operas, psychoanalysis and cheap novelettes) upon which I drew for my characters and she for her mode of expression" (82). Dolores is her mother's progeny in regard to reading, though she is even more the lineal descendent of Gerty

136   *The Reader in Modernist Fiction*

MacDowell: "She believed, with a kind of celestial trust, any advertisement or advice that appeared in *Movie Love* or *Screen Land* . . . The words 'novelties and souvenirs' simply entranced her by their trochaic lilt. If some café sign proclaimed Ice Cold Drinks, she was automatically stirred, though all drinks everywhere were ice-cold. She it was to whom the ads were dedicated: the subject and object of every foul poster" (150). She uses books like *Treasure Island* as repositories for hiding dollar bills from Humbert (186).

The most elaborate attempt at reading concerns the most prominent set of clues in the book, the ever-changing fictitious names and addresses that Humbert's nemesis provides in the motel guest books as he follows Humbert and Dolores around America. This "cryptogrammic paper chase" (252) haunts Humbert, who is never able to accurately decipher his antagonist: "His main trait was his passion for tantalization. Goodness, what a tease the poor fellow was! . . . I noticed that whenever he felt his enigmas were becoming too recondite, even for such a solver as I, he would lure me back with an easy one" (252). But Humbert is never able to decipher this private, taunting code; he does not learn the name until he wrests it from Dolly years later. This encounter is revealing, as I will discuss later: "she emitted, a little mockingly, somewhat fastidiously, not untenderly, in a kind of muted whistle, the name that the astute reader has guessed long ago" (273–74).

There is an interesting interplay between reading and misreading within this text, as poor readers are able to make major discoveries and the most sophisticated reader ("Well-read Humbert" [72]) is regularly confounded. Charlotte Haze does find and read Humbert's diary and ignores his attempts to narrativize the entries in a less incriminating manner by pretending they were part of a novel he was writing. Humbert and Dolores engage in their own dynamic of deliberate and unintended misreading, which reveals Dolores's growing interpretive abilities as she helps plot what she believes will be her rescue. When Humbert takes out the piece of paper on which he has written the number of the license plate of the car that has been following them, he finds "erasures revealing the hurried shuttle smear of a pencil's rubber end, and with parts of numbers obliterated or reconstructed in a child's hand" (228), leaving an impenetrable hieroglyph; Dolores thus helps disguise the identity of their pursuer. After a hostile conversation with her, Humbert picks up the book she was reading ("some trash for young people," he notes), and sees that it contained a powerful scene about a dying mother who wished to mitigate the devastation of her death on her daughter. After she leaves the room, Humbert belatedly realizes that Dolores had seen this narrative as a figuration of her life and her dead mother's (288). Near the end of the novel, Dolores claims that the supreme interpreter was, in fact, Quilty: "He saw—smiling—through everything and everybody, because he was not like me and her but a genius . . . Had rocked with laughter when she confessed about me and her, and said he had thought so" (277). Humbert, not surprisingly, treats this claim with contempt, despite the fact that it is, in its broadest outlines, correct: Quilty saw through Humbert's pose, lured Dolly away from him, successfully concealed his identity despite the many clues he offered. In addition, he was (unlike Humbert) a successful author.

In his nonfiction, Nabokov has discussed the subject of his intended audience: "I think the audience an artist imagines . . . is a room full of people wearing his own mask," *Strong* 18). He explicitly excludes certain types of reader ("all my books should be stamped, Freudians, Keep Out" [introduction to *Bend Sinister* xviii]); he has tried to direct the reception of his own works, most obviously, in "On a Book Entitled *Lolita*" (*Annotated* 313–19). He has expatiated on the subject of quality readers: "a good reader, a major reader, an active and creative reader is a rereader," he states (*Lectures* 3). In this lecture, he contrasts two kinds of readers (as we can also see in Wharton and Woolf). The "lowly kind" of reader turns to a book for support of simple, personal emotions. Subvarieties of this kind of reader include those who feel intensely because the book reminds them of a personal experience, a familiar country, or mode of living, or because of the possibility of identifying with a character. The superior reader instead utilizes "impersonal imagination" and seeks "aesthetic delight." Nabokov urges us "to remain a little aloof and take pleasure in this aloofness while at the same time we keenly enjoy—passionately enjoy, enjoy with tears and shivers—the inner weave of a given masterpiece" (4). The stance he advocates is distanced, contemplative, and intersubjective, rather than involved or subjective; these injunctions correspond nicely with the contemporary approach outlined by the New Criticism, including Wimsatt and Beardsley's denunciation of what they called the "affective fallacy" around the same general period.

In *Lolita*, we find not just these two but also a third type of implied reader; I will call them the pornographic, the humanist, and the aesthetic readers of the text.[2] The first group, Nabokov explains in his essay on *Lolita*, "expected the rising succession of erotic scenes; when they stopped, the readers stopped, too, and felt bored and let down" (315). Consequently, the pornographic reader is not merely ignored,

138   *The Reader in Modernist Fiction*

he—I deliberately employ the masculine pronoun—is regularly frustrated. This is most theatrically demonstrated in the non-description of Humbert's long-desired copulation with Lolita. Instead of an account of it, we are offered the following disclaimer: "but really these are irrelevant matters; I am not concerned with so-called 'sex' at all. Anybody can imagine those elements of animality" (136).

Tzvetan Todorov has asserted that "a text always contains within itself directions for its own consumption" ("Reading" 77); in this case, however, the directions are potentially misleading and the penalties for misuse are rather severe. The often fatuous "Foreword" by Dr. John Ray that precedes Humbert's confessions serves as a kind of guide for the reader, if read with appropriate detachment and skepticism. Humanist readers who are overly serious, literally minded, ideologically committed, sociologically oriented, or unfamiliar with the duplicities of narrators are offered an implicit warning. Potential readers should not, like Dr. Ray, read fiction for what it says about ideas or the social world and thereby misread the text, mistake its irony, confuse parody for sincerity, or inappropriately employ the expectations suitable for a "committed" work of realism. It is an audience that Nabokov simultaneously teases and rebuffs, convinced in his belief that "what some call the Literature of Ideas" is very often mere "topical trash coming in huge blocks of plaster that are carefully transmitted from age to age until somebody comes along with a hammer and takes a good crack at Balzac, at Gorki, at Mann" (*Annotated* 317).

This type of audience is identified by Ray as the "old-fashioned" reader who wishes "to follow the destinies of 'real' people beyond the 'true' story" (6)—red flags to more formalist-minded readers who were trained to scoff at such "How-many-children-had-Lady-Macbeth"-type questions. Interestingly, Nabokov here has stopped mocking Ray and is instead using him as an unlikely mouthpiece for his own literary beliefs. Paradoxically, after scorning the desire to follow the destinies of the characters beyond the covers of the book, Ray (and through him, Nabokov) does just that by obliquely indicating the final fates of Humbert and Dolores. Nabokov goes on to lay cunning traps for this, his "most inimical reader" (*Lolita* 274). Humbert's worst plans are intolerably offensive to all who thoroughly suspend their disbelief in the fictionality of the text; the author goes to great lengths to ensure that such readers will be both chastised and ultimately assuaged: "Gentlewomen of the jury! Bear with me! Allow me to take just a tiny bit of your precious time!" he exhorts (125). His plotting fails, Humbert is left frustrated in the

Reading Ruins: Postmodernism   **139**

story, and the humanist reader presumably continues on, awaiting further provocations.

The pornographic and humanist readers are opposed by what Nabokov, as we have seen, refers to as "a major reader, an active and creative reader" (*Lectures* 3). There is a kind of test offered in the first paragraph of Humbert's narration which, answered correctly, rewards and validates the efforts of the aesthetic reader. Encountering the oddly phrased rhetorical question, "Did she have a precursor?" (11), audiences must make an interpretive choice and determine whether the word is used in the unusual, though expected sense of forerunner or predecessor, or in the strictly literary meaning of textual antecedent. The first choice will yield a search for earlier individuals, originary moments, and psychological repetition; the latter will encourage one to look instead for intertextual echoes of earlier works.

Nabokov partially maintains the plausibility of the first reading by having Humbert recount the story of his first, adolescent love; that girl's name however turns out to be Annabel Leigh, and Poe's poem of the same name (though spelled differently) is parodied in the very beginning of Humbert's memoir: "there might have been no Lolita at all had I not loved, one summer, a certain initial girl-child. In a princedom by the sea" (11). Nabokov's aesthetic reader is presumably intended to discern that Dolores's precursor was not a human being but a series of literary texts, and would not have existed without Poe's prior text.

Lolita is of course saturated with allusions, many to Poe, many others to *Carmen*, and there is also a sustained homage to Proust's *Recherche*.[3] The realm of intertextuality often calls for a different, partially nonrepresentational construal, one that in this case can contest and supplant the work's ostensible mimetic aspects as the reader identifies a literary reincarnation rather than identifying with a character's action. Nabokov's imagined aesthetic reader will, he postulates, be more intrigued by the author's play with motifs and manipulation of earlier texts than by any purported representation of salacious or criminal acts, and will in fact read the latter *as* themes and motifs. For a Nabokovian character, after all, "death is but a question of style, a mere literary device, a musical resolution" (*Portable* 246). The aesthetic reader can both enjoy the pseudo-Dostoyevskian "confessions" of the narrator, and appreciate that intertextual nature of the fictional world: "As in a Turgenev story, a torrent of Italian music came from an open window" (290, this alludes to a significant image from Turgenev's *Torrents of Spring*). Nabokov wants us to believe that the characters are merely figures in a novel, not people in

140   *The Reader in Modernist Fiction*

the world. His aesthetic reader likewise should perceive the metafictional ramifications of Humbert's plea, "Imagine me; I shall not exist if you do not imagine me" (131): while humans can be alive without being perceived by others, a character only exists by being read. Art is "the only immortality" that characters can share (311); this thesis is one that Humbert must learn.

The dialectic of readerly contestation outlined above permeates the novel. The pornographic reader, presumably identifying with Humbert, continues to be invoked and disappointed ("the coarse reader" is explicitly addressed as late as page 287), though there is little for him to enjoy in the last half of the novel. The clash between humanist and aesthetic readers occurs more insistently throughout the book, as opposite interpretive stances are differentially rewarded: one of the more tantalizing instances being the hermeneutical drama over the identity of Humbert's antagonist. The narrator, as we have noted, praises "the astute reader" who has "long ago" guessed the identity of his enemy—even as he continues to withhold the name from other, less perspicacious readers (274).

But there is a contradiction in the "aesthetic" stance, and it's one that seems to have snared Nabokov. The author firmly claims he is "neither a reader nor a writer of didactic fiction, and despite John Ray's assertion, *Lolita* has no moral in tow" (316). While Nabokov is not a didactic writer, he regularly asserts social and political positions throughout his fiction, such as his hatred of totalitarian regimes and contempt for psychoanalysis. It is revealing to examine the language he employs to oppose his own aestheticism to committed works of realism: "For me a work of art exists only insofar as it affords me with what I shall bluntly call aesthetic bliss, that is a sense of being somehow, somewhere, connected with other states of being where art (curiosity, tenderness, kindness, ecstasy) is the norm" (316–17). The parenthetical explanation of art is curiously centered on ethical qualities (tenderness, kindness) and surrounded by generally approved human qualities (curiosity, ecstasy). This is a surprisingly—in fact, stunningly—ethical definition of art. An ending that would satisfy moralizing middlebrow readers (the kind who might well belong to an old fashioned book club) is also provided: Humbert, for all his monstrous egotism and decadent posturing, finally concurs with the ethical verdict of liberal humanism. The book flaunts its aesthetic amorality throughout, but in the end is wrapped up in a snug moral frame—rather too snugly to be entirely convincing for some readers (284–89, 309–10). With *Lolita*, Nabokov attempts to have his cake and eat it, too.

In addition to the narratees and implied readers addressed within it, there are also significant communities excluded by this text. As already noted, those most flamboyantly expelled are the advocates of literary realism and, by extension, politically committed fiction and the literature of ideas; specific opprobrium is reserved for reductive psychoanalytic exegesis. Several distinct groups of actual readers— women, gays, and working-class men—are also denigrated by this novel. Critically, the most contested audience response to this text is that of women: Linda Kauffman argues persuasively that Nabokov's attempt to create an exclusively aesthetic, self-referential totality fails, as the text despite its apparent intentions remains painfully representational (see also Patnoe; Rabinowitz "*Lolita*").[4] To articulate this in another way, fictional characters typically have both an artificial component as verbal creations of a fictional story, and a mimetic or referential component that draws on our knowledge of the actual world. Nabokov, despite brilliantly reproducing numerous realistic traits, settings, and sensibilities, pretends that the avowedly fictional aspect of his work reduces everything else to artifice, and therefore is immune to real-world ethical judgements. But the more realistic a scenario is, the more appropriate it is to judge it by our ethical values. Nabokov fails because he has made his figures too plausible, too verisimilar, too realistic.

It is safe to say that the work's implied aesthetic reader is gendered as male, and is also cis, white, and upper or upper-middle class, or what Hannah Kubowitz has called the "default reader." Gay characters like Gaston Godin are deprecated in the novel ("a glum, repulsive fat old invert" 185, see also 217) and the implied primary audience is expected to share these values. Similarly, workingmen are generally presented as buffoons. The routinely mocked humanist reader, by contrast, can be male or female ("ladies and gentlemen of the jury" are frequently addressed, 105). In practice, it can be invidious to ask for an aesthetic reading to be produced by the people the work excludes and derides. These groups of readers will presumably read at least in part oppositionally, against some of the dominant aspects of this text. Here too the work produces a response that is multiple and opposed.

Lolita repeats, re-enacts, extends, and at times parodies the strategies we have seen being employed since the early works of Conrad and Joyce. In particular, it both makes explicit and exaggerates the quest for hidden design as the reader, like the central characters of the work, searches the text for patterns, allusions, and clues. At times, however, the text seems to parody the search for submerged meanings

142   *The Reader in Modernist Fiction*

that, as we have seen, is a repeated theme and trope of high modernist composition. Nabokov may very well have created a novel that simultaneously invites and refuses such exegesis: David L. Cooper has argued convincingly that "the text undermines both naive and sophisticated first readings" and instead rewards only "strategies that depend upon rereading" (27). It is as if Nabokov can only extend the high modernist practice by partially subverting it. The critical reader constructed by modernism is not able to solve these mysteries on a first reading.

We can see the full extent and effect of this hermeneutical ambivalence by looking more closely into the patterns of intertextuality woven into the book. As previously noted, its most salient references point back to the work of Edgar Allan Poe, to *Carmen*, and to Proust's *Recherche*. The allusions to Poe form a cluster that refer to several works as well as to Poe's life (he married his thirteen-year-old cousin); they develop related themes rather than reproduce the arc of a single text. The allusions to Proust, though clearly important, are fairly intermittent; they are also quite general and basically suggest that Humbert will, like Marcel, lose his object of desire, pursue her, and finally try to attain by art what has proven impossible to obtain in life. But the numerous allusions to *Carmen* are another matter. They are ubiquitous, even appearing in a popular song heard on the radio, which Humbert imperfectly remembers: "O my Carmen, my little Carmen, something, something, those something nights, and the stars, and the bars, and the barmen" (61; see Appel's annotations, 357–58). These are ultimately red herrings. Mérimée's novella and Bizet's opera do indeed involve a love triangle that ends in death, but Humbert is no Don José who kills his lover in his passion and despair. In fact, this very possibility is mocked within the novel. When Humbert finally catches up with Dolly in her new home, at the end of their conversation he asks her if there is any possibility she would return to him. As he narrates this exchange, he repeats Don José's words, "*Carmencita, lui demandais-je*" (282). She tells him no, and he continues, "Then I pulled out my automatic—I mean, this is the kind of fool thing a reader might suppose I did. It never even occurred to me to do it" (282). This denial is not merely a Nabokovian repudiation of the melodramatic imagination but also a contravention of the logic of intertextuality as deployed by the modernists. Why keep alluding to *Carmen* if it is not a model of the trajectory of the plot? And why castigate readers who have carefully followed the allusions to this point? Michael Riffaterre explains that the "intertext is one or more texts which the reader must know in order to

Reading Ruins: Postmodernism   143

understand a work of literature in terms of its overall significance" (56), but this intertext leads more to mistaken expectations than to a better understanding. Nabokov here seems to be moving instead toward a more postmodern pastiche of source texts that casually reconfigures them in any way that might be desired.

In *Lolita* we also see dramatized a modernist contempt for the inaccuracies of journalism: Humbert creates a fictitious biography for the local newspaper, complete with a false name and misleading vocation, "Edgar H. Humbert, writer and explorer" (77), that is published without any fact checking and includes new errors. It has been observed that the detective novel is a kind of inverted specimen of the modernist hermeneutical text; this text combines a modernist quest for hidden meaning with a parodic incarnation of a detective novel. In a similar manner, Nabokov takes the early modernist opposition of art and life to its pathological conclusions by having Humbert attempt to achieve through criminal pedophilia the arresting of time and change that can only come from the achievement of art, as Proust's Marcel is replaced by Nabokov's maniac.

There is another partial difference between *Lolita* and the many other works that dramatize reading which I have discussed in the rest of this book: while being the victim of naïve, uncritical interpretive strategies still causes pain or failure for those who believe what they read, in *Lolita* the ability to read critically does not produce any significant enlightenment, as Humbert's experience attests to. It may even be that his very skills as a literary reader help him delude himself into denying the terrible damage he is inflicting on his step-daughter. Developing further a position that reaches back to Mansfield and Bowen, Nabokov intensifies the opposition between good people and good readers: Charlotte Haze may be naïve, credulous, romantic, fatuous, and deluded, but she does not hesitate for an instant to save her daughter from Humbert's horrid designs. Combined with Nabokov's other interpretive stances, this seems yet another move away from the common modernist interpretive paradigm.

Finally, we might note the curious fact that, despite the near ubiquity of each term, the themes of reading and sexual desire do not intersect much. The few points of connection usually indicate something different, and often lead away from sex. We can note Mrs. Haze's temporary use of books to try to impress Humbert, Humbert's corollary deployment of the language of cheap romance novels to ensnare her in turn, and finally his exposure due to her reading his diary. Lo dismissively tells Humbert, "you talk like a book" (116), and we see her obscuring Humbert's scrawled attempt

144   The Reader in Modernist Fiction

to record the figures of Quilty's license plate. Humbert refers to Dante falling in love with Beatrice when she was nine and Petrarch adoring the twelve-year-old Laura (21), but these references, like the allusions to Poe, concern the authors' lives rather than their writing per se. Similarly, we observe many literary, and especially dramatic, false names that Quilty leaves in the motel registers, such as Donald Quix of Sierra Nevada, Arthur Rainbow (i.e. Rimbaud), Morris Schmetterling (Maurice Maeterlinck), N. S. Aristoff (Aristophanes), and many others (250–54). Though some of the names and places have sexual associations, most do not. In a rare case of nonconjunction, Nabokov seems to be keeping these two themes apart; reading does not seem to be especially sexual, unlike the practice of most of the authors we have discussed and will continue to encounter in the pages that follow—and, we might add, unlike the practice of lurid playwright Clare Quilty, whose sexual desires fuel and interpenetrate his various productions.

In the 1960s and 1970s Nabokov would write in an increasingly postmodern mode, evident in *Pale Fire* (1962), *Ada* (1969), *Transparent Things* (1972), and *Look at the Harlequins!* (1974). Of these, the most interesting for our purposes is *Pale Fire*, a text so constructed that it may well be impossible to definitively interpret. The book consists of a 999-line poem by John Shade, a murdered poet, along with a foreword, an obsessive 200-page commentary, and an index by his volunteer literary executor, the unbalanced professor, Charles Kinbote. The book frames itself as a modernist work with a wildly unreliable narrator; a guide to its interpretation is presented in some of the poem's early lines that invite semiotic speculation and promise satisfactory answers:

> Whose spurred feet have crossed
> From left to right the blank page of the road?
> Reading from left to right in winter's code:
> A dot, an arrow pointing back; repeat:
> A dot, arrow pointing back . . . A pheasant's feet! (lines 20–24)

The hermeneutic drama seems straightforward: here are all the requisite signs; deduce the action and agents from them. The book itself, however, has proven much more difficult to interpret; its pages are crossed and recrossed by too many potential signifiers, and they may be read in too many directions, yielding differing and opposite interpretations. Because of the extent of Kinbote's delusions (and the instability of postmodern fiction), very little is agreed upon about the narrative. Describing the transition from modernism to postmodernism in Nabokov's work, Brian McHale points out that "in *Pale Fire* [the] familiar convention of narratorial unreliability has been pushed to the limit. Here we can be sure that the narrator is radically unreliable, but without being able to determine (as we still can in the case of Humbert Humbert) *in what ways* he is unreliable, or *to what degree*" (18). *Pale Fire* is thus "a text of absolute epistemological uncertainty"; furthermore, "epistemological doubt as total as this has ontological consequences as well" (18).

The modernist drama of reading is now made undecidable: there are incorrect readings, but we cannot know what they are. This extends to the most basic aspects of the story and include the real identity of Kinbote (Botkin? King Charles of Zembla? Shade in disguise?), the nature of the fictional world (does Zembla exist?), what actually happens (is Shade actually dead? who really killed him?), and the identity of the poem's author (could Kinbote have written it?). As time passed, even more extreme critical interpretations were offered (for a brief account of this interpretive labyrinth, see Coutourier, "Master"). By pushing the modernist hermeneutic too forcefully, Nabokov produces a postmodern collage of signs that cannot be reduced to any convincing, consistent interpretation. John Shade's epigrams prove too accurate: "Life is a message scribbled in the dark" (41); or the mise-en-abyme "Man's life as commentary to abstruse/ Unfinished poem" (67). Near the end of his commentary Kinbote constructs extravagant metaphors to depict the miraculous act of literary communication: "fireflies were making decodable signals on behalf of stranded spirits, . . . a bat was writing a legible tale of torture in the bruised and branded sky" (289). The impossible aspects of such preternatural images of communication point to the difficulty of recuperating this work within the modernist interpretive model. Nabokov has moved on to a different narrative paradigm and his template of reading has changed.

Postmodern Illegibility

With the development of postmodern fiction, the trajectory we have been following up to this point begins to alter substantially. As texts become increasingly destabilized, the drama of misreading tends to wither away since there are no firm grounds on which to distinguish between accurate and inaccurate interpretations. As Paul de Man wrote, "There is no room . . . for notions of accuracy and

146   *The Reader in Modernist Fiction*

identity in the shifting world of interpretation" (110). Other postmodern techniques include exaggeration and parody; both will be prominent in postmodern scenes of reading, depictions of books, and accounts of the effects of reading. Borges is the obvious precursor that this analysis invites us to evoke. Many of his works from the 1940s employ this alternative paradigm, most obviously his evocation of the infinite, labyrinthine library of Babel with its unreadable books; there are also the volumes describing the world of Tlön that appear to materially generate the fictional objects they describe. The literature of Tlön's northern hemisphere is "filled with ideal objects, called forth and dissolved in an instant, as the poetry requires"; there one also finds famous poems composed of a single, enormous word (73). In this land where individual identity does not exist, "books are rarely signed, nor does the concept of plagiarism exist. It has been decided that all books are the work of a single author who is timeless and anonymous. Literary criticism often invents authors: It will take two dissimilar works—the *Tao Te Ching* and the *1001 Nights*, for example—attribute them to a single author, and then in all good conscience determine the psychology of that most interesting *homme de lettres*" (76–77). Likewise, their books all have only a single plot, but with every imaginable permutation.

In a later work, "The Book of Sand" (1975), the narrator is approached by a bookseller who offers him a volume like none he has ever encountered. Every time the narrator looks at it, the writing has changed; no page once read will ever appear again. Neither can he find the beginning or the end of the work; other pages always intervene between the cover and what seems to be the first or last page. It is an infinite book. The narrator barters a Wiclif Bible [*sic*] for the volume and spends more and more time with it. Gradually, he becomes its prisoner, unwilling to leave his house and dreaming of the book at night. He grows to feel "it was a nightmare thing, an obscene thing, and that it corrupted reality" (483). He considers burning the book, but fears its smoke might also be infinite and suffocate the planet. Finally, he achieves his escape from it by hiding the Book of Sand in the one place where it would never be found again—in an obscure spot in a library.

Many other examples that defy earlier models of reading can be adduced here; I will briefly summarize their depictions of the act of reading, which is often physically dangerous. In Julio Cortázar's "The Continuity of Parks" (1956), a man is reading a novel, fully immersing himself in it. The story ends as a character in the novel he is enjoying is about to murder him. Nathalie Sarraute's *Les Fruits d'or* (1963) is composed of a number of unmarked dialogues by critics and lay persons about a new work of fiction. Some have read the book, read part of the book, plan to read the book, or have have formed judgments based on what they have heard about the work. This discourse proves to be a congeries of incompatible interpretations that keep changing and cannot be adjudicated. Brigid Brophy's *In Transit* (1969) is set within an airport; there a revolution breaks out and soon it "becomes a revolution of the word, an updated battle of the books in which hundreds of volumes fall off the bookstall shelves, bombarding (and even killing) the travelers with words," as Karen Lawrence (*Penelope* 235) summarizes a scene that almost appears to exaggeratedly re-enact the killing of Leonard Bast in *Howards End*. Czech author Bohumil Hrabal's *Too Loud a Solitude* (1976) narrates the dystopian story of an ordinary man whose job it is to destroy excess books and papers in a hydraulic compactor. His monthly average is two tons of books. He begins to develop an affection for rare books, classics of philosophy and literature, and the reproductions of paintings by Old Masters, and he builds up a substantial library of rescued books in his basement. There, he indulges a new desire for literature and displays a marked preference for Goethe and Schiller in morocco bindings—a preference that is also shared by the many mice in his building. As the novel continues, the pace of the destruction becomes faster; soon, books that have been printed but never distributed come straight to the compactor, unread and unopened. New machines, able to destroy more books even more quickly, are introduced; the protagonist realizes his days of employment will soon end. In despair, clutching a volume of Novalis, he climbs into the mouth of the compactor and presses the start button. Though to a large extent this text is a critique of Communist deprecation of imaginative literature, its allegory resonates far beyond the Iron Curtain.

Orhan Pamuk's *The New Life* (1994) follows the adventures of characters whose lives have been utterly disrupted and radically transformed after having read a particular, charismatic book. A more playful and provocative story of the ends of reading appears in Steven Millhauser's "The People of the Book" (2011). A narrative is given that provides the history of the people. When the earth was without form and darkness ruled the face of the deep, the Creator breathed the breath of life into the Twelve Tablets. Then, as one tablet lay upon another, they copulated and produced new tablets. This was the origin of books, though each copy was fainter that the one it reproduced. One day, a maiden lay down in the grass with a tablet

148 *The Reader in Modernist Fiction*

on her lap; this parody of the immaculate conception produced the first of the People of the Book. These persons devote their lives to reading at long tables in communal libraries, and hope to attain in the next life the Paradise of Books. The parodic defamiliarization of the Judeo-Christian story draws attention to its artificiality, and shows how easily key elements can be substituted. This in turn may obliquely suggest that many of the early Hebrew stories (the creation, the flood, the Tower of Babel) were taken from much earlier Babylonian sources and then transformed to suit the newer religion and culture.

Ishmael Reed's *Flight to Canada* (1977), a postmodern rewriting of the genre of the slave narrative, takes up and signifies on a number of earlier African-American works. Reading is central to this text in many ways and has divergent and opposed valences. The enlightenment notion of reading is substantially validated throughout the book: "Raven was the first one of Swille's slaves to read, the first to write and the first to run away" (14). Swille also notes that Raven "fooled around with my books, so every time I bought a new slave he'd destroy the invoices and I'd have no record of purchase; he was also writing passes and forging freedom papers. We gave him Literacy . . . and what does he do with it? Uses it like that old Voodoo" (36). At the same time, the liberatory virtues of reading are opposed to the reactionary power of certain authors: early in the book, Swille, dining with Lincoln, encourages him to indulge in the poetry of Tennyson. Taking up a copy of *Idylls of the King*, Swille affirms: "This book tells you about aristocratic rule, Lincoln. How to deal with inferiors. How to handle the help. How the chief of the tribes is supposed to carry himself" (27). Still later, the narrator observes, extending sentiments expressed by Faulkner and Porter, that "the South is dandyish, foppish, pimpish; its writers are Scott, Poe, Wilde, and Tennyson" (141). These authors appeal to and help create the romantic culture of the slave-owning South. Some literature is liberating, other forms lend themselves to repressive sensibilities.

Other paradoxes of reading are explored in the novel. Raven pens a poem, "Flight to Canada," which is published and brings him various rewards: "it made him famous but also tracked him down. It pointed to where he [and two friends] were hiding. It was their bloodhound, this poem 'Flight to Canada.' It had tracked him down just as his name had" (13). He now has to elude those who would capture him and return him to slavery. This dilemma, by the way, was not uncommon in the period; Frederick Douglass, for example, published his autobiography in 1845 to help establish the veracity of his account of his experiences. Later, the author fled to England at the behest of his friends and supporters who feared his recapture as long as he lived in the United States under the Fugitive Slave Laws. The more effective his testimony became, the more endangered his freedom was. In these circumstances, being read by the wrong audience could easily destroy the author.

Flight to Canada also addresses concerns involving books and the ownership of a person's life story. The novel begins with a reference to Harriet Beecher Stowe, discusses the detrimental effect of Stowe's negative comments about Lincoln, and goes on to explain how Stowe appropriated an autobiography, *The Life of Josiah Henson, Formerly a Slave*, for her novel, *Uncle Tom's Cabin*. "Seventy-seven pages long. It was short, but it was his. It was all he had. His story" (8). Reed's novel is intended to reauthorize the story, restore its original source, and correct the inaccuracies introduced into later versions. At the end of the novel, Stowe telephones Uncle Robin and asks to interview him for a book she is writing; Robin responds by saying that Raven Quickskill will be writing the narrative of his life.

Christian Moraru explains a key feature of postmodern reading: "The postmodern environment overflows . . . with texts and signals, with a symbolic glut that threatens our ability to read." In the work of DeLillo, Pynchon, and others, there is a "deceptive overabundance of legibility, of readable objects calling out to us, a befuddling surplus that turns before you know it into its opposite, into the illegible, the impossible-to-read" (206).[5] This statement nicely describes the overabundance of signs in *Pale Fire*; we also find this situation dramatized and extended further in Italo Calvino's *Il castello dei destini incrociati* (*The Castle of Crossed Destinies*, 1973). Looking at the tarot cards which the mute characters use to delineate their stories, the narrator remarks: "The square is now entirely covered with cards and with stories. My story is also contained in it, though I can no longer say which it is, since their simultaneous weaving has been so close . . . Each story runs into another story, . . . and the same cards, presented in a different order, often change their meaning" (41).

Calvino has always been intrigued by reading and interpretation. His story "The Count of Monte Cristo" (1967) transforms Dumas's account of the Abbé Faria's attempt to reconstruct half a missing page of the paper that reveals the site of a treasure. In Calvino's version, Edmond Dantès is in his cell trying to imagine possible ways out of the prison. At one point he compares his quest to that of Dumas penning possible variants of his story: "Another bundle of papers is awaiting the final touches: Dumas is still revising the chapters of the

150   *The Reader in Modernist Fiction*

imprisonment in the Chateau d'If; Faria and I are struggling inside there, inkstained, in a tangle of revisions" (157): Dantès's imagination of his future bleeds into Dumas's writing of it.

In *Se una notte d'inverno un viaggiatore* (*If on a winter's night a traveler* 1977 [1979]), Calvino provides his ultimate story of reading and interpretation; intriguingly, it is one that is ambivalent in its recasting of the indeterminacy displayed in *Crossed Destinies*. The first words are famously addressed to the actual reader: "You are about to begin reading Italo Calvino's new novel, *If on a winter's night a traveler*. Relax. Concentrate. Dispel every other thought. Let the world around you fade" (1), as Calvino's dialectical narrative of books, interpretation, and desire begins. There are many readers in the book: the actual person physically holding the book turns imperceptibly into one of many potential readers who might be reading the work at a different time: "Find the most comfortable position: seated, stretched out, curled up, or lying flat" (3)—clearly, if we have read this far in the book, we have already found a position and don't need to be told, a few pages later, "So here you are now, ready to attack the first lines of the first page" (9). At the same time, these lines emphasize the bodily act of reading a book and typically engender corresponding sensations in the actual reader's own body.

The narratee identified as the reader soon becomes the protagonist of a fictional narrative. In it, he is trying to find a complete copy of the novel he is (and we are) trying to read; despite the most assiduous attempts, he keeps getting the first chapter of a different novel. And all the readers are addressed as "you" ("*tu*"); this increases the merging of the disparate readers even as it simultaneously highlights the differences among them. The narrator notes: "This book has so far been careful to leave open to the Reader who is reading the possibility of identifying himself with the Reader who is read" (141). But as Brian McHale has pointed out, Italian grammar forces Calvino to identify the number and gender of the Reader (singular, masculine; 256). Soon, the Reader meets another reader in the same situation as himself; she is a young woman named Ludmilla and referred to as the Other Reader. From this point on, the act of reading assumes a sexual tinge: "your reading is no longer solitary: you think of the Other Reader, who, at the same, is also opening the book; and there, the novel to be read is superimposed [upon] a possible novel to be lived" (32).

A romance between the two readers develops gradually; by the seventh chapter the readers become lovers. Each explicitly reads the other like a book, complete with the language of hidden meanings, signs, and codes, in a passage that nicely encapsulates high modernist reading practices:

> Ludmilla, now you are being read. Your body is being subjected to a systematic reading, through channels of tactile information, visual, olfactory, and not without some intervention of the taste buds. Hearing also has its role, alert to your gasps and your trills. It is not only the body that is, in you, the object of reading: the body matters insofar as it is part of a complex of elaborate elements, not all visible and not all present, but manifested in visible and present events: the clouding of your eyes, your laughing, the words you speak, your way of gathering and spreading your hair, your initiatives and your reticences, and all the signs that are on the frontier between you and usage and habits and memory and prehistory and fashion, all codes, all the poor alphabets by which one human being believes at certain moments that he is reading another human being (155).

The male gaze, which has dominated the novel up to now, is briefly bracketed as male reader's body is read by Ludmilla: "And you too, O Reader, are meanwhile an object of reading: the Other Reader now is reviewing your body as if skimming the index, and at some moments she consults it as if gripped by sudden and specific curiosities" (155). She lingers on certain aspects as her gazing continues: "Now she dwells on negligible details, perhaps tiny stylistic faults, for example the prominent Adam's apple" (155). He largely enjoys the feeling of being read by her, until he wonders whether she is engaging in a different, antithetical kind of reading, one that strays from the text and incorporates other, alien elements: "she is not reading you, single and whole as you are, but using you, using fragments of you detached from the context to construct for herself a ghostly partner, known to her alone, in the penumbra of her semiconsciousness, and what she is deciphering is this apocryphal visitor, not you" (156). A perfect reading remains difficult, elusive, and suspect—and so, for that matter, is a merely informed reading.

Calvino goes on to differentiate the interpretation of amorous bodies from the conventional consumption of traditional narratives: lovers' reading each other's bodies "differs from the reading of written pages in that it is not linear. It starts at any point, skips, repeats itself, goes backward, insists, ramifies in simultaneous and divergent messages, converges again, has moments of irritation, turns the page, finds its place, gets lost. A direction can be recognized in it, a route to an end, since it tends toward a climax, and with this end in view it arranges rhythmic phases, metrical scansions, recurrence

152   *The Reader in Modernist Fiction*

of motives. But is the climax really the end?" (156). Here, sexual congress becomes a model for the experimental narrative technique that describes it, as Calvino's text becomes and provides an erotics of reading.

If on a winter's night a traveler offers a sustained and almost encyclopedic investigation of different aspects of reading. We are presented with the idea of an innocent precritical reading ruined by professional authors who use books only to produce other books (93). We encounter the reading of anonymous books, plagiarized works, collective tomes, and ghost-written volumes. When apprised of an unfinished novel by the writer Silas Flannery, a company promises that their "computers would be capable of completing it easily, programmed as they are to develop all the elements of a text with perfect fidelity to the stylistic and conceptual models of the author" (118). There is also a corresponding digital reader who can only respond to a work after it has been analyzed by a computer (186). We receive a report of a blind, illiterate old Native American known as the Father of Stories who uninterruptedly tells competent stories that take place in countries and times completely unknown to him (117). A rather Borgesian literature is imagined "made entirely of apocrypha, of false attributions, of imitations and counterfeits and pastiches" (159). In nearly all of these examples, we see that the romantic ideal of the distinctive work by an individual author with a unique voice is under assault from every direction.

Calvino regularly castigates what would later be called "paranoid" or "symptomatic" modes of reading, as ideologically based strategies of reading are denounced, whether they center on the means of production, processes of reification, sublimation of repression, or the transgression of personal or political norms (74–76, 91). The ultimate insult to reading comes from a nonreading sculptor who uses books as raw material for his artworks: "I fix the books with mastic, and they stay as they were. Shut, or open, or else I give them forms, I carve them, I make holes in them. A book is a good material to work with; you can make all sorts of things with it" (149). In a final irony, images of the sculptor's works are about to be collected together and published in a book.

Calvino's novel continually frustrates and simultaneously depends upon the idea of a linear sequence in both reading and life; this is evident in the book's two components. The inner "story" is nothing but a series of the opening chapters of ten different novels, thereby celebrating multiplicity, multilinearity, and the endless possibilities of narrative: as Silas Flannery observes in a mise-en-abyme of the novel that circumscribes him: "the romantic fascination produced in the pure state by the first sentences of the first chapter of many novels is soon lost in the continuation of the story: it is the promise of a time of reading that extends before us and can comprise all possible developments. I would like to write a book that is only an *incipit*, that maintains for its whole duration the potentiality of the beginning, the expectation still not focused on an object" (177). One may read these inner chapters in any order; their sequencing in the text is largely arbitrary. At the same time, the book's frame narrative moves relentlessly forward in a traditional linear fashion as both Readers search for the continuation of this manuscript, a quest that culminates in (what else?) the marriage of the two at the end of the text.

The fusion of premodern and postmodern narrative progressions is partially mirrored in the kind of implied reader called for by the text and dramatized within it. In the novel's final chapter, the reader goes to a library to find complete copies of all the books he has been reading the first chapter of. This quest is frustrated, but he does encounter several readers there who provide a symposium of ideas about the nature and goals of reading. In addition to those who prefer beginnings or endings or prefer to read a few sentences and then gaze away from the book in deep thought, he encounters several who make different cases for poststructuralist indeterminate reading positions. One asserts, somewhat like Roland Barthes on the *text*, "at every rereading I seem to be reading a new book, for the first time"; this reader speculates that reading is "a construction that assumes form, that assembles a number of variables, and therefore something that cannot be repeated twice according to the same pattern" (255). For another, a different pattern of subjectivity prevails: every new book he reads comes to be part of that "overall and unitary book" that is the sum of his readings; to compose that general book, each individual book must be transformed, and enter into a relationship with other books he has previously read (255–56). We have here something like a kind of personalized version of T. S. Eliot's idea of literary tradition. Another reader seeks to read an eternal and inexhaustible book that exists outside of himself, while yet another employs a deconstructive rhetoric to describe his search for an elusive meaning: "reading is a discontinuous and fragmentary operation"; nevertheless he seeks passages that "possess an extremely concentrated density of meaning" (254). Our protagonist, the Reader, gets the last word and, sounding rather like Wolfgang Iser, states, "I like to read only what is written, and to connect the details with the whole, and to consider certain readings as definitive; and I like to keep one book distinct from another" (256). The tension between the two models of reading is not bridged; after all, one must have a somewhat determinate sensibility if one is to establish that one text is not another. Calvino's fascinating dialectic of reading finally refuses to move beyond or otherwise transcend the modernist position. His narrative practice partially contradicts the many postmodern stances he alludes to and affirms. As Inge Fink observes, "although he seems to share the postmodernist notions of the self-conscious text, the death of the author, absence of any univocal textual message, Calvino undercuts contemporary theories and reestablished the hierarchies of literary discourse" (94). When it comes to defending a theory of reading, Calvino, in this work, reaffirms the critical, modernist one.

Many of the elements we find in Calvino also appear in David Toscana's novel, *El últímo lector* (*The Last Reader*, 2005 [2009]), a narrative about a librarian in a village in the Mexican desert whose inhabitants do not read books. The librarian is a sophisticated and critical reader, and routinely discards novels that do not meet his aesthetic standards: "Lucio opens *Autumn in Madrid* again and runs his eyes briefly over the next few sentences. Natalia, my Natalia, I have mentioned to you a hundred and one times that the city is a shop window that displays my sadnesses, my need for you . . . Mentioning it once would be enough for me, says Lucio, reaching into his desk drawer for the WITHDRAWN stamp. Another of those oily Spaniards with more guile that style" (19). Of the first shipment of 507 books, only 130 were allowed to appear on the shelves. The novel thus offers a kind of aesthetic education for its reader—a particularly vivid one since the most offending volumes are thrown into an adjacent room to be consumed by cockroaches. An interesting feature of the book is its absence of typographical markers to indicate quoted speech, thoughts, or texts; this provides a number of defamiliarizing experiences as the reader is situated within the mind of the reading character without being aware of it. A mystery soon develops once a body is found in the well on the property of the librarian's son; an unusual twist emerges once he realizes that the dead girl bears a number of resemblances to a dead girl in an Italian novel on his shelves. He later encounters the girl's mother, who has also read the novel and who similarly conflates the two girls.

As the narrative continues, fiction seems to be increasingly imposing itself on reality, and Lucio uses it more and more to understand the events around him. Other readers hardly exist; the librarian, looking down at a fossilized trilobite, imagines what a future paleontologist would say of his own bones a million years hence: "carnivorous,

Reading Ruins: Postmodernism 155

walked on four feet, mated once a year and laid eggs; he was a reader, the last of his species; a temperature change killed him" (176). In the end he realizes that none of the books in his library depict a woman like his dead wife; he starts to cut words out of books and paste them together to fix her in language. One needs high modernist strategies of suspicious reading to follow the development of the murder plot; at the same time, the book is thoroughly postmodern in many ways, including its double ending—one an exaggerated tragedy, the other an impossible comic resolution. Here too, there is fusion of high modernist and postmodern interpretive stances, a dialectic of determinate (though hidden) and multivalent (and irreducible) meanings. The battle over rival hermeneutics continues unresolved; this may be because each position can only define itself in relation to its opposite, and can only exist in a continuous relation to the other that it nevertheless seeks to refute and deny. We can see in this a critical allegory of poststructuralist accounts of reading: there are fixed meanings in parts of the text, but only in parts; the rest of the elements can be recombined, perhaps endlessly. And where there are assertions of the impossibility of genuine communications, these assertions are made in unambiguous, unmistakable language. This is less a battle for interpretive authority than a continuing dialectical struggle that is ultimately unresolvable.[6]

Generally speaking, the scenes of reading are much rarer in postmodern fiction than in modernism, where they appear with a compulsive regularity. For the most part, the postmodern scenes tend to be exaggerated or inconsequential; books are unread or unreadable, lost or unobtainable, overwhelming or insipid. They incite violence, kill people, overwhelm readers, and upset the boundaries between fiction and reality. The fictional displaces the actual and books are hidden in libraries, made into sculptures, destroyed in compactors, and fed to cockroaches. Reading resembles dreaming and narratives turn self-reflexive. Both classical and modernist reading practices tend to be shunned, except in the cases of Nabokov, Calvino, and Toscana, where they act as a foil to the postmodern elements that seek to transcend the earlier paradigm. Because of these exaggerations, it may be that their stakes are not nearly as high and their dramas ultimately less intense; in any event, the failures of reading and the destruction of books form ready allegories of other larger, more insistently social positions.

The crisis in the modernist story of the uncritical reader exemplified in *Lolita* and exacerbated in *Pale Fire* produces several different trajectories, leading to a narrative of the present that has several distinct

156   *The Reader in Modernist Fiction*

strands and that resists any simple closure. In addition to the proliferation of postmodern stances discussed in this chapter, we also see a somewhat surprising and widespread continuation of modernist strategies as well as some interesting, vestigial recurrences of the earlier, enlightenment paradigm. In all of these analytical arenas, we regularly find compelling associations of reading with sexual passion; the two concepts have nearly become bound together.

The Return of the Enlightenment Model

Narratives of the effects of reading did not cease after the arrival of postmodernism; we also find survivals of the older, liberal humanist stance. This is not surprising: the twentieth century has seen a sustained suppression of books and frequent assaults on authors and readers in a variety of forms and in differing degrees of severity, including European control of the books allowed in their colonies, the public book burnings of the Nazis, Communist censorship, religious bannings and fatwahs against books and authors, and right-wing censorship and self-censorship in the United States during the Cold War and again in public schools today. Though of greatly different magnitude and barbarity, these are all about the suppression of books by authoritarian leaders (see Cummings 370–86). Naturally, there have always been books like Ray Bradbury's *Fahrenheit 451* that strongly opposed censorship and advocated the widespread dissemination of books and other forms of writing. We see this tradition continuing to manifest itself in works like Pearl Abraham's *The Romance Reader* (1995), Bernhard Schlink's *Der Vorleser* (*The Reader*, 1995), Dai Sijie's *Balzac and the Little Chinese Seamstress* (2001), Azar Nafisi's *Reading Lolita in Tehran* (2003), and Jhumpa Lahiri's *The Namesake* (2003). Some of these works are in fact among the most dramatically compelling stories of reading that have been set forth.

The limitations of the enlightenment model are especially evident in Bernhard Schlink's *Der Vorleser* (*The Reader*, 1995). This book also explores reading and eroticism as it takes the theme of the morally deficient reader, which we found in *Lolita*, to its furthest limits. An older woman, Hanna, and a teenage boy develop a sexual attraction for each other in postwar Germany. Soon they start having a passionate affair; their sexual routine is usually prefaced by the boy reading literary narratives (Homer, Tolstoy, Chekhov) to the woman as a kind of verbal foreplay: "reading to her, showering with her, making love to her, and lying next to her afterward—that became the ritual of our meetings" (43). After a few happy years, she vanishes without a trace. Some time later, he learns that she was a concentration camp guard during the war and is being tried for the deaths of several women in her charge. He learns that she had a practice of selecting a woman prisoner to read to her for a month or so; then she would send the woman to the gas chambers. It also emerges that she is illiterate; during her trial for allowing a group of Jewish prisoners to be burned alive, she accepts most of the blame rather than admit her inability to read. While in jail, she learns to read and goes on to read accounts of Holocaust survivors. After her death, her money is rejected by its designated heir, a survivor of the fire, and it winds up in a Jewish charity to help illiterates learn to read. The book is drenched in allegories of reading, intentional and unintentional, such as the "moral illiteracy" of Germany under Hitler and the irony of Hanna standing in for the country with the highest literacy rate in Europe that went on to commit its worst atrocities. Since Conrad created the figure of Kurtz, whose splendid knowledge and eloquence were surpassed only by his acts of savagery, it has been apparent that reading and ethics are distinct activities that may have little or no effect on each other. This conclusion is evident in the story told by this novel as well, perhaps more baldly than its author intended it to be.

Jhumpa Lahiri's *The Namesake* presents the story of the Ganguli family; many of its most important events turn on books and the numerous consequences that reading them produces. As a young man in India, Ashoke Ganguli learns to love literature from his grandfather, a professor of European literature at Calcutta University, who, each day at tea time, reads aloud to him. Ashoke is soon devoted to English and European literature; he becomes known for his habit of reading as he walks through Calcutta. Like his grandfather, he particularly adores Russian literature; his favorite author is Gogol. Many years later after he has moved away, he takes a train to visit his grandfather, who has become blind and is going to give him his library. There is an accident at night; the train is derailed and many of the passengers die. Ashoke is badly injured and cannot draw the attention of the emergency workers in the darkness: "The lantern's light lingered, just long enough for Ashoke to raise a hand, a gesture he believed would consume the small fragment of life left in him. He was still clutching a single page of 'The Overcoat,' crumpled tightly in his fist" (18). As he raises his hand upwards, the paper falls and catches the eyes of the workers; his life is saved by a fragment of the material book.

158 *The Reader in Modernist Fiction*

Ashoke and his wife, Ashima, move to the United States, but Ashima finds assimilation difficult. She keeps a tattered copy of *Desh* magazine that she cannot bring herself to throw away, even though she has read each of the stories, poems, and essays several times. "The printed pages of Bengali type, slightly rough to the touch, are a perpetual comfort to her" (6). The two have a child who, through a series of cultural accidents, is named Gogol. Gogol always dislikes his first name and legally changes it as soon as he is able to. He becomes an architect and never reads much literature of any kind. As a young adult, he becomes attracted to a graduate student, Moushumi, who is studying French literature. He had known her as a girl; he remembers she had aways had her nose in a book. When he meets her again for their first date, she is reading a book in French. They grow fond of each other and get married, but their marriage gradually disintegrates. Eventually, Moushumi finds herself back in contact with an old flame, a lover of the arts who used to send her books. About to see him again for the first time in several years, she finds the old volume of *The Red and the Black* he had once sent her and devours it "within days, reading it at her desk in the department, and her carrel in the library. In the evenings, at home. She reads it in bed until [Gogol] comes home. Then she puts it away and opens something else" (262). The two soon begin an affair; their shared sexual passion is mirrored and fueled by the similar contents of their libraries: "The same edition of *Mimesis*. The same boxed set of Proust" (267).

Gogol finally acts. He goes to a bookstore and decides to buy a travel guide to Italy; he will take her there to rekindle their love. But the marriage is over: Gogol is too late and he has bought the wrong book. At the end of the novel he finally takes up the stories of his namesake and is about to read them carefully for the first time. Lahiri's novel can be read as an allegory of the power of books to enhance lives and to weave them together; Ashoke curled up against his grandfather's side is an extension of the feelings of affection that bring the fraught Ramsays closer together at the end of the first and third parts of *To the Lighthouse*. Sadly, Gogol is never able to experience this connection with his own father; tragically, he is equally unable to share and arouse his wife's passion, which is both produced and symbolized by the French literature she adores. In this work, it is reading that brings knowledge, enjoyment, love, and even saves the life of Ashoke; it is thus a kind of mirror image of the modernist model, in which misreading brings confusion and suffering.

The Neomodernism of John Banville and Ian McEwan

In the twenty-first century, the modernist model continues to be deployed, though often with certain variations. We find it animating John Banville's *Eclipse* (2000), a novel that traces the struggles of a once successful actor, Alexander Cleave, who in the middle of a performance, freezes up and becomes unable to perform. He retreats to the house of his deceased mother to try to recover his sense of self and discern the pattern of his life: "I told myself this is the way I shall be condemned to pass my days, turning over words, stray lines, fragments of memory, to see what might be lurking underneath them, as if they were so many flat stones, while I steadily faded" (19). Continuing the opposition noted in the introduction to this book, the protagonists' difficult struggle to correctly interpret recalcitrant signs is inversely mirrored by those around him, particularly his emotionally troubled daughter who, like the child in "Signs and Symbols," claims to find a singular meaning present in ordinary objects and events: "Everything that happens, she is convinced, carries a specific and personal reference to her. There is nothing, not a turn in the weather, or a chance word spoken on the street, that does not covertly pass on to her some profound message of warning or encouragement" (71). Such perceptions, he is careful to note, were once universal, especially when applied to unusual events such as the eclipse that takes place during the narrative. Most people "yearn for a sign, a light in the sky, a darkness, even, to tell them that things are intended, that all is not blind happenstance" (117). The narrator goes on to wonder what they would do with the ghostly figures he perceives on occasion: "Now there is a sign, a portent, of what, I am still not sure" (118).

The protagonist's desire to discover his own identity is complemented by his attempts to understand the infirmity of his daughter. This too involves reading; this too is futile. After learning of her death he analyzes her writing pads: "largely illegible, they seemed a chaos, at first, out of all sequence, with no rhyme or reason to them I could discern. Then, gradually, a pattern began to emerge, no, not a pattern, nothing so definite as a pattern—an aura, rather, a faint, flickering glow of almost-meaning" (208). In the end, he is unable to read either his self or the social world around it. "I feel for the gaps, the empty places, moving my mind like a blind man's fingers over the words, which still refuse to give up their secret" (209). The tone of this conclusion is more of a piece with Beckett than with the earlier modernists' challenge to the reader to find the solution to

160   *The Reader in Modernist Fiction*

the text's enigma. Suspicious readers, however, take this claim to be yet another evasion to be seen through. Robin Wilkinson argues persuasively for an incestuous relationship between father and daughter that culminates in her suicide, concluding: "Cleave realizes that had he read all the signs, he would have understood" (361). This later modernist path flirts with and employs the kind of unreadability associated with postmodernism as one more ruse to be exposed.[7]

The classic modernist position is reanimated in Ian McEwan's *Atonement* (2001), a work devoted to questions of interpretation and misinterpretation. Martin Jacobi writes, "*Atonement* can be read, and by a number of critics has been read, as an attempt to show readers typical and recurrent reasons for why we misread, ways in which we do misread, and consequences resulting from misreading" (66). The novel's protagonist, Briony Tallis, is obsessed with reading and writing literature. By the age of thirteen, "she had written her way through a whole history of literature" (38). She dives into a river and waits beneath the surface to be rescued by her neighbor, Robbie Turner; this prank, he observes, came "surely from one of her books, one she had read lately, or one she had written" (218). This scene does in fact have a direct analogue in another novel about a confused reader, Arabella in Charlotte Lennox's *The Female Quixote*, as Kathleen D'Angelo points out in her essay on reading in the novel.[8] Robbie, it should be observed, also thinks of lives in terms of narratives: deciding on the trajectory of his existence, he muses, "there was a story he was plotting with himself as a hero, and already its opening had caused a little shock among his friends" (85).

Throughout the narrative there are frequent and occasionally spectacular associations of reading and sex between Robbie and Celia, Briony's older sister. As Dorothee Birke observes in her discussion of this theme, "their fondness of books is closely linked to the development of their love story and especially their sexual passion" (197). Alone in his room, Robbie holds a book Cecelia had handed him, reflecting that "somewhere on its leather surface were her fingerprints. Willing himself not to, he raised the book to his nostrils and inhaled. Dust, old paper, the scent of soap on his hands, but nothing of her. How had it crept up on him, this advanced stage of fetishizing the love object? Surely Freud had something to say about that in *Three Essays on Sexuality*. And so did Keats, Shakespeare and Petrarch, and all the rest" (79). Early on, Cecelia tells Robbie that she would rather read Fielding than Samuel Richardson any day; she then wonders on how this statement might be interpreted: "He might be thinking that she was talking to him in code,

Reading Ruins: Postmodernism   **161**

suggestively conveying her taste for the full blooded and sensual. That was a mistake, of course, and she had no idea how to put him right" (24). But of course this was no mistake, and reveals feelings she does not yet recognize herself.

Cecilia's situation is piquantly paralleled by Robbie's own error, as he unwittingly sends her a graphically erotic draft instead of the polite note lying near it. Ironically, Robbie tries to elude a Freudian reading of this slip: "No need for Freudian smart-aleckry—the explanation was simple and mechanical—the innocuous letter was lying across figure 1236," an image of a vagina in his open copy of *Gray's Anatomy*, "with its bold spread and rakish crown of pubic hair, while his obscene draft was on the table, within easy reach" (89). One hardly needs Freud to account for this example of poorly repressed desire.

Unfortunately, Briony, who delivers the letter, opens it and reads it first. She is stunned by the crude Anglo-Saxon word for vagina in the missive; she is staggered by its full import, which she tries to shield herself against: "the word: she tried to prevent it sounding in her thoughts, and yet it danced through them obscenely, a typographical demon, juggling vague insinuating anagrams—an uncle and a nut, the Latin for next, an Old English king attempting to turn back the tide. Rhyming words took their form from children's books—the smallest pig in the litter . . . the flat bottomed boats on the Cam" (107). Despite the fact that she had never "heard the word spoken, or seen it in print, or come across it in asterisks," she knows what it refers to. She is disgusted; something repulsive and dangerous had now been introduced to her experience.

When Robbie sees Cecilia next at her house, it is quickly apparent that he need not refer to D. H. Lawrence to explain his vocabulary. Cecilia leads him into the library, where their intimacy begins. Embracing, they press each other "into the corner, between the books" (127); Robbie moves on to kiss "her throat, forcing her head against the shelves" (127); as their copulation is about to begin, Robbie "guided her foot onto the lowest shelf" (128). Then "they began to make love against the library shelves which creaked with their movement" (129). It is as if McEwan were inverting the death scene of Leonard Bast, killed by a falling bookshelf in *Howards End*, even as the working-class Robbie would go on to experience a much worse fate than his upstart literary predecessor did. Later, languishing in jail and diagnosed as being morbidly oversexed, any signs of affection in his correspondence with Cecilia are deemed dangerous and are promptly confiscated. "So they wrote about literature, and

162   The Reader in Modernist Fiction

used characters as codes . . . Mention of 'a quiet corner in a library' was a code for sexual ecstasy" (192). As Birke observes, "in the representation of their relationship, the novel celebrates literary reading as forging an intellectual as well as emotional and also intensely physical bond" (198).

Briony's immersion in fiction (along with her youth and naïveté) causes her to misinterpret the amorous scene she observes between her sister and Robbie—with fatal consequences for the two. Not understanding Robbie's actions and intentions, she finds a narrative pattern for him from her reading: "Surely it was not too childish to say there had to be a story; and this was the story of a man whom everybody liked, but about whom the heroine always had her doubts, and finally she was able to reveal he was the incarnation of evil" (108). Misreadings abound in the novel, though Briony's are the most literary and the most harmful. Brian Finney refers to the "succession of misinterpretations" in this novel and notes, "every time a character misinterprets the situation it proves to be the consequence of a faulty projection on his or her part onto another character" (80). At the same time, it is important to recognize the modernist difference between this narrative and *The Female Quixote*, the one it appears to reinscribe: in Charlotte Lennox's work, Arabella is almost entirely inexperienced in the world and has little reason (at first) to doubt the veracity of the romances she reads, despite their obvious fictitiousness to everyone else. Briony's confusions are much more realistically motivated and involve class prejudice as well as childish naïveté.

The long search for the true identity of the man who raped Briony's cousin, Lola, has more than a hint of a Nabokovian quest; the name of the victim invites the reader, finding in it a suggestion of Lolita, to discover the identity of the actual perpetrator. This search continues the rich drama of intertextuality in this novel, as earlier works are often invoked or alluded to only to be revealed to be somewhat accurate but much too tame in their earlier form to genuinely depict the rapacious, mercenary, or delusory situations McEwan recreates. Thus Robbie, who has a photo of himself playing Malvolio, will later reflect on the line he once spoke on stage, "Nothing that can be can come between me and the full prospect of my hopes" (123), little guessing that his fall from anticipated bliss will be far more painful than Malvolio's, and will end in his death.

Briony will later try to make atonement for her catastrophic misreadings by replotting in fiction the lives that she has ruined in actuality. This attempt too fails; life and literature remain incommensurable. A further irony is that she cannot publish the novel she has finally

Reading Ruins: Postmodernism   163

completed without engendering a libel suit brought by the actual criminal. The book's potential effects are so powerful that they necessitate its suppression. Though McEwan critiques Woolf's disdain for plot within this novel, he does not neglect to reinscribe the drama of reading found throughout her fiction. It is evident that modernist stories of reading and misreading remain timely and powerful and show themselves to be capable of new embodiments and transformations.

Notes

1. Subsequent references to *Lolita* will be to this edition.
2. For some of the implications of this dialectic of contestation, see the studies of Rowe (61–72), Toker (198–227), Tamir-Ghez, and, especially, Tammi (241–86). Rowe explores the ways in which readers participate in the creation of Nabokov's worlds; Tamir-Ghez documents interpretive conflicts between the reader and novel's various narratees; Tammi provides an excellent and comprehensive overview of the role of the reader in Nabokov's fiction and poetry. Sara Mills also notes that "even when we have identified a dominant reading within the text, it is not necessarily the case that we are aware . . . of all the ideological positionings taking place. We may also decide that, even having recognized the dominant reading, we will take pleasure as readers in elements which seem at first sight to be regressive" (43).
3. For extended discussions of the role of allusion in *Lolita*, see Appel, "Parody"; for an overview of Nabokov's deployment of parody, see Stuart.
4. It is also the case that Nomi Tamir-Ghez meticulously shows how a woman can be one of the text's aesthetic readers; furthermore, as Leona Toker remarks, repeated readings generally produce "the serener aesthetic enjoyment" (199) Nabokov intends.
5. For more on reading and decoding in Pynchon and DeLillo, see Moraru 129–44 and 205–23.
6. Unfortunately, the sexism of this novel creates another divided audience.
7. A similar interpretive drama pervades Julian Barnes's *The Sense of an Ending*, which employs a modernist structure of the quest for the real meaning of a series of partially inexplicable events along with a recalcitrant text that resists the explanation it seems to call for. I explore this in a forthcoming essay.
8. Birke also insightfully discusses the relation between these novels (177–78). For an extended discussion of the many intertextual strands of this highly allusive narrative, see Finney.

Conclusion: The Stories of Modern Fiction, the End(s) of Misreading, and the Other Reader's Response

This study has assembled and analyzed the numerous accounts of the effects of reading that modern writers have constructed in work after work. At the conclusion of this book, I must admit to a certain degree of amazement at the insistence of this subject, its proliferation, and the number of tasks it performs. In its modernist form, it often functions as a kind of hidden narrative or figure in the carpet of twentieth- and twenty-first-century fiction, commenting reflexively on a broad range of interconnected issues. The typical consequence for overly credulous readers is failure, frustration, or destruction; this association thereby functions as an important allegory of the dangers of naïve and uncritical reading practices, whether they are applied to a book or to the world. At the same time, more skeptical characters are shown to be more successful interpreters, despite their typically modest social status in the fictional world. The drama of reading expresses an aesthetic, performs ideological critiques, and transforms the role of the reader. Its lesson is one of critical scrutiny and general skepticism and of the need to question received opinions and conventional ideas. It reminds us that the narratives surrounding us are regularly duplicitous and it urges us to perceive genuine patterns hidden among misleading or illusory trappings. This is especially the case with official, political, and religious narratives as well as many journalistic and historical accounts. All ostensible knowledge is suspect, and should be treated as warily as dubious personal or social communications. The poetics is similarly devoted to careful reading that can discern important but obscured or disguised progressions. The successful modernist reader implied by these works is a close reader who is alert to correspondences and contradictions, who does not take the perception of any character or narrator as inherently truthful, and who is alert to statements involving self-interest and ideological conformity. The kind of relationship between the writer and the reader presupposed by this interaction helped give rise to theories like those of the implied author and the implied reader, though these terms are insufficient to describe the full range of responses modernist authors produce. One version of the poetics such texts embody has been articulated by Virginia Woolf in her essays "Modern Fiction," "The Russian Point of View," "How Should One Read a Book?," and "Mr. Bennett and Mrs. Brown," each of which advocates creating new methods of fictional representation as they elude traditional, formulaic patterns, methods best apprehended by close, critical, and at times suspicious reading.

The new social world of the earlier twentieth century required a different, at times challenging, narrative engagement. Vicki Mahaffey observes that "modernist writers took the view that since we understand the world through stories, we needed to change the way stories are told . . . [Changing social relations] called into being more complex, dynamic, contradictory, and even seemingly nonsensical stories designed to resist and expose the extent to which interpretation had become a maladaptive habit. Through its changing forms, but also in its historical context, modernist literature reminds readers to respect the difficulty and unpredictability of reading" (200). This drama grounds and informs the high modernist mode of reading, and thus helps construct the modernist reader. The modernist reader is one regularly presented with unusual or unmarked details or trivial-seeming events, and who must determine the nature and meaning of these often obscure and unlikely signs. I have called this figure the critical reader, and she is the counterpart of the familiar unreliable narrator and suspiciously anodyne text. A poetics always requires a corresponding hermeneutics.[1]

Even as I mention the considerable extent of the effects and tropes of reading in the works I have discussed, I also note still other scenes and texts that could have been included in a larger study: Miriam Henderson's belief that books were poisoned and her wish to burn all the volumes in response to their denigration of women in chapter twenty-four of *The Tunnel* (1919); the scene in Radclyffe Hall's *The Well of Loneliness* (1928) where Stephen Gordon encounters Krafft-Ebing and other works of early sexology in her deceased father's study and, after poring over them for hours, pick up his Bible and throws it away in anger (186, see Rohy 120–30); the fate of Paul Henty who, in Evelyn Waugh's "The Man Who Liked Dickens" (1933) is kept captive in the Amazon jungle and forced to read aloud the works of Dickens to an illiterate settler (see my "The Trope of the Book in the Jungle" 3–4, 10–12); the opposed colonial responses to the burning of works of literature after the death of their English owner in Jean Rhys's "The Day They Burned the Books" (1953, see Sue Thomas). Most of these works are beyond the parameters of this study; fortunately, most of these scenes involving books and reading have received critical attention.

We can sketch a general progression of dramas of reading over the past century and a half. In the background of this study there is the enlightenment model that simply and unproblematically affirms the value of books and reading, and a romantic tradition that is dubious of Western industrial culture in general and of reading in particular. The distinctive modernist stance emerges as an extension of the model of *Madame Bovary* in the earlier stories of *Dubliners* and the early work of Conrad, as naïve characters mistake improbable scenarios in romantic or popular fiction for usable guides to contemporary life. This model is extended and developed to encompass a critical suspicion of most modes of reading; it continues with impressive variations throughout the 1920s and 1930s and continues to make itself present in contemporary works. Postcolonial and US ethnic works depict the antithetical valences of reading, which can be used as a tool of subjugation or liberation. The rise of postmodernism reiterates the modernists' fascination with scenes of reading but tends to parody it in brief pastiches and allegorical satires. This is an extensive model, as what are thought of as postmodern modes of reading and accounts of reception extend from Kafka and Borges to the present; here, reading is questioned, communication denied, and images of destroyed books abound. Central postmodern texts by Nabokov, Calvino, and Toscana are unable to fully free themselves from the modernist model of critical reading as modernist positions undergird or oppose numerous postmodern impulses. But this is not the end of the story; other branches continue to persist, such as the return of the enlightenment model.

One of the most compelling results of this study is the recognition of the central strand of modern literary history that has been documented here: a continuous chain of distinctively modernist works running from Flaubert into the twenty-first century; the postmodern paradigm has not superseded the modernist one but continues to do battle with it. This suggests the need for a more flexible, revised model of modern literary history. Modernist strategies extend from 1857 to the present day, while postmodern models stretch back for over a century (see my "Re-mapping the Present"). At the same time, we need to be wary of lumping all antirealist narrative poetics together into a loose, baggy, and undifferentiated modernism: the poetics of

Kafka or the historical avant garde is radically different from that of Conrad, Ford, Woolf, and (most of the time) Joyce; Thomas Mann has nothing in common with Gertrude Stein.

Frequently, the interpretive dilemmas experienced by the characters are restaged for the reader to experience, as reading takes on a more active, performative function. Linda Hutcheon has observed that metafictional works place explicit demands on the reader and make him or her a kind of co-creator of "intellectual and affective responses comparable in scope and intensity to those of his life experience. In fact, these responses are shown to be a *part* of his life experience" (*Narcissistic* 5). This is most prominently the case when scenes of reading are staged and then adjudicated. As David Spurr comments on modernist works' interpretive self-situating: "a characteristic feature of the literary text in the twentieth century is this preemptive strike at reception, this tactic of including within the context of the text the range of possible interpretations to which the text might be subjected. It is a strategy that often takes the form of representing within the frame of the text—whether ironically or in some other mode—the scene in which the text is to be read" (88). What has emerged is an entire history of character-readers who figure prominently in the fiction of the most significant modernists: James, Conrad, Joyce, Ford, Mansfield, Wharton, Woolf, Faulkner, Bowen, Ellison, and others, who guide, directly or indirectly, our responses to the narrative.

Looking back over the texts that perform the modernist drama of misreading, we usually find a privileged interpreter who is able to see through the illusions that ensnare the other characters. Typically, that person is a social outsider or part of a marginalized group, female, proletarian, or a member of a racial or sexual minority: the African bookkeeper, Makola, in "An Outpost of Progress," the crewmen on board Conrad's *Sephora*; the impoverished, freethinking Stephen Dedalus in *A Portrait*; the Jewish outsider Leopold Bloom in *Ulysses*; the displaced and dependent Ellen Olenska in *The Age of Innocence*; Faulkner's adolescent Ike McCaslin; the marginalized suffragette, Eva, in "Old Mortality," and the working-class Robbie in *Atonement*. In societies controlled by adult white upper-class Christian heterosexuals, these individuals, each existing outside the structures of power, also elude the interpretive strictures that power attempts to impose. Each sees through significant aspects of the social master narrative governing society and thereby becomes a model of the kind of critical, demystified reader that modernism seeks to enable.

Throughout these works, we see a vigorous though subtle defense of a number of radical or progressive political positions as writers

168 *The Reader in Modernist Fiction*

critique and attack traditional beliefs and practices such as Victorian marriage conventions, normative heterosexuality, and gender hierarchies; national, class, and ethnic discriminations; the ideology of imperialism; assertions of a Eurocentric teleology of history; and the false claims of organized religion.[2] A related conclusion revealed by this study is that of pervasive modernist battles over interpretation. In the analysis of many works, I have moved to the extreme end of skeptical readings that invert the ostensible or less disruptive meaning of the text in question; I side with the gay reading of James's "The Figure in the Carpet," offer a radically skeptical interpretation of Joyce's "The Dead," provide a suspicious, subaltern reading of Conrad's "The Secret Sharer," suggest a reconfigured feminist explanation for the story of "The Fisherman and His Wife," curiously embedded within *To the Lighthouse*, and advocate a skeptical feminist reading of Porter's "Old Mortality." In each case the narrator is less reliable or transparent and the actual facts more crassly material, unwittingly ignored, and deliberately obscured than most critics discern. We find a profound and sustained investigation of the act and effects of reading and interpretation throughout the works of Conrad, Joyce, Woolf, and Faulkner, the entire extent of which is not fully recognized. A focus on characters as readers and the implications of the effects of their reading suggests that high modernist works are more intricately constructed, more skeptically oriented, and more ideologically critical than is often assumed.

We also see that the relations between reading and sex are almost as polymorphous as sex itself. At the most general level, we can affirm that reading arouses sexual desire, yet often makes that desire unattainable. Frequently, romantic reading leads to sexual relations that turn out to be unfortunate because they are modeled on the conventions of romantic fiction rather than being grounded in actual human relations (*Madame Bovary, The Good Soldier*). The varieties of miscognition among readers enamored of each other (and, at times, those who observe them) are also vast, and often harmful, even deadly (*The Heart of the Matter, Atonement*). Feigned reading can be a badly staged performance while the genuine activity is a method of deep emotional connection (*To the Lighthouse*). Reading can provide knowledge of dangerous desires lurking within oneself (*Dorian Gray*) or can trigger powerful, lustful passions (*Portrait of the Artist as a Young Man*).

Among other things, this book identifies a literary tradition of divided audiences that is a characteristic or even a defining feature of modernism. Audiences determined to read a modernist work as

Conclusion   **169**

if it were a Victorian novel are invariably frustrated; often, their expectations are written into the text precisely to be frustrated. At other times, modernist authors, imitating the practice of African-American or gay authors, write a double-voiced narrative, one directed to the dominant audience, the other in a kind of code that, though easily missed by the first audience, is readily comprehended by their own. In order to publish in the conservative though prestigious *Blackwood's* magazine, Conrad partially had to mask his anti-imperial critique so that powerful, conventional readers could find the message they expected. And his strategy worked: as noted in Chapter One, an early reviewer of "Heart of Darkness" for the *Manchester Guardian* commented that "It must not be supposed that Mr Conrad makes attack upon colonisation, expansion, even Imperialism." In "The Secret Sharer," the hidden subtext, I have argued, is one that can be discerned most readily by skeptical critics or by experienced seamen. This text, like other works of Conrad, also includes a homosocial subtext that is readily perceived by readers alert to such signs. *Ulysses* is directed to those with an uncompromisingly modern sensibility, especially in regard to sexuality, as well as those who appreciate the furthest reaches of a modernist poetics of narrative. His anti-colonialism is so subtle that it was entirely overlooked by generations of Joyce scholars, though since the work of Vincent Cheng and others writing in the 1990s it has now become impossible to miss. In the 1920s, Woolf famously claimed to write for the "common" reader, but by the later 1930s she was asserting that most readers do not really read at all, something which she had already documented in her portraits of the various non- and pseudo-readers in *To the Lighthouse*. Ralph Ellison speaks to both black and white audiences in *Invisible Man*, though the divide between these audiences is perhaps most evident in the book's final sentences, clearly addressed to a Euro-American narratee: "Who knows but that, on the lower frequencies, I speak for you?" (568). What is a revelation for this reader is common knowledge for a Black audience. And Nabokov, as I have argued, constructs and divides several different audiences: high-, middle- and lowbrow readers, modernist and postmodern, and elite and minority audiences.

This study produces some significant implications for narrative and critical theory, especially concerning the theory of the reader. Since 1980, this theory has been at an impasse, with two rival conceptions in place, neither of which has been able to definitively displace the other. One of these is what may be called the monist conception which emphasizes a single, intended correct reading

170 The Reader in Modernist Fiction

performed by the ideal, implied, model, or encoded reader (Booth, Iser, Eco, Brooke-Rose) or "authorial audience" (Rabinowitz).[3] This first wave of reader response theory seemed designed to explain the effects of processing a modernist text. We can easily see how this model would appeal to those attempting to articulate the subtle ironies, revealing parallels, and hidden patterns cached within so many modernist works of fiction. But modern works are also notoriously polysemic, ambiguous, vague, and obscure; the subterranean nature of such cached meanings invariably produces alternative readings that seem equally plausible. Many reader response theorists of this type often seemed guilty of the charge that they took their own readings and attributed them to the implied or ideal reader. There is also the fact that after producing numerous works with hidden interpretations, many authors went on to produce works with largely indeterminable meanings, such as in *Finnegans Wake, Absalom, Absalom!* or *Pale Fire*. As they were scrutinized more closely, the idea of a single, definitive implied reader became less practical to apply to the complex modernist narratives that had helped to generate the concept.

Thus, many of the texts that seem to reward a monist reading also perversely assisted in giving rise to its opposite, an inherently indeterminate model of reading. This opposed approach has been variously set forth by Norman Holland, David Bleich, Jacques Derrida, Stanley Fish, and others. Such radically indeterminate, subjective, or relativistic criticism would deny in theory the possibility of any model, ideal, or authorial reading. There is no autonomous textual meaning there to be recovered; the reader creates the text even as he or she reads it. As Fish claims in a well-known statement, "Interpreters do not decode poems; they make them" (327).[4] Indeterminism also has its problems. It cannot explain how shared, seemingly incontrovertible meanings are routinely written into and regularly retrieved from texts. Such a perspective, examined rigorously, cannot explain why audience members spontaneously laugh at the same points while watching a comedy, in many cases, centuries after it was written. Neither can it in theory adequately account for basic, unavoidable concepts of reading and criticism that are particularly salient for modernism, such as investigations into "difficult" reading (Diane Elam, Ellen Spolsky), "the distracted reader" (Paul Fry), and naïve "incompetent readers," unaware of their ignorance when appropriating culturally different texts and unwilling to allow subaltern narrators the right to silence when they refuse to tell key aspects of their stories (Doris Sommer).

Conclusion   171

The last concept points to a third wave of studies of reader responses: those that focus on various types of Other readers excluded from standard models. Monist theorists never seem to discuss the fact that their implied or ideal reader is almost always implicitly informed by white, usually male, invariably Western, and typically heterosexual sensibilities. Subjectivist and relativist accounts are no help to oppositional readers; as Patrocinio Schweickart explains: "Feminists insist that the androcentricity of the text and its damaging effects on women readers are not figments of their imagination. These are implicit in the 'schematized aspects' of the text" (49). Equally inadequate is Fish's strangely gender-neutral interpretive community: "unlike Fish, the feminist reader is also aware that the ruling interpretive communities are androcentric, and that this androcentricity is deeply etched in the strategies and modes of thought that have been introjected by all readers, women as well as men" (50).[5] Robert B. Stepto has also critiqued the strangely deracinated models of interpretive communities and conventions set forth by Fish and Steven Mailloux; only a social model of interpretation can hope to include the range of African-American responses, but their specimens ultimately remain "insufficiently social" (205–07).[6] In addition, as Paula Bennett has demonstrated, feminists can themselves form a divided or antithetical readership when lesbian and heterosexual readers fall into two opposed interpretive camps.[7]

Our best approach to modernism's ideal reader may be through the perspective of Umberto Eco. Discussing a surrealist text, Alphonse Allais's "Un drame bien Parisien," he observes that the text "can be read in two different ways, a naïve way and a critical way, but both types of reader are inscribed within the textual strategy. The naïve reader will be unable to enjoy the story (he will suffer a final uneasiness), but the critical reader will succeed only by enjoying the defeat of the former" (10). This is a good description of the way many modernist texts work, though we need to add a larger social component: the critical reader also is enjoined to see through official and idealistic fabrications; in fact, the critical reading of the text is often an allegory for a critical reading of accepted social dogmas.

We find a similar dynamic in texts that include but hide a gay reading; as noted in the introduction, Nella Larsen's novel *Passing* actually has "two different authorial audiences, two assumed, intended and *necessary* targets for the text"; the first one is ignorant of the work's lesbian subtext, while the other "realizes, and even relishes, the ignorance of the first audience" (Rabinowitz, "Betraying" 203). Similar dual authorial audiences are present in works produced under

172   *The Reader in Modernist Fiction*

political censorship or a de facto socio-economic set of prohibitions. As Raymond Hedin wrote concerning the hidden, deeper meanings of Charles W. Chesnutt's fiction, at the time he was writing, "a white listener cannot plausibly be asked to embrace the full implication of such tales, but he can become a strategically placed misreader . . . through whose gaps in perception the tales can seep, damaged but recoverable" (193). The concept of a dual (or multiple) implied reader is very effective in clarifying the multiple audiences that are addressed by modernist authors and others writing for opposed audiences. This general position is adumbrated in a statement by Italo Calvino (which probably alludes to Sartre's rhetorical questions on the subject and object of literature). He clearly identifies the conflict inherent in any serious work that appears in a class society: "whom is the writer writing for? Answer: he writes for the one side and the other. Every book—not only of literature, and even if 'addressed' to someone— is read by its addressees and by its enemies" (*Uses* 86). Overall, we conclude that high modernist works typically have dual or multiple implied readers, and add the important caveat that the implied readers must always be understood in relation to the excluded readers of a work.

In this book I have attempted to utilize aspects of all of these approaches in constructing what I have termed the critical reader of modernism. In some cases there are fixed, determinate meanings: in "An Outpost of Progress," Kayerts and Carlier are ignorant, incompetent, and susceptible to imperial propaganda. No one can seriously question this. Rather more hidden but readily discernible to those who are able to perceive it is a larger critique of imperialism in Africa—the men are not just a couple of poor performers, but representatives of an entirely corrupt enterprise; this general position and its articulation are repeated in "Heart of Darkness." Sometimes there are crucial facts that are hidden in the text, as we have seen throughout this study, and the most comprehensive interpretation of the relevant evidence is the one that explains the most, and the most thoroughly. In "Old Mortality," the family's version of the story of Aunt Amy is incorrect, while cousin Eva's version, augmented by the critical reader, explains the situation much more plausibly. Other questions are more difficult. It is undeniable that, in "Bliss," Harry Young and Pearl Fulton are having an affair, and may well have just arrived from an assignation in the same taxi, but what precisely is Bertha's sexuality? The best arguments, I believe, can be made for her having an unacknowledged lesbian desire for Pearl Fulton, though other possibilities are also available, as the critical literature on the

Conclusion 173

subject attests. We can only give our best interpretation, and marshal the most convincing evidence in support of our theory. Other issues are objectively unknowable: we will never determine where Stephen sleeps at the end of *Ulysses*, and we will probably never have a full, entirely convincing account of the status of the figure in the carpet in James's tale. In these cases, all we can do is speculate. Much of Kafka is suggestive but unresolvable; several of the works of Gertrude Stein offer many possible meanings, and at times no meaning at all. In her case, the concept of an implied reader may not be much help at all.

The modernist reader is often constructed by a *via negativa*: we learn how to interpret correctly by observing the ends of those who misinterpret, as well as by the quiet success of more skeptical interpreters in the text. Looking back at the various faulty or failed readers of the texts we have examined, we can get a better sense of the stakes and effects of these dramatizations. Assembled together in this book is an amazing collection of egregious misreaders: Conrad's pathetic Kayerts and Carlier and in a different way, Lord Jim; Joyce's naïve schoolboys in "An Encounter"; Gerty MacDowell in *Ulysses*; Faulkner's tall convict in "Old Man"; and Charles Kinbote in *Pale Fire*. Among the more poignant are those whose lives turn out to be tragic once the protagonists realize the extent of their misreading: Gabriel Conroy in "The Dead," Bertha in "Bliss," Dowell in *The Good Soldier*, Archer in *The Age of Innocence*, and Briony Tallis in *Atonement*. Naïve reading can hurt a character in a number of different ways.

In *Time, Narrative, and History*, David Carr extends the narrative analysis of history by pointing out that not only do we comprehend experience in the form of a narrative, we also live our lives in order to fulfill certain narratives: "we are at once the spectators of, agents in, and tellers of . . . a life-story" (78). Such an insight would not come as any surprise to modernists who disclosed these and related types of narrative self-fashioning. Conrad devotes considerable attention to the ways people's lives are read and the ways in which they attempt to direct a particular reading of their nature. Lord Jim spends his days vainly trying to elude the characterization that his one rash act invariably produces, and Nostromo devotes his life to the creation of a specific kind of personal narrative that will result in his being "well spoken of" up and down the seaboard. Once he sees that four ingots are missing from the silver he was guarding, he knows the squalid incriminating narrative that would inescapably be constructed by all who learned of it. Ironically, this situation forces Nostromo into a secret and doomed life as he keeps the silver hidden.

174   *The Reader in Modernist Fiction*

In "The Secret Sharer," Leggatt is most deft in juggling events to provide the most effective reading that can be given to his life story as he maneuvers the story of his recent past out of one familiar trajectory (not a "nice tale for a quiet tea party"103) and into another, more acceptable (in fact, heroic) version.[8]

In *Ulysses*, Stephen is intent on imagining, staging, and guiding public readings of his life. In the third episode he mentally reviews several such strategies from his recent past, including the following specimens: "You bowed to yourself in the mirror, stepping forward to applause earnestly, striking face" (34); "Just say in the most natural tone: when I was in Paris, *boul' Mich'*, I used to" (35). He is also interested in the reception of works he has not yet written. Archer at the end of *The Age of Innocence* abruptly discovers that many of his actions, real and imagined, have been constructed into a communal narrative that has been incorrectly glossed and unfairly judged. As Mr. Ramsay despairs of being read at all in the future, his wife is actively plotting to situate herself into the future narratives of those around her: "however long they lived," the Rayleys would "come back to this night; this moon; this house: and to her too. It flattered her, where she was most susceptible of flattery, to think how, wound about in their hearts, however long they lived she would be woven" (113). She is finally woven into the narratives of her friends, especially Lily Briscoe, but not in the manner she imagines. Faulkner (especially in *Absalom, Absalom!*) takes pains to document the self narratives carefully fabricated by many of his more memorable characters; Porter shows the distance between the circulating family narratives and the actual persons in the family dramas. The anonymous narrator of *Invisible Man* learns how limited, exclusive, and wayward the historical narratives that surround him actually are.

Most of the works analyzed in this book focus on faulty reading of novels, but many other dubious texts are also invoked. These include the jingoistic newspaper in "An Outpost of Progress," popular histories in *Nostromo*, the New Testament in "Grace," true crime stories in "Old Man," the poetry of Tennyson and a magazine of sensationalistic stories in *Light in August*, family ledgers in "The Bear," a diary in *The Death of the Heart*, and the hotel registers in *Lolita*. We also note the insistently material presence of many of the books and other writings that are present in the fictions: the "torn books" and "wrecks of novels" picked up by Kayerts and Carlier in Africa (94); the typesetter's letters in reverse sequence, the line of "bitched type" later read by Leopold Bloom, and the page of *Tit-Bits* he uses to wipe himself with in *Ulysses*; and the "cheap, paper-covered edition" of *Anna Lombard*,

Conclusion 175

"tear-spattered by the rain" that Mansfield's Rosabel archly views. In *To the Lighthouse*, books are offered as a gesture of politeness (41), banged on the floor (116), left unread on the grass (191), forgotten on a train (98), or sit in storage, "breeding pale mushrooms and secreting furtive spiders" (140). There are also the old ledgers, written in brown thin ink on yellowed pages, bound in scarred, cracked leather bindings, that chronicle the fates of the enslaved in Faulkner's "The Bear"; the poem on Amy's gravestone in "Old Mortality"; the revealing letter set on fire that the narrator uses to read the others he has carried in his briefcase in *Invisible Man*; the physically incomplete and incorrectly bound books in Calvino that keep the Readers searching for the subsequent chapters; the crumpled page of Gogol's writing that saves Ashoke on the night of the train derailment in *The Namesake*; the leather surface of the borrowed book in *Atonement* that Cecelia had handed to Robbie and which he later raises to his nose, hoping to discern her smell (79) and, as they make love in the library, the physical books themselves: "One elbow was resting on the shelves, and she seemed to slide among them, as though to disappear between the books" (133; see Birke 197–98).

This study has also traced out what I believe is a distinctive modernist mode of intertextuality: specifically, the allusion to an anterior text by characters who are unaware of its actual pertinence to the narrative of their lives and which foreshadows significant events they are about to experience. The secret sharer's allusion to Cain undercuts his own self-fashioning and suggests a much more sinister reading of his fate than the narrator is able to conceive. In "The Dead," Gabriel invokes the mythic origin of the Trojan war without ever imagining that he is himself acting out a central role in a different Greek myth—that of the vengeance of the Furies. In "Bliss," Bertha's pert statement that her modern friends' conversation is just like that in a play by Chekhov can prepare the critical reader for the typically Chekhovian frustrations and adulterous desires that will soon reveal themselves. The fairy tale read aloud to James in *To the Lighthouse* discloses Mrs. Ramsay's situation better than she can imagine it, and the tableau of unspoken and immobilized love in *The Shaughraun* vividly foretells Archer's inability to act in *The Age of Innocence*. Nabokov, as usual, embodies and parodies this tradition: the repeated references to Poe prepare us for the death of Dolores, and the many allusions to Proust suggest a radical implementation of his ideas of the incommensurability between art and life, fiction and reality, but the many references to Mérimée's *Carmen* are largely a red herring: Humbert/Don José does not kill Lolita/Carmen, but

176   *The Reader in Modernist Fiction*

instead puts to death the other member of the sexual triangle, Quilty/Escamillo. By contrast, the numerous invocations of Ralph Waldo Emerson in *Invisible Man* only serve to underscore the inadequacy of self-reliance in a thoroughly racist society. In text after text, we find an opposition between the misreading by the characters and the possibility of accurate comprehension by a more perceptive modernist reader who is able to discern the relevant allusions and understand their import.

Walter Scott emerges as the uncontested villain of this study, functioning synecdochically as the representative of a false, idealistic, and mystified presentation of human society and interpersonal relations that, if applied to life, will produce unfortunate or disastrous results. It is the operatic version of Scott's *The Bride of Lammermoor* that triggers Emma Bovary's romantic obsessions. Scott's works are roundly scorned in Joyce's texts, his novels are a partial source of some of Ashburham's folly in *The Good Soldier*, he is the symbol of the older, retrogressive Victorian generation in *To the Lighthouse*, and his fiction stands for the repressive values of the old order in Porter's *Old Mortality*, as they helped produce the confused, deadly romanticism of the old South there and in the work of Faulkner and Reed.

Sexualized fiction can point to a world of sensual pleasure that characters may find unattainable or discover too late (*The Age of Innocence*, *The Namesake*), or it can be a temporary, deceptive aphrodisiac that leads to marriage but vanishes quickly after the ceremony is performed (May Welland, Charlotte Haze). Reading can be an effective tool of emancipation and seduction (*The Reader*, *The Namesake*) but is no guarantee of a successful union. Sex and reading also can be exquisitely complementary, as one fuels the desires occasioned by the other (*Ulysses*). It can also disclose how good readers can be very unethical or immoral agents who commit a range of sexual and personal betrayals ("Marriage à la Mode," *The Death of the Heart*, *Lolita*). There is even one case in which reading can prevent or preclude sexual pleasure. The passionate, illicit love in Stefan Zweig's *Widerstand der Wirklichkeit* (*Journey into the Past* 1942) was propelled in part by the beloved's reading of a poem by Verlaine, "Colloque sentimentale." When, after many years have passed, the two are reunited and finally able to physically fulfill their love, the protagonist recalls this act of reading but it has a prophylactic effect; strangely, he no longer desires bodily love. The affair ends without any consummation. Reading kindled their desire, but re-reading appears to have extinguished it. This work seems to be a negation of the Paolo and Francesca story.

Conclusion   **177**

At one point in "Youth," Marlow thinks he sees the ship's carpenter trying to tilt the bench; he "immediately became aware of a queer sensation, an absurd delusion,—I seemed somehow to be in the air. I heard all around me like a pent up breath released . . . and felt a dull concussion which made my ribs ache suddenly" (*Youth* 22–23). After we are given Marlow's perceptions, we are told what has actually happened: "No doubt about it—I was in the air, and my body was describing a short parabola" after an explosion in the ship's hold. Here we see another instance of Conradian "delayed decoding" in which the reader experiences the same sensations as the character and must, like the character, determine how to interpret them. The modernist works that thematize interpretation frequently restage the characters' hermeneutical dilemmas and their acts of reading for the reader to experience simultaneously. We have Stephen's phenomenological skimming of Deasey's letter in *Ulysses*, the description of Mr. Ramsay finishing reading his book as we finish reading *To the Lighthouse*, and Calvino's statement at the beginning of his novel, "You are about to begin reading Italo Calvino's new novel, *If on a winter's night a traveler*. Relax" (3). We similarly have numerous interpretations set forth that the critical reader is invited to question or contest. In each case the interpretive issues involving the characters are restaged for the reader to experience as well, as the reception and the representation are substantially fused. And in many cases, these are not just questions concerning fictional figures and events, but the ways in which we interpret people and actions in the world.

At this point, I wish to make a few disclaimers to help prevent misinterpretation of my positions in this book—an unavoidable task for a book on misreading. I am not claiming that all prose writers called modernist used the same methods or produced the same textual drama of interpretation, and readily point out that James, Proust, Kafka, and others also wrote frequently about reading and interpretation though they did so in different ways than the main authors I focus on in this study. I do claim instead that a very large number of modern and modernist authors chose to include depictions of the effects of reading in their work, and that there is a remarkable continuity in the stories of uncritical reading that lead to failure, suffering, or death in Conrad, Joyce, Ford, Mansfield, Wharton, Faulkner, Porter, Greene, Ellison, Banville, McEwan, and partially in Woolf. I have focused on what I have called "the modernist reader," that is, the critical or skeptical reader constructed by many of the high modernists; I readily acknowledge that rather different implied readers

178   *The Reader in Modernist Fiction*

were configured by Kafka, Mina Loy, and others. I am not offering a revived conception of the old monolithic implied reader that fully comprehends a work's meaning and design, but instead suggesting that the idea of dual or multiple implied readers is a useful tool in understanding many parts of many modernist texts.

I fully understand that many contemporary critics are somewhat allergic to the idea of misreading, and prefer to think of all interpretations as rather plausible. I would only caution that this is a twenty-first-century sentiment that was not current a hundred years ago; we need to historicize our own perspectives and not impose them on earlier figures who would have repudiated them. Joyce's "Grace" is one of many works that centers on misreading, in this case an egregious misreading of a biblical passage. The text makes no sense without acknowledgement of the misreading; with it, we find a characteristic Joycean attack on clerical hypocrisy. With texts like this, epistemological relativists need to resist the urge to universalize relativism. In addition, as noted in the Preface, I am not offering a new theory of modernism here but identifying what I feel is a very interesting and underappreciated strand of modernism—almost, in fact, a subgenre. At the same time, I suggest that high modernist texts are often more suspicious, critical, and complex than many critics recognize, with numerous salient or crucial features partially hidden but nevertheless fully discernable. I also challenge restrictive definitions of modernism that attempt to confine it to narrow historical boundaries; instead, we see these practices running from Flaubert to McEwan.

Concerning modernism, we can conclude that dramas of reading were and remain central to fiction. Many major modernist authors in the English-speaking world seemed compelled to stage such dramas, often repeatedly, in order to represent (and often to reenact for the reader) the necessity of critical reading in a world filled with mistakes, illusions, and deceptions at every level. Stephen Dedalus wants to escape from the power of the Church and the state; to do so he, like most modernists, must see through their falsehoods and deceptions. The modernist poetics of the authors I have studied here (as opposed to the poetics of the historical avant garde) require a careful, wary, close reader who can see through the errors and misprisions of less alert characters and narrators.[9] The stories of failed readings point toward an alternative poetics based on original orderings that may confuse traditional readers as they instead reward those who perceive the works' cached meanings, patterns, suggestive parallels, and revealing allusions. They require an active reader and frequently counterpoise themselves to the predictable patterns of formulaic fiction,

Conclusion   179

whether popular or Victorian. The unprecedented ordering of *To the Lighthouse* is intimately conjoined to the scenes of reading, misreading, and nonreading within the novel. We are still fighting the battles that the early modernists fought: for gender equality, sexual freedom, gay rights, economic fairness, racial justice, antimilitarism, freedom from religion-based coercion, anti-imperialism, and for democracy itself. As long as ideological structures and media support regressive positions, we will continue to need to read critically and skeptically.

Notes

1. As Paul Ricoeur notes in a larger intellectual context: "the distinguishing characteristic of Marx, Freud, and Nietzsche is the general hypothesis concerning both the process of false consciousness and the method of deciphering. The two go together, since the man of suspicion carries out in reverse the work of falsification of the man of guile" (34).
2. Walter Benjamin notes that a modernist poet like Mallarmé "no longer undertakes to support any of the causes that are pursued by the class to which he belongs" (82). This is, as it were, the political implication of the sensibility expressed by Flaubert's famous statement that hatred of the bourgeois is the beginning of all wisdom. As Benjamin astutely observes, "Baudelaire was a secret agent—an agent of the secret dissent of his class with its own rule" (83).
3. These and other positions are outlined and contrasted by Tompkins, by Freund (69–151), and by Martin (153–62). For Iser's own differentiation between his "implied reader" and other comparable terms, see *The Act of Reading*, 27–38; for Rabinowitz's, see *Before* 20–29. Rabinowitz, as we will see, does make space for the dual audience of Nella Larsen's *Passing*.
4. Roland Barthes was one of the few theorists to include both concepts; he claimed there were two models of production and reception, one treating the book as a "readerly" work that conformed to the pre-existing expectations of the reader, the other a "writerly" text that is partially constructed by the reader, and different readers will construct the same work differently. Barthes's conceptualizations point to a potentially very significant "third way" that leads to one route beyond the determinate/indeterminate impasse.
5. A thorough study of a particular female interpretive community appears in Janice Radway's *Reading the Romance*. For additional, more general work on this subject, see Bridget Fowler.
6. Another, more sustained critique of Fish's position from an African-American vantage point (as well as from the perspective of cognitive psychology) has been made by David R. Anderson; for a more general political criticism of Fish, see William E. Cain.

7. In this context, see Hannah Kubowitz' concept of the "Default Reader."
8. For an extended account of characters' construction and manipulation of their own narratives, see my article, "The Use and Abuse of Narrative in Conrad's Fiction."
9. Understandably, such a drama of reading rarely appears in modernist poetry or plays of the period. Intriguingly, however, they tend to be rather rare in European fiction after Flaubert. In Elias Canetti's expressionist novel, *Die Blendung* (*Auto da Fé*, 1935), however, we do find an obsessive scholar and book collector whose specialty is classical Chinese writings. As the story unfolds, the protagonist becomes ever more impoverished, deranged, and exploited until he and his magnificent library are destroyed by a fire he has set.

Bibliography of Works Cited

Acheraïou, Amar. *Joseph Conrad and the Reader: Questioning Modern Theories of Narrative and Readership.* New York: Palgrave Macmillan, 2009.

Ammons, Elizabeth. *Edith Wharton's Argument with America.* Athens: U of Georgia P, 1980.

Anderson, David R. "Razing the Framework: Reader-Response Criticism after Fish." *After Poststructuralism: Interdisciplinarity and Literary Theory.* Eds. Nancy Easterlin and Barbara Riebling. Chicago: Northwestern UP, 1993. 155–76.

Anspaugh, Kelly. "Circe Resartus: *To the Lighthouse* and William Browne of Tavistock's *Circe and Ulysses* Masque." *Virginia Woolf: Reading the Renaissance.* Ed. Sally Greene. Athens: Ohio University Press (1999) 161–91.

Appel, Alfred, Jr. "*Lolita*: The Springboard of Parody." *Wisconsin Studies in Contemporary Literature* 8 (1967). 106–43.

——. "Introduction." *The Annotated Lolita.* By Vladimir Nabokov. New York: McGraw Hill, 1970. xv–lxxi.

Armstrong, Paul B. *The Challenge of Bewilderment: Understanding and Representation in James, Conrad, and Ford.* Ithaca: Cornell UP, 1987.

Arnim, Elizabeth von. *The Enchanted April.* London: Virago, 1986.

Banville, John. *Eclipse.* New York: Vintage, 2000.

Barthes, Roland. *Image-Music-Text.* Trans. Stephen Heath. New York: Hill and Wang, 1977.

Bauer, K. Jack. *A Maritime History of the United States.* Columbia: U of South Carolina P, 1988.

Beaty, Jerome, Ed. *The Norton Introduction to the Short Novel.* 3rd Edition. New York: W. W. Norton, 1982.

Benjamin, Walter. "Addendum to The Paris of the Second Empire in Baudelaire." *Marxist Literary Theory: A Reader.* Eds. Terry Eagleton and Drew Milne. Oxford: Blackwell, 1996. 80–83.

Bennett, Paula. "The Pea That Duty Locks: Lesbian and Feminist-Heterosexual Readings of Emily Dickinson's Poetry." *Lesbian Texts and Contexts: Radical Revisions.* Eds. Karla Jay and Joanne Glasgow. New York: New York UP, 1990. 104–25.

Berbinau-Dezalay, Agnès. "Reading and Readers in Edith Wharton's Short Stories." *Journal of the Short Story in English* 58 (June 2012) 93–108 journals.openedition.org/jsse/1242. Online.

Bessel, Richard. "European Society in the Twentieth Century." *The Oxford History of Modern Europe*. Ed. T. C. W. Blanning. Oxford: Oxford UP, 1996. 234–59.

Best, Stephen and Sharon Marcus. "Surface Reading: An Introduction." *Representations* 108 (2009) 1–21.

Birke, Dorothee. *Writing the Reader: Configurations of a Cultural Practice in the English Novel*. Berlin: DeGruyter, 2016.

Birmingham, Kevin. *The Most Dangerous Book: The Battle for James Joyce's Ulysses*. New York: Penguin, 2014.

Blanchot, Maurice. "Reading," *The Siren's Song: Selected Essays by Maurice Blanchot*. Trans. Sacha Rabinovitch. Bloomington: Indiana UP, 1982. 249–55.

Bonney, William. *Themes and Arabesques: Contexts for Conrad's Fiction*. Baltimore: Johns Hopkins UP, 1980.

Booth, Wayne C. *The Rhetoric of Fiction*. Rev. ed. Chicago: U Chicago P, 1983 (1961).

Borges, Jorge Luis. *Collected Fictions*. Trans. Andrew Hurley. New York: Penguin, 1999.

Bowen, Elizabeth. *The Death of the Heart*. New York: Knopf, 1955.

Brantlinger, Patrick. *Reading Lessons: The Threat of Mass Literacy in Nineteenth-Century British Fiction*. Bloomington: Indiana UP, 1998.

Briggs, Julia. *Reading Virginia Woolf*. Edinburgh: Edinburgh University Press, 2006.

Brown, Richard. *James Joyce and Sexuality*. Cambridge: Cambridge UP, 1985.

Browne, William, "The Inner Temple Masque." http://spenserians.cath. vt.edu/TextRecord.php?textid=33142

Cain, William E. "Constraints and Politics in the Literary Theory of Stanley Fish." *Theories of Reading, Looking and Listening*. Ed. Harry R. Garvin. Lewisburg: Bucknell UP, 1981. 75–88.

Callahan, John F. "The Historical Frequencies of Ralph Ellison." *Chants of Saints: A Gathering of Afro-American Literature, Art, and Scholarship*. Eds. Michael S. Harper and Robert B. Stepto. Urbana: U of Illinois P, 1979. 33–52.

Calvino, Italo. *The Castle of Crossed Destinies*. Trans. William Weaver. New York: Harcourt, Brace Jovanovich, 1979 (1973).

——. "The Count of Monte Cristo." *t zero* trans. William Weaver. New York: Harcourt, Brace, and World, 1969 (1967). 145–60.

——. *If on a winter's night a traveler*. Trans. William Weaver. New York: Harcourt, Brace Jovanovich, 1979 (1977).

——. *The Uses of Literature*. Trans. Patrick Creagh. New York: Harcourt, Brace Jovanovich, 1986 (1982).

Carabine, Keith. "'A very charming old gentleman': Conrad, Count Szembek, and 'Il Conde." *Conradiana* 37.1–2 (2005) 57–77.

Bibliography of Works Cited 183

Caraher, Brian. "Protocols of Reading *Ulysses.*" *Joyce's Audiences*. Ed. John Nash. *European Joyce Studies* 14. Amsterdam: Rodopi, 2002. 153–78.

Carr, David. *Time, Narrative and History*. Indianapolis: Indiana UP, 1991.

Chambers, Ross. *Story and Situation: Narrative Seduction and the Power of Fiction*. Minneapolis: U of Minnesota P, 1984.

Choi, Tina Young. "Writing the Victorian City: Discourses of Risk, Connection, and Inevitability." *Victorian Studies* 43.4 (2001) 561–89.

Cohen, Margaret. "Narratology in the Archive of Literature." *Representations* 108.1 (2009) 51–75.

Conley, Tim. "Misquoting Joyce." *Joycean Unions: Post-Millennial Essays from East to West*. Eds. R. Brandon Kershner and Tekla Mecsnóber. Rodopi, 2013. 209–24.

Conrad, Jessie. *Joseph Conrad and his Circle*. London: Jarrolds, 1935.

Conrad, Joseph. *The Collected Letters of Joseph Conrad*. Vol. 5. Eds. Frederick R. Karl and Laurence Davies. Cambridge: Cambridge UP, 1996.

——. *Lord Jim*. In *Collected Works*. New York: Doubleday, 1928.

——. *Nostromo*. In *Collected Works*. New York: Doubleday, 1928.

——. *Notes on Life and Letters*. In *Collected Works*. Doubleday, 1928.

——. *An Outcast of the Islands*. In *Collected Works*. New York: Doubleday, 1928.

——. *The Secret Agent*. In *Collected Works*. New York: Doubleday, 1928.

——. "The Secret Sharer." *Twixt Land and Sea*. In *Collected Works*. New York: Doubleday, 1928. 91–143.

——. *Tales of Unrest*. In *Collected Works*. New York: Doubleday, 1928.

——. *Under Western Eyes*. In *Collected Works*. New York: Doubleday, 1928.

——. *Youth and Two Other Stories*. In *Collected Works*. New York: Doubleday, 1928.

Cooper, David. "*Lolita*: A Text for Rereading." *The Reader* 37 (1997) 27–37.

Corser, Sophie. *The Reader's Joyce*: Ulysses, *Authorship, and the Authority of the Reader*. Edinburgh: Edinburgh UP, 2022.

Couturier, Maurice, "'Which is to be master' in *Pale Fire*." *Zembla*. Criticism, http://www.libraries.psu.edu/nabokov/coutpf2.htm.

Craft, Christopher. "Alias Bunbury: Desire and Representation in *The Importance of Being Earnest*." *Representations* 31 (1990) 190–46.

Cuddy-Keane, Melba. *Virginia Woolf, the Intellectual, and the Public Sphere*. Cambridge: Cambridge UP, 2003.

Culler, Jonathan. *On Deconstruction: Theory and Criticism after Structuralism*. Ithaca: Cornell UP, 1982.

Cummings, Brian. *Bibliophobia: The End and Beginning of the Book*. Oxford: Oxford UP, 2022.

Daleski, H. M. *Joseph Conrad: The Way of Dispossession*. New York: Holmes, 1976.

D'Angelo, Kathleen, "'To Make a Novel': The Construction of a Critical Readership in Ian McEwan's *Atonement*," *Studies in the Novel* 41.1 (2009) 88–105.

184 The Reader in Modernist Fiction

Daugherty, Beth Rigel. "'There She Sat': The Power of the Feminist Imagination in *To the Lighthouse*." *Twentieth Century Literature* 37, 1991. 289–308.

De Man, Paul. *Blindness and Insight: Essays in the Rhetoric of Contemporary Criticism*. Oxford: Oxford University Press, 1971.

Dettmar, Kevin. *The Illicit Joyce of Postmodernism*. Madison: U of Wisconsin P, 1996.

——. "*Ulysses* and the Preemptive Power of Plot." *Pedagogy, Praxis, Ulysses: Using Joyce's Text to Transform the Classroom*. Ed. Robert Newman. Ann Arbor: U of Michigan P, 1996. 21–46.

DiBattista, Maria. *Fables of Anon: Virginia Woolf's Major Novels*. New Haven: Yale UP, 1980.

Dubino, Jeanne. "Creating 'the conditions of life': Virginia Woolf and the Common Reader." *Re: Reading, Re: Writing, Re: Teaching Virginia Woolf*. Eds. Eileen Barrett and Patricia Cramer. New York: Pace UP, 1995. 129–36.

DuPlessis, Rachel Blau. *Writing beyond the Ending: Narrative Strategies of Twentieth-Century Women Writers*. Bloomington: Indiana University Press, 1985.

Dussere, Erik. *Balancing the Books: Faulkner, Morrison, and the Economies of Slavery*. New York: Routledge, 2003.

Eco, Umberto. *The Role of the Reader: Explorations in the Semiotics of Texts*. Bloomington: Indiana UP, 1984 (1979).

Eide, Marian. "Joyce, Genre, and the Authority of Form." *Palgrave Advances in James Joyce Studies*. Ed. Jean-Michel Rabaté. New York: Palgrave Macmillan, 2004. 97–120.

Elam, Helen Regueiro. "The Difficulty of Reading." *The Idea of Difficulty in Literature*. Ed. Alan C. Purves. Buffalo: State U of New York P, 1991. 73–89.

Ellis, John M. *Against Deconstruction*. Princeton: Princeton UP, 1989.

Ellison, Ralph. *Invisible Man*. New York: Random: 1995 (1952).

Ellmann, Richard. *James Joyce*. 2nd edition. New York: Oxford UP, 1982.

Emre, Merve. *Paraliterary: The Making of Bad Readers in Postwar America*. Chicago: U of Chicago P, 2017.

Epstein, Hugh. *Hardy, Conrad and the Senses*. Edinburgh: Edinburgh UP, 2022.

Facknitz, Mark A. R. "Cryptic Allusions and the Moral of the Story: The Case of Joseph Conrad's 'The Secret Sharer.'" *The Journal of Narrative Technique* 17 (1987) 115–30.

Faulkner, William. *Go Down, Moses*. In *Novels, 1942–1954*. New York: Library of America. 1984. 1–281.

——. *Light in August*. In *Novels, 1930–1935*. New York: Library of America, 1985. 399–774.

——. *Novels, 1936–1940*. New York: Library of America, 1990.

Fernald, Anne E. *Virginia Woolf: Feminism and the Reader*. New York: Palgrave Macmillan, 2006.

Bibliography of Works Cited   185

Fetterly, Judith. *The Resisting Reader: A Feminist Approach to American Fiction*. Bloomington: Indiana UP, 1978.

Fink, Inge. "The Power behind the Pronoun: Narrative Games in Calvino's *If on a winter's night a traveler*." *Twentieth Century Literature* 37.1 (1991): 93–104.

Finney, Brian. "Briony's Stand against Oblivion: The Making of Fiction in Ian McEwan's *Atonement*." *Journal of Modern Literature* 27.3 (2004) 68–82.

Fish, Stanley. *Is There a Text in This Class? The Authority of Interpretive Communities*. Cambridge: Harvard UP, 1980.

Flaubert, Gustave. *Bouvard and Pecuchet*. Trans. Mark Polizzotti. Funks Grove IL: Dalkey Archive P, 2005.

——. *Madame Bovary*. Trans. Eleanor Marx Aveling, revised by Paul de Man. New York: Norton, 1965.

——. *A Sentimental Education*. Trans. Robert Baldick. New York: Penguin, 1964.

Flint, Kate. *The Woman Reader 1837–1914*. Oxford: Oxford UP, 1993.

——. "Reading Uncommonly: Virginia Woolf and the Practice of Reading." *Yearbook of English Studies* 26 (1996) 187–98.

Fogarty, Anne. "'I think He Died for Me': Memory and Ethics in 'The Dead.'" *Memory Ireland: James Joyce and Cultural Memory*, eds. Oona Frawley and Katherine O'Callaghan. Syracuse: Syracuse UP (2014) 46–61.

Ford, Ford Madox. *Critical Writings of Ford Madox Ford*. Ed. Frank McShane. Lincoln: U of Nebraska P, 1964.

——. *The Good Soldier*. Oxford: Oxford UP, 1999 [1915].

——. *The Soul of London: A Survey of a Modern City*. London: Alston Rivers, 1905.

Forster, E. M. *A Room with a View*. New York: Random, 1986 [1908].

——. *Howards End*. New York: Random, 1990 [1910].

Fowler, Bridget. *The Alienated Reader: Women and Popular Romantic Literature in the Twentieth Century*. London: Harvester Wheatsheaf, 1991.

Fox, Alice. *Virginia Woolf and the Literature of the English Renaissance*. Oxford: Clarendon Press, 1990.

Free, Melissa. "'Who is G. C.?': Misprizing Gabriel Conway in 'The Dead.'" *Joyce Studies Annual* (2009) 277–303.

Freud, Sigmund. *Gesammelte Werke*. Frankfurt a M: Fischer Verlag, 1972.

——. *The Standard Edition of the Complete Psychological Works of Sigmund Freud*. Vol 6. *The Psychopathology of Everyday Life*. Trans. James Strachey. London: Hogarth Press, 1960.

Freund, Elizabeth. *The Return of the Reader: Reader-Response Criticism*. London and New York: Methuen, 1987.

Friedman, Alan W. *Party Pieces: Oral Storytelling and Social Performance in Joyce and Beckett*. Syracuse: Syracuse UP, 2007.

Friedman, Susan Stanford. "Virginia Woolf's Pedagogical Scenes of Reading: *The Voyage Out, The Common Reader*, and Her 'Common Readers.'" *Virginia Woolf: An MFS Reader*. Ed. Maren Linett. Baltimore: Johns Hopkins UP, 2009. 60–86.

186   The Reader in Modernist Fiction

Frost, Laura. *The Problem with Pleasure: Modernism and Its Discontents*. New York: Columbia UP, 2013.

Froula, Christine. "Out of the Chrysalis: Female Initiation and Female Authority in Virginia Woolf's *The Voyage Out*." In Margaret Homans, Ed. *Virginia Woolf: A Collection of Critical Essays*. Englewood Cliffs NJ: Prentice Hall, 1993. 136–61.

Fry, Paul H. "The Distracted Reader," *Criticism* 32 (1990) 295–308.

Fullbrook, Kate. "Freedom and Confinement," *Katherine Mansfield's Selected Stories*. Norton Critical Edition. Ed. Vincent O' Sullivan. New York: Norton, 2006. 379–85.

Garrington, Abbie. *Haptic Modernism: Touch and the Tactile in Modernist Writing*. Edinburgh: Edinburgh University Press, 2013.

Gates, Henry Louis, Jr. "Criticism in the Jungle." In *Black Literature and Literary Theory*. Ed. Henry Louis Gates, Jr. New York and London: Methuen, 1984. 1–24.

Gifford, Don, with Robert J. Seidman. Ulysses *Annotated: Notes for James Joyce's* Ulysses. Rev. ed. U of California P, 1988.

Gissing, George. *The New Grub Street*. New York: Random, 2002.

Goldberg, Joseph P. *The Maritime Story: A Study in Labor-Management Relations*. Cambridge: Harvard UP, 1958.

Goldman, Jane. *The Feminist Aesthetics of Virginia Woolf*. Cambridge: Cambridge UP, 1998.

Greene, Graham, *The Heart of the Matter*. New York: Penguin, 1982 [1947].

Guttridge, Leonard F. *Mutiny: A History of Naval Insurrection*. Annapolis MD: Naval Institute P, 1992.

Harper, Howard. *Between Language and Silence: The Novels of Virginia Woolf*. Baton Rouge: Louisiana State UP, 1982.

Hawthorn, Jeremy. *Sexuality and the Erotic in the Fiction of Joseph Conrad*. London: Continuum, 2007.

Hedin, Raymond. "Probable Readers, Possible Stories: The Limits of Nineteenth Century Black Narrative." *Readers in History: Nineteenth-Century American Literature and the Contexts of Response*. Ed. James L. Machor. Baltimore: Johns Hopkins UP, 1993. 180–205.

Herr, Cheryl. "Art and Life, Nature and Culture, *Ulysses*." *James Joyce's* Ulysses*: A Casebook*. Ed. Derek Attridge. Oxford: Oxford UP, 2004. 55–81.

Herzog, Dagmar. *Sexuality in Europe: A Twentieth Century History*. Cambridge: Cambridge UP, 2011.

Hodges, Robert. "Deep Fellowship: Homosexuality and Male Bonding in the Life and Fiction of Joseph Conrad." *Journal of Homosexuality* 4.4 (1979) 159–75.

Hussey, Mark. "Introduction" to Virginia Woolf, *To the Lighthouse: Annotated and with an Introduction by Mark Hussey*. Harcourt, 2005.

Hutcheon, Linda. *Narcissistic Narrative: The Metafictional Paradox*. Waterloo, Ontario: Wilfrid Laurier UP, 1980.

Bibliography of Works Cited   187

Iser, Wolfgang. *The Act of Reading: A Theory of Aesthetic Response*. Baltimore: Johns Hopkins UP, 1978.

——. *The Implied Reader: Patters of Communication in Prose Fiction from Bunyan to Beckett*. Baltimore: Johns Hopkins UP, 1974.

Jacobi, Martin. "Who Killed Robbie and Cecelia? Reading and Misreading Ian McEwan's *Atonement*." *Critique* 52 (2011) 55–73.

James, Henry. *Eight Tales from the Major Phase*. New York: Norton, 1969.

——. *Stories of Artists and Writers*. Ed. F. O. Matthiessen. New York: New Directions, nd.

——. *Theory of Fiction: Henry James*. Ed. Miller. Lincoln: U of Nebraska P, 1972.

Johnson, James Weldon. "The Dilemma of the Negro Author." *The American Mercury*, vol. 15, no. 60 (December 1928) 477–81.

Jones, Suzanne W. "Reading the Endings in Katherine Anne Porter's 'Old Mortality.'" *Famous Last Words: Changes in Gender and Narrative Closure*. Charlottesville: U of Virginia P, 1993. 280–99.

Joyce, James. *Dubliners: Texts, Criticism, and Notes*. Eds. Robert Scholes and A. Walton Litz. Penguin, 1996 [1914].

——. *A Portrait of the Artist as a Young Man: Text, Criticism, and Notes*. Ed. Chester G. Anderson. New York: Viking Penguin, 1968 [1916].

——. *Ulysses*. Ed. Hans Walter Gabler. New York: Random House, 1986 [1922].

Kaplan, Fred. *Henry James: The Imagination of a Genius*. Baltimore: Johns Hopkins UP, 1999.

Kappeler, Suzanne. *Writing and Reading in Henry James*. New York: Columbia UP, 1980.

Karl, Frederick. *A Reader's Guide to Joseph Conrad*. Rev. ed. New York: Farrar, Straus and Giroux, 1969.

Kauffman, Linda. "Framing *Lolita*: Is There a Woman in the Text?" *Refiguring the Father: New Feminist Readings of Patriarchy*. Eds. Patricia Yaeger and Beth Kowaleski-Wallace. Carbondale: Southern Illinois UP, 1989. 131–52.

Keating, Peter. *The Haunted Study: A Social History of the English Novel, 1875–1914*. London: Grange, 1991.

Kelleher, John V. "Irish History and Mythology in James Joyce's 'The Dead.'" *Review of Politics* 27 (1968) 414–33.

Kenner, Hugh. *Joyce's Voices*. Berkeley: U of California P, 1978.

Kerr, Douglas. "The Secret Secret Sharer." *The Conradian* 39.2 (2014) 19–30.

Kershner, R. Brandon. *The Culture of Joyce's* Ulysses. Palgrave, 2010.

——. *Joyce, Bakhtin, and Popular Literature: Chronicles of Disorder*. Chapel Hill: U of North Carolina P, 1989.

Krause, David, "Reading Bon's Letter in Faulkner's *Absalom, Absalom!*" *PMLA* 99 (March 1984) 225–41.

Kubowitz, Hannah. "The Default Reader and a Model of Reading and Writing Strategies." *Style* 46.2 (2012) 201–28.

Lahiri, Jhumpa. *The Namesake*. Boston: Houghton Mifflin, 2004.

188 *The Reader in Modernist Fiction*

Lamos, Colleen. *Deviant Modernism: Sexual and Textual Errancy in T. S. Eliot, James Joyce, and Marcel Proust*. Cambridge: Cambridge UP, 1998.

Lawrence. D. H. *Lady Chatterley's Lover*. London: Penguin, 2000 [1928].

——. *Selected Literary Criticism*. Eds. Brian Crick and Michael DeSanto. Corbridge UK: Brynmill, 2009.

Lee, Hermione. *Virginia Woolf*. New York: Random, 1999.

Leinwand, Theodore. *The Great William: Writers Reading Shakespeare*. Chicago: U of Chicago P, 2016.

Linge, David E., "Introduction," Hans-Georg Gadamer, *Philosophical Hermeneutics*. Berkeley: U of California P, 1976. xi–lviii.

Lothe, Jakob. *Conrad's Narrative Method*. Oxford: Oxford UP. 1989.

Luey, Beth. "Modernity and Print III: The United States 1890–1970." In *A Companion to the History of the Book*. Eds. Simon Eliot and Jonathan Rowe. Malden MA: Blackwell, 2007. 368–80.

Mahaffey, Vicki. *Modernist Literature: Challenging Fictions*. Maldon MA: Blackwell, 2007.

Mailloux, Steven. *Interpretive Conventions: The Reader in the Study of American Fiction*. Ithaca: Cornell UP, 1982.

Mansfield, Katherine. *The Edinburgh Edition of the Collected Works of Katherine Mansfield*: Vols I and II, *The Collected Fiction*. Eds. Gerri Kimber and Vincent O'Sullivan. Edinburgh: Edinburgh UP, 2012.

Marcus, Jane. "Other People's I's (Eyes): The Reader, Gender and Recursive Reading in *To the Lighthouse* and *The Waves*." *The Reader* 22 (1989) 53–67.

——. *Virginia Woolf and the Languages of Patriarchy*. Bloomington: Indiana UP, 1987.

Martin, Wallace. *Recent Theories of Narrative*. Ithaca: Cornell UP, 1986.

Maugham, W. Somerset. *Rain and Other South Sea Stories*. Minneola NY: Dover, 2005 [1921].

May, Brian. *The Modernist as Pragmatist: E. M. Forster and the Fate of Liberalism*. Columbus: U of Missouri P, 1997.

McCarthy, Patrick A. "Joyce's Silent Readers," *New Alliances in Joyce Studies*. Ed. Bonnie Kime Scott. Newark DE: U of Delaware P, 1988. 73–78.

——. "Reading in *Ulysses*." *Ulysses: Portals of Discovery*. Boston: Twayne, 1990, 94–112.

——. "*Ulysses*: Book of Many Errors," *Joycean Unions: Post-Millennial Essays from East to West*. Eds. R. Brandon Kershner and Tekla Mecsnóber. Rodopi, 2013. 195–208.

McEwan, Ian. *Atonement*. New York: Random, 2001.

McHale, Brian. *Postmodernist Fiction*. Methuen, 1987.

McLaren, Angus. *Twentieth-century Sexuality: A History*. Oxford: Blackwell, 1999.

Menton, Allan W. "Typical Tales of Paris: The Function of Reading in *The Ambassadors*." *The Henry James Review* 15 (1994) 286–300.

Miller, J. Hillis. *Reading Narrative*. Norman: U of Oklahoma P, 1998.

Bibliography of Works Cited 189

Mills, Sara. "Reading as/like a Feminist." *Gendering the Reader*. Ed. Sara Mills. New York: Harvester Wheatsheaf, 1994. 25–46.

Moi, Toril, "'Nothing is Hidden': From Confusion to Clarity; or, Wittgenstein on Critique." *Critique and Postcritique*. Eds. Elizabeth S. Anker and Rita Felski. Durham: Duke UP, 2017. 31–49.

Moraru, Christian. *Reprise and Representation in Postmodernism*. Madison NJ: Fairleigh Dickinson UP, 2005.

Murphy, Michael. "'The Secret Sharer': Conrad's Turn of the Winch." *Conradiana* 18 (1986) 193–200.

Nabokov, Vladimir. *The Annotated Lolita*. Ed. Alfred Appel, Jr. New York: McGraw Hill, 1970 (1955).

——. *Lectures on Literature*. Vol. I. Ed. Fredson Bowers. New York: Harcourt, Brace, Jovanovich, 1980.

——. *Pale Fire*. New York: G. P. Putnam's Sons, 1962.

——. *The Portable Nabokov*. Ed. Page Stegner. New York: Viking, 1978.

——. *Stories of Vladimir Nabokov*. New York: Knopf. 1995.

——. *Strong Opinions*. New York: McGraw Hill, 1973.

Nash, John. *James Joyce and the Act of Reception: Reading, Ireland, Modernism*. Cambridge: Cambridge UP, 2006.

Nohrnberg, Peter. "'I wish he'd never been to school': Stevie, Newspapers, and the Reader in *The Secret Agent*." *Conradiana* 35.1–2 (2003) 49–62.

Norris, Margot. *Suspicious Readings of Joyce's Dubliners*. Philadelphia: U of Pennsylvania P, 2003.

Norris, Margot and Vincent P. Pecora. "Dead Again." *Collaborative Dubliners: Joyce in Dialogue*. Ed. Vicki Mahaffey. Syracuse: Syracuse University Press, 2012. 343–75.

O'Hara, J. D. "Unlearned Lessons in 'The Secret Sharer.'" *College English* 27 (1965) 444–50.

Onion, Rebecca. "Nineteenth-Century Classified Ads for Abortifacients and Contraceptives." *Slate*, August 6, 2014, https://slate.com/human-interest/2014/08/history-of-contraception-19th-century-classified-ads-for-abortifacients-and-contraceptives.html.

Orlando, Emily J. "'We'll look, not at visions, but realities': Women, Art, and Representation in The Age of Innocence." *Edith Wharton and the Visual Arts*. Tuscaloosa: U of Alabama P, 2007. 170–200.

Owens, Coílín. *James Joyce's Painful Case*. Gainesville: U of Florida P, 2008

Peterson, Carla. *The Determined Reader*. New Brunswick: Rutgers UP, 1987.

Phelan, James. "Sharing Secrets." *Joseph Conrad: The Secret Sharer*. Case Studies in Contemporary Criticism. Ed. Daniel Schwarz. New York: Bedford, 1997. 128–44.

Pinkney, Tony. *D. H. Lawrence and Modernism*. Iowa City: U of Iowa P, 1990.

Pioro, Tadeusz. "Representation and Fear in Ralph Ellison's *Invisible Man*." *Acta Philologica* 41 (2012) 60–65.

Porter, Katherine Anne. *Collected Stories and Other Writings*. New York: Library of America, 2008.

Power, Arthur. *Conversations with James Joyce*. New York: Barnes and Noble, 1974.

Price, Leah. *How to Do Things with Books*. Princeton: Princeton UP, 2012.

Proulx, François. *Victims of the Book: Reading and Masculinity in Fin-de-Siècle France*. Toronto: U of Toronto P, 2019.

Queirós, Eça de. *The City and the Mountains*. Trans. Margaret Jull Costa. New York: New Directions, 2008.

Rabaté, Jean-Michel. "From the Erotic to the Obscene: Joyce's *Ulysses*." *Modernist Eroticisms: European Literature after Sexology*. Eds. Anna Katharina Schaffner and Shane Weller. New York: Palgrave Macmillan, 2012. 123–33.

Rabinowitz, Peter J. *Before Reading: Narrative Conventions and the Politics of Interpretation*. Ithaca: Cornell UP, 1987.

——. "'Betraying the Sender': The Rhetoric and Ethics of Fragile Texts." *Narrative* 2 (1994) 201–13.

Radway, Janice A. *Reading the Romance: Women, Patriarchy, and Popular Literature*. Chapel Hill: U of North Carolina P, 1984.

Rainey, Lawrence. "The Cultural Economy of Modernism." *The Cambridge Companion to Modernism*. 2nd Edition. Ed. Michael Levinson. Cambridge: Cambridge UP, 2011. 33–68.

Reed, Ishmael. *Flight to Canada*. New York: Atheneum, 1989 [1976].

Reynolds, Mary. *Joyce and Dante*. Princeton: Princeton UP, 1982.

Rice, Thomas Jackson. "I Do Mince Words, Don't I? *Ulysses in Tempore Belli*." *Joycemedia: James Joyce, Hypermedia and Textual Genetics*. Ed. Louis Armand. Prague: Litteraria Pragensia, 2004. 146–51.

Richardson, Alan. *Literature, Education, and Romanticism: Reading as a Social Practice, 1780–1832*. Cambridge: Cambridge University Press, 1994.

——. "Reading Practices." *Jane Austen in Context*. Ed. Janet Todd. Cambridge: Cambridge UP, 2005. 397–405.

Richardson, Brian. "Misreadings, Self-Misconstruals, and Fabricated Resolutions in Joyce's 'The Dead.'" *Partial Answers* 22.1 (2024) 55–70.

——. "The Real Ending of Julian Barnes' *The Sense of an Ending*" (forthcoming).

——. "Re-Mapping the Present: The Master Narrative of Modern Literary History and the Lost Forms of Twentieth-Century Fiction." *Twentieth Century Literature* 43 (1997) 291–309.

——. "The Trope of the Book in the Jungle: Colonial and Postcolonial Avatars." *The Conradian* 36.1 (Spring 2011) 1–13.

——. *Unnatural Voices: Extreme Narration in Modern and Contemporary Fiction*. Columbus: Ohio State UP, 2006.

——. "The Use and Abuse of Narrative in Conrad's Fiction." *The Conradian* 47.2 (2022) 8–20.

Bibliography of Works Cited   191

Ricoeur, Paul. *Freud and Philosophy: An Essay on Interpretation*. New Haven: Yale UP, 1977.

Riffaterre, Michael. "Compulsory Reader Response: The Intertextual Drive." *Intertextuality: Theories and Practices*. Eds. Michael Wooten and Judith Still. Manchester: Manchester UP, 1990. 56–78.

Rimmon, Shlomith. *The Concept of Ambiguity—The Example of James*. Chicago: U of Chicago P, 1977.

Rohy, Valerie. *Lost Causes: Narrative, Etiology, and Queer Theory*. Oxford: Oxford UP, 2015.

Rosenberg, Joseph Elkanah. *Wastepaper Modernism: Twentieth-Century Fiction and the Ruins of Print*. Oxford: Oxford UP, 2019.

Rowe, William Woodin. *Nabokov's Deceptive World*. New York: New York UP, 1971.

Ruppel, Richard. *Homosexuality in the Life and Work of Joseph Conrad: Love between the Lines*. New York: Routledge, 2008.

Said, Edward W. *Joseph Conrad and the Fiction of Autobiography*. Cambridge: Harvard UP, 1966.

Savoy, Eric. "Embarrassments: Figure in the Closet." *The Henry James Review* 20.3 (1999) 227–36.

Schleiermacher, Friedrich. *Hermeneutik*. Ed. H. Kimmerle. Heidelberg: Karl Winter, 1959.

Schwarz, Daniel. "'The Secret Sharer' as an Act of Memory." *Joseph Conrad: The Secret Sharer*. Case Studies in Contemporary Criticism. Ed. Daniel Schwarz. New York: Bedford, 1997. 95–111.

Schweickart, Patrocinio P. "Reading Ourselves: Toward a Feminist Theory of Reading." In Flynn and Schweickart, 31–62.

Sedgwick, Eve Kosovsky. "'Paranoid Reading and Reparative Reading, Or, You're So Paranoid, You Probably Think This Essay Is About You." https://www.ias.edu/sites/default/files/sss/pdfs/Critique/sedgwick-paranoid-reading.pdf.

Senn, Fritz. "'All the errears and erroribosse': Joyce's Misconducting Universe." *International Perspectives on James Joyce*. Ed. Gottleib Gaiser. Troy NY: Whitson, 1986. 161–70.

Shaffer, Brian W. "The Role of Marlow's *Nellie* Audience in 'Heart of Darkness.'" *Approaches to Teaching "Heart of Darkness" and "The Secret Sharer*. Eds. Hunt Hawkins and Brian Shaffer. New York: MLA (2002) 67–73.

Silver, Brenda R. "'Anon' and 'The Reader': Virginia Woolf's Last Essays." *Twentieth Century Literature* 25 (1979) 356–441.

Smith, Valerie. "The Meaning of Narration in *Invisible Man*." *Ralph Ellison's Invisible Man: A Casebook*. Ed. John F. Callahan. Oxford: Oxford UP, 2004. 189–220.

Sommer, Doris. "Resisting the Heat: Menchu, Morrison, and Incompetent Readers." *Cultures of US Imperialism*. Eds. Amy Kaplan and Donald E. Pease. Durham: Duke UP, 1993.

Spolsky. Ellen. "The Uses of Adversity: The Literary Text and the Audience That Doesn't Understand." *The Uses of Adversity: Failure and Accommodation in Reader Response*. Ed. Ellen Spolsky. Lewisburg PA: Bucknell UP, 1990. 17–35.

Spurr, David. "Scenes of Reading." *Joyce and the Scene of Modernity*. Gainesville: U of Florida P, 2002. 88–103.

Stephens, John Russell. *The Censorship of English Dramas: 1824–1901*. Cambridge: Cambridge UP, 1980.

Stepto, Robert Burns. "Distrust of the Reader in Afro-American Narratives." *From Behind the Veil: A Study of Afro-American Narrative*. 2nd Ed. Urbana: U of Illinois P, 1991. 195–215.

Stevenson, Randall and Jane Goldman. "'But what? Elegy?': Modernist Reading and the Death of Mrs. Ramsay." *Yearbook of English Studies* 26 (1996) 173–86.

Stuart, Dabney. *Nabokov: The Dimensions of Parody*. Baton Rouge: Louisiana State UP, 1978.

Tamir-Ghez, Nomi. "The Art of Persuasion in Nabokov's *Lolita*." *Poetics Today* 1 (1979) 65–83.

Tammi, Pekka. *Problems of Nabokov's Poetics: A Narratological Analysis*. Helsinki: Academia Scientiarum Fennica, 1985.

Thomas, Mark Ellis. "Doubling and Difference in Conrad: 'The Secret Sharer,' *Lord Jim*, and *The Shadow Line*." *Conradiana* 27 (1995) 222–34.

Thomas, Sue. "Genealogies of Story in Jean Rhys' 'The Day They Burned the Books.'" *Review of English Studies* 72 (2021) 565–76.

Todorov, Tzvetan. *The Poetics of Prose*. Trans. Richard Howard. Ithaca: Cornell UP, 1977.

——. "Reading as Construction." *The Reader in the Text: Essays on Audience and Interpretation*. Eds. Susan R. Suleiman and Inge Crosman. Princeton: Princeton UP, 1980. 67–82.

Toker, Leona. *Nabokov: The Mystery of Literary Structures*. Ithaca: Cornell UP, 1989.

Tomkins, Jane P. "An Introduction to Reader-Response Criticism." *Reader-Response Criticism: From Formalism to Post-Structuralism*. Ed. Jane Tomkins. Baltimore: Johns Hopkins UP, 1980.

Toscana, David. *The Last Reader*. Trans. Asa Zatz. Lubbock: Texas Tech UP, 2009.

Travis, Molly Abel. *Reading Cultures: The Construction of Readers in the Twentieth Century*. Carbondale: Southern Illinois UP, 1998.

Trotter, David. *The English Novel in History, 1895–1920*. London: Routledge, 1993.

Tyson, Helen. "Reading Childishly? Learning to Read Modernism: Reading the Child Reader in Modernism and Psychoanalysis." *Textual Practice* 31:7 (2017) 1435–57.

Valle, James E. *Rocks and Shoals: Order and Discipline in the Old Navy, 1800–1861*. Annapolis MD: Naval Institute P, 1980.

Bibliography of Works Cited 193

Wadlington, Warwick. *Reading Faulknerian Tragedy*. Ithaca: Cornell UP, 1987.

Walker, Nancy A. *The Disobedient Writer: Women and Narrative Tradition*. Austin: U of Texas P, 1995.

Warner, Michael. "Uncritical Reading," *Polemic: Critical or Uncritical*, edited by Jane Gallop. New York: Routledge, 2004. 13–38

Watt, Ian. *Conrad in the Nineteenth Century*. Berkeley: U of California P, 1979.

Watts, Cedric. "The Mirror Tale: An Ethico-Structural Analysis of Conrad's 'The Secret Sharer.'" *Critical Quarterly* 19 (1977) 25–37.

Wegner, Phillip E. "Spatial Criticism: Critical Geography, Space, Place and Textuality." *Introducing Criticism at the 21st Century*, edited by Julian Wolfreys. Edinburgh: Edinburgh University Press, 2002. 179–201.

Weinstein, Philip. *Unknowing: The Work of Modernist Fiction*. Ithaca NY: Cornell UP, 2005.

Wexler, Joyce Piell. *Who Paid for Modernism? Art, Money, and the Fiction of Conrad, Joyce, and Lawrence*. Fayetteville: U of Arkansas P, 1997.

Wharton, Edith. *Four Novels*. New York: Library of America, 1996.

——. "The Vice of Reading." *The Uncollected Critical Writings*. Ed. Frederick Wegener. Princeton: Princeton UP, 1996. 99–105.

White, Harry and Irving L. Finston. "Conrad's Incompetent Secret Sharer." *Conradiana* 44.1 (2012) 51–70.

Wilde, Oscar. *The Importance of Being Earnest*. Ed. Michael Patrick Gillespie. New York: Norton, 2006.

——. *The Picture of Dorian Gray and Three Stories*. New York: Signet, 2007.

Wilkinson, Robin. "Echo and Coincidence in John Banville's *Eclipse*." *Irish University Review* 33 (2003) 356–70.

Wilson, Deborah. "Fishing for Woolf's Submerged Lesbian Text." *Re: Reading, Re: Writing, Re: Teaching Virginia Woolf*. Eds. Eileen Barrett and Patricia Cramer. New York: Pace Univ Press, 1995. 121–28.

Wollaeger, Mark A. *Joseph Conrad and the Fictions of Skepticism*. Stanford: Stanford UP, 1990.

——. "Reading *Ulysses*: Agency, Ideology, and the Novel." *James Joyce's Ulysses: A Casebook*. Ed. Derek Attridge. Oxford: Oxford UP, 2004. 129–54.

Wood, Michael. *The Magician's Doubts: Nabokov and the Risks of Fiction*. Princeton: Princeton UP, 1994.

Woolf, Virginia. *The Common Reader. First Series*. New York: Harcourt, Brace and World, 1925.

——. *The Common Reader. Second Series*. New York: Harcourt, Brace and World, 1932.

——. *The Diary of Virginia Woolf*. 5 volumes. Ed. Anne Oliver Bell. New York: Harcourt, 1977–84.

——. *The Essays of Virginia Woolf*. 4 volumes. Ed. Andrew McNellie. London: Hogarth, 1986–88.

—. *Jacob's Room*. New York: Harcourt, Brace and World, 1978 [1922].
—. *Mrs. Dalloway*. New York: Harcourt, Brace and World, 1981 [1925].
—. *To the Lighthouse*. New York: Harcourt Brace, 1981 [1927].
Wyatt, David. "Faulkner and the Reading Self." *Faulkner and Psychology*. Eds. Donald M. Kartiganer and Ann J. Abadie. Jackson: U of Mississippi P, 1994. 272–87.
Wyatt, Robert D. "Conrad's 'The Secret Sharer': Point of View and Mistaken Identities." *Conradiana* 12–26.
Zender, Karl F. "Reading in 'The Bear.'" *Faulkner Studies* 1 (1980). 91–99.

Index

Acheraïou, Amar, 32
Allan, Maude, 7
allusion, modernist, 42, 55–6,
    83, 89–91, 109–10, 127–8,
    139, 142–3, 162, 175–6
Ammons, Elizabeth, 108
archeology, 8–9
Arnim, Elizabeth von, *The
    Enchanted April*, 80
Austin, Jane, *Northanger
    Abbey*, 13

Banville, John, *Eclipse*, 159–60
Barthes, Roland, 71, 153
Beaty, Jerome, 120
Bennett, Paula, 171
Berbinau-Dezalay, Agnès, 106
Bessel, Richard, 10
Birke, Dorothee, 16, 160, 162
Bizet, Georges, *Carmen*, 142
Blanchot, Maurice, 1
books, physical, 3–5, 23, 31–2,
    61, 62–3, 78, 92–3, 96,
    112–14, 116, 129–30,
    146–8, 150, 152, 154, 157,
    160–1, 174–5
Borges, Jorge Luis, 146
    "The Book of Sand," 146
Bowen, Elizabeth, *The Death of
    the Heart*, 120–3

Brantlinger, Patrick, 11,
    14–15
Briggs, Julia, 84–5
Brophy, Brigid, 147
Brown, Richard, 5

Calvino, Italo, 149–54, 172
    *The Castle of Crossed
        Destinies*, 149
    "The Count of Monte
        Cristo," 149–50
    *If on a winter's night a
        traveler*, 150–4
Canetti, Elias, *Auto da Fé*,
    180n9
Carabine, Keith, 44
Carr, David, 173
Cervantes, Miguel de, *Don
    Quixote*, 13
Chekhov, Anton, 83–4
Cohen, Margaret, 35
Conrad, Jesse, 46
Conrad, Joseph, 3–5, 7, 31–47,
    169, 177
    "The Black Mate," 43
    "Il Conde," 44
    "Heart of Darkness," 33–4,
        129, 169
    Lord Jim, 34–5
    Nostromo, 32, 173

196 *The Reader in Modernist Fiction*

Conrad (*cont.*)
  An Outcast of the Islands,
    31–2
  "An Outpost of Progress"
    3–5, 32
  The Secret Agent, 32
  "The Secret Sharer," 35–47,
    174
  "Youth," 32–3, 177
Corser, Sophie, 71
Cortázar, Julio, 146
Coutourier, Maurice, 145
Craft, Christopher, 6

D'Angelo, Katherine, 160
Dante Alighieri, *Inferno*, 5
Daugherty, Beth Rigel, 90
de Man, Paul, 145–6
Detmar, Kevin, 53
DiBattista, Maria, 89–90
Dumas, Alexandre, 3, 57
Dussere, Eric, 116

Eça de Queirós, José Maria de,
    19
Eco, Umberto, 47, 170, 171
Eide, Marian, 68
Ellison, Ralph, 125–9
Ellmann, Richard, 71
Epstein, Hugh, 7

Faulkner, William, 112–17
  Absalom, Absalom!, 114–15
  "The Bear," 115–17
  Light in August, 113–14
  "Old Man," 112–13
Felski, Rita, 19
Fernald, Anne, 84
fiction, incommensurability with
    life, 13–15, 43, 107, 109,
    117–20, 124–5, 129–30,
    133–4, 155, 162–3

Fink, Inge, 154
Finney, Brian, 162
Fish, Stanley, 170, 171
"The Fisherman and His Wife,"
    (Grimm), 89–90
Flaubert, Gustave, 13–14
  Bouvard et Pécuchet, 14
  L'Education Sentimentale,
    13–14
  Madame Bovary, 5–6, 13
Flint, Kate, 85
Fogarty, Anne, 56
Ford, Ford Madox, 7, 12, 47–9
  The Good Soldier, 47–9
Forster, E. M., 12, 23–4
  "Ansell," 20–1
  Howards End, 22–4
  A Room with a View, 22
Fox, Alice, 90–1
Free, Melissa, 56
Freud, Sigmund, 8, 160–1
Friedman, Alan, 70
Friedman, Susan Stanford, 86
Frost, Laura, 63
Froula, Christine, 85
Fullbrook, Kate, 79

Garrington, Abbie, 98
Gates, Henry Louis, 125
Gissing, George, 10, 11
Goldberg, Joseph, 38
Goldman, Jane, 99
Greene, Graham, *The Heart of
    the Matter*, 123–5

Hall, Radclyffe, 165
Hardy, Thomas, *Jude the
    Obscure*, 15
Harper, Howard, 89
Hedin, Raymond, 172
hermeneutics, 8
hermeneutics of suspicion, 8

Herr, Cheryl, 66
Hrabel, Bohumil, *Too Loud a Solitude*, 147
Hussey, Mark, 89
Hutcheon, Linda, 167

interpretive challenges shared by character and reader, 1, 4, 5, 40–1, 54–6, 102, 118–19, 167, 177
intertextuality *see* allusion, modernist
Iser, Wolfgang ix, 71, 72, 170

Jacobi, Martin, 160
James, Henry, 10, 11, 26–31
  "The Figure in the Carpet," 28–30
  "In the Cage," 28
  "The Middle Years," 27–8
Johnson, James Weldon, 128
Jones, Suzette W., 119, 120
journalism, 3–4, 11–12, 32, 143
Joyce, James, 1, 11, 55–76
  "The Dead," 55–6
  Dubliners, 52–6
  A Portrait of the Artist as a Young Man, 56–9
  Ulysses, 1, 10, 59–75, 174

Kafka, Franz, xv, 16
Kappeler, Suzanne, 30, 31
Karl, Frederick, 44
Kaufmann, Linda, 141
Keating, Peter, 10
Kenner, Hugh, 53, 55
Kershner, R. Brandon, 11, 52
knowledge, transformation in conception of, 9
Krause, David, 115
Kubowitz, Hannah, 141

Lahiri, Jhumpa, *The Namesake*, 157–8
Lamos, Colleen, 66
Larsen, Nella, *Passing*, 6–7, 171
Lawrence, D. H., 21, 161
Lawrence, Karen, 73, 147
Lee, Hermione, 92
Leinwand, Theodore, 85
Lennox, Charlotte, *The Female Quixote*, 13, 160
literacy, 10
Lurz, John, 61

McCabe, Colin, 71
McCarthy, Patrick, 61
McEwan, Ian, *Atonement*, 160–3
McHale, Brian, 145, 150
McLaren, Angus 7
Mahaffey, Vicki, 2, 56, 165
Mallarmé, Stéphane, 11–12
Mansfield, Katherine, 77–84
  "Bliss," 83–4
  "A Cup of Tea," 79–80
  "The Little Governess," 80–2
  "Marriage à la Mode," 82–3
  "Miss Brill," 78
  "The Tiredness of Rosabel," 78–9
Marcus, Jane, 89, 97
Maugham, W. Somerset, 20
meaning, spectrum of, 172–3, 178
Menton, Allen W., 27
Mill, John Stuart, 7
Miller, J. Hillis, 29
Millhauser, Steven, "The People of the Book," 147–8
misreading, 1, 65–8, 81, 86–7, 90, 96–7, 111–12, 135–7, 159–60, 160–2, 164, 173, 174–5, 177–8

modernism, ix–x, xv, 1–6, 159, 164–9, 172–3, 175–9
historical range, 166–7, 178
modernisms, multiple, xv, 177–8
Murphy, Michael, 40

Nabokov, Vladimir, 133, 137, 144
Despair, 44
Lolita, 135–45, 162
Pale Fire, 144–5
Real Life of Sebastian Knight, 133
"Signs and Symbols" 3, 133–4
"The Vane Sisters," 134–5
narrative, self, 43, 128, 173–4
Nash, John, 71
newspapers *see* journalism
Nohrnberg, Peter, 32
Norris, Margot, 53–4

Orientalism, 32–3, 53, 66–7, 129, 131
Orlando, Emily, 108

Peterson, Carla, 15
Phelan James, 45
phenomenalism, 7
Poe Edgar Allan, 142
Porter, Katherine Anne, "Old Mortality," 117–20
postmodernism, 144–7, 153–5
Price, Leah, 92
Proust, Marcel, 25n11

Rabaté, Jean Michel, 63
Rabinowitz, Peter 6–7, 170, 171
race, 114–16, 126–8, 129, 148–9, 170–2

reader
critical *see* reading models, modernist
dual *see* reader, multiple
feminist, 67–8, 79, 85–6, 89–91, 97, 101, 118–20, 141, 167, 170–1
minority and disempowered, 4, 125–9, 130, 141, 148–9, 167–9; *see also* reading, class inflected; reader, feminist
mistaken *see* misreading
multiple, 6–7, 47, 73–4, 128, 131, 168–72
pornographic, 139
postcolonial, 124, 129–31, 169
resisting *see* reader, feminist; reader, minority and disempowered
see also misreading
reader response criticism, 72, 169–73
reading, class inflected, 22–4, 28, 37, 40–2, 101
ethical concerns, 84, 98–9, 143, 156–7
phenomenological, 60–1, 82, 91, 150, 154
queer, 6–7, 30, 45–6, 171
reading and interpretation, theories of
indeterminate, 114–15, 154–6, 170
paranoid and reparative, 18
postcritical, 19
surface and symptomatic, 17–18, 35, 46, 72–3, 152
reading models
conservative, 19–20
enlightenment, 19, 156–8

modernist, x, 1–5, 47, 114–15, 139–42, 152–4, 159–62, 164–9, 178–9
postmodern, 144–9, 153, 155–6
romantic, 20–2, 80
Reed, Ishmael, *Flight to Canada*, 148–9
reflexivity, 43, 70–1, 89, 140
Rhys, Jean, 166
Rice, Thomas Jackson, 60
Richards, Thomas, 67
Richardson, Dorothy, 165
Richter, David, 134
Rimmon, Shlomith, 29
Rohy, Valerie, 6
Rosenberg, Joseph Elkanah, 122
Ruppel, Richard, 45–6

Salih, Tayeb, *Season of Migration to the North*, 129–31
Savoy, Eric, 30
Schleiermacher, Friedrich, 8
Schlink, Bernhard, *The Reader*, 156–7
Schwarz, Daniel, 41
Schweickart, Patrocinio, 171
Scott, Walter, 13, 14, 52, 53, 58, 92, 93–4, 120, 148, 176
Sedgwick, Eve Kosovsky, 18
Senn, Fritz, 66
sex and reading, 5–6, 21, 47–9, 52, 58, 62–5, 68–9, 74, 99–100, 108, 117–19, 123–5, 143–4, 147–8, 150–2, 160–2, 168, 176
Shaffer, Brian, 33–4
signs, 74–5, 95, 110, 125, 136, 159

Smith, Valerie, 127
Spencer, Harold 7
Spurr, David, 69, 167
Stepto, Robert, 128–9, 171
symbols, dubious, 2–3, 55, 74–5, 83–4

Tennyson, Alfred Lord, 96–7, 113, 148
theater imagery, 77–8, 111–12
Tit-Bits, 10
Todorov, Tzvetan, 29
Toscana, David, *The Last Reader*, 154–5
Travis, Molly, 132–3
Trotter, David, 10

USS Somers (ship), 38, 40

Valle, James E., 40
Voltaire, François Marie Arouet, 9

Wadlington, Warwick, 115
Warner, Michael, 18
Watt, Ian, 4–5
Watts, Cedric, 41–2
Waugh, Evelyn, 165
Wegner, Philip, 35
Weinstein, Philip, 15–16
Wells, H. G., 12, 19
Wharton, Edith, *The Age of Innocence*, 106–12
Wilde, Oscar, 6–7
  The Importance of Being Earnest, 6
  The Picture of Dorian Gray, 6
  Salome, 7
Wilkinson, Robin, 160
Wollaeger, Mark, 43, 71
Wood, Michael, 134

Woolf, Virginia, 10–11, 84–103, 165
   Jacob's Room, 86
   Mrs. Dalloway, 2–3, 86–7
   To the Lighthouse, 5, 9, 87–102, 174
   The Voyage Out, 85–6

Wordsworth, William, 20
Wyatt, David, 115

Zender, Karl F., 116
Zweig, Stefan, "Journey into the Past," 176